CAMDEN MISCELLANY
VOL. XXVII

CAMDEN FOURTH SERIES
VOLUME 22

LONDON
OFFICES OF THE ROYAL HISTORICAL SOCIETY
UNIVERSITY COLLEGE LONDON, GOWER STREET, WC1E 6BT
1979

ISBN 0 901050 47 4

Made and Printed in Great Britain by Butler & Tanner Ltd
Frome and London

CONTENTS

I

THE DISPUTED REGENCY OF THE KINGDOM OF JERUSALEM 1264/6 AND 1268

edited by

P. W. EDBURY, M.A., Ph.D.

Of the surviving sources for the internal history of the Latin King-dom of Jerusalem in the 1260s, the collection of materials on the regency (*bailliage*) disputes of 1264 (or 1265 or 1266) and 1268 is among the most important. It helps explain the rise to power of Hugh of Antioch-Lusignan (King Hugh III of Cyprus) and also sheds much light on contemporary legal concepts and procedures.

This collection has been printed three times before: by Labbe in 1651,[1] by La Thaumassière in 1690,[2] and, from La Thaumassière's edition, by Comte Beugnot in 1843.[3] The present edition is based on the text in Codex Vaticanus latinus 4789, an early fifteenth-century manuscript which is the ancestor of all other surviving copies of the collection.[4] This manuscript belonged to James of Floury, count of Jaffa in the second quarter of the fifteenth century,[5] and contains a version of the legal treatise by the thirteenth-century count of Jaffa,

[1] P. Labbe, *L'Abrégé royal de l'alliance chronologique de l'histoire sacrée et profane,* ... *avec le Lignage d'outre-mer, les assises de Jérusalem et un recueil historique de pièces ancienne* (Paris, 1651), i, pp. 514–41.

[2] G. Thaumas de La Thaumassière, *Coustumes de Beauvoisis, par Messire Philippes de Beaumanoir Bailly de Clermont en Beauvoisis. Assises et bons usages du royaume de Jerusalem, par Messire Jean d'Ibelin Comte de Japhe & d'Ascalon, S. de Rames & de Baruth. Et autres anciennes coutumes Le tout tiré des Manuscrits* (Bourges, 1690), pt 1, pp. 195–208.

[3] 'Documents relatifs à la successibilité au trône et à la régence', *R[ecueil des] H[istoriens des] C[roisades.] Lois,* ii, pp. 401–19.

[4] See M. Grandclaude, 'Classement sommaire des manuscrits des principaux livres des Assises de Jérusalem', *Revue historique de droit français et étranger,* sér. 4, v (1926), 450, 462–3, 475; E. Brayer, P. Lemerle, V. Laurent, 'Le Vaticanus latinus 4789: histoire et alliances des Cantacuzènes aux XIVᵉ–XVᵉ siècles', *Revue des études byzantines,* ix (1951), 47–50.

[5] See J. Richard, *Chypre sous les Lusignans. Documents chypriotes des archives du Vatican (XIVᵉ et XVᵉ siècles)* (Paris, 1962), pp. 123–32. Someone, presumably a member of his family or household, has marked all the references to members of the Floury family in the manuscript. See below, p. 28, n. *d* and p. 30, n. *e,* and also fos. cclxxxvᵛ, cclxxxviijʳ, ccxcᵛ, ccxcjʳ.

John of Ibelin, and a fourteenth-century recension of the 'Lignages d'Outremer'. The version of John of Ibelin's treatise is thought to be that commissioned in Cyprus in 1369 to be an official work of reference in the High Court.[6] We are told that various additions were inserted into the treatise at that time,[7] and it would seem that the collection relating to the 1260s was among them. Beugnot appears to have been the first to realize that the materials for the regency disputes were not part of John of Ibelin's original treatise, and he published them separately with three other texts under the title of 'Documents relatifs à la successibilité au trône et à la régence'.[8] It is on his edition that all subsequent scholars have hitherto relied.[9]

The need for a new edition arises from the fact that Labbe and La Thaumassière based theirs on seventeenth-century manuscripts which were markedly inferior to their fifteenth-century prototype. Interest in the work of John of Ibelin had been awakened in France in the early part of the seventeenth century largely through the activities of the distinguished antiquarian and virtuoso, Nicolas-Claude Fabri de Peiresc (1580–1637). In 1627 Peiresc arranged for a copy of Vaticanus latinus 4789 to be made, and this copy is now to be found in the collection of his manuscripts in the Bibliothèque Inguimbertine at Carpentras (MS. Carpentras 1786). Labbe used a copy made from Peiresc's manuscript and La Thaumassière a manuscript at two removes from Labbe's.[10] Grandclaude pointed out that Peiresc's manuscript shows signs of having been executed carelessly,[11] but no one seems to have realized the full extent of its

[6] See Grandclaude, 'Classement sommaire', 450, 453, 462.

[7] John of Ibelin, 'Livre', *RHC. Lois*, i, p. 6.

[8] The 'Documents relatifs' consists of (a) part of the first chapter of the legal treatise by James of Ibelin (*RHC. Lois*, i, pp. 453–4) which had also been inserted into the 1369 version of John of Ibelin's treatise (Cod. Vat. lat. 4789, fo. ccxxxv^r–v); (b) a treatise on the *bailliage* by John of Ibelin (see Grandclaude, 'Classement sommaire', 460 ('un fragment d'une consultation donnée par Jean d'Ibelin'); (c) the materials for the regency disputes of the 1260s (Cod. Vat. lat. 4789, fo. ccxliiij^r–fo. cclxij^v); (d) an account of the accession of King Hugh IV of Cyprus, also from the 1369 version of John of Ibelin's treatise (Cod. Vat. lat. 4789, fo. cclxiij^v–fo. cclxvi^v).

[9] In particular: L. de Mas Latrie, *Histoire de l'île de Chypre sous le règne des princes de la maison de Lusignan* (Paris, 1852–61), i, pp. 339–408, 424–8; J. L. La Monte, *Feudal Monarchy in the Latin Kingdom of Jerusalem, 1100 to 1291* (Cambridge, Mass., 1932), pp. 51, 75–9; G. F. Hill, *A History of Cyprus* (Cambridge, 1940–52), ii, pp. 152–4, 161–3; J. S. C. Riley-Smith, *The Feudal Nobility and the Kingdom of Jerusalem, 1174–1277* (London, 1973), pp. 218–22 and *passim*.

[10] See Grandclaude, 'Classement sommaire', 450–2, 471–4.

[11] Ibid., 451.

defects. It is clear from a comparison of Vaticanus latinus 4789 and Carpentras 1786 that the copyist of the latter deliberately omitted passages from some of the longer chapters, sometimes concealing his omissions with a précis so that the passage still made sense. Beugnot was able to supply the passages omitted from John of Ibelin's treatise from manuscripts of other recensions of that work, but as he had made no use of Vaticanus latinus 4789 he was unaware of the missing passages from the materials for the regency dispute.[12] The value of Beugnot's edition of this collection is further reduced by errors in the transmission of the text between Peiresc's manuscript and La Thaumassière's edition and in Beugnot's own transcription from La Thaumassière.

The materials for the disputes of the 1260s comprise fifteen chapters of which the first nine relate to 1264/6 and the remaining six to 1268. At the end of the last chapter there is a reference to a *vidimus* of documents concerned with the pleading in both disputes, together with some account of what action had been taken. This instrument had been drawn up at the instance of King Hugh III and sealed by the papal legate and other church dignitaries. Probably the contents of the *vidimus* were substantially the same as the collection of materials preserved in our manuscript. If so, the collection dates from Hugh's lifetime, and, as the last chapter describes him as having been crowned king of Jerusalem and enjoying his kingdom in peace, it presumably belongs to the period between his coronation in 1269 and his departure from Acre in 1276. Possibly the account of the proceedings in these disputes was compiled for Hugh's procurators to lay before Pope Gregory X who, in 1272, had cited Hugh to defend himself at the Curia against the claims of Maria of Antioch, the unsuccessful contestant of 1268.[13]

Whether or not the collection of materials was identical with the contents of the *vidimus*, there is no reason to doubt that these documents were assembled as justification for Hugh III's title to the crown of Jerusalem: in both 1264/6 and 1268 he had been recognized by the feudatories, the Military Orders and other important elements in society as the rightful regent; his rule was therefore both legal and popular. But if the collection was intended as propaganda

---

[12] For important instances, see below, pp. 33–4, 36. Beugnot was similarly ignorant of a section from the 'Lignages d'Outremer' also omitted by the copyist of Carpentras 1786. See P. W. Edbury, 'The Ibelin counts of Jaffa: a previously unknown passage from the "Lignages d'Outremer"', *English Historical Review*, lxxxix (1974), 604–9.

[13] See Riley-Smith, *Feudal Nobility*, p. 222.

for Hugh III, the question arises of how far it gives a distorted account of what happened. It is necessary to distinguish two types of material in the collection: what purports to be the verbatim record of the pleading (chapters 1–8 and most of chapters 11, 12, 13 and 14), and the narrative description of the decisions of the court and the political developments (chapters 9, 10, 15 and the rest of 11, 12, 13, 14). There is no evidence whatever that the transcriptions of the pleadings have been tampered with to bolster Hugh's case: in both disputes Hugh used arguments which may not have withstood careful scrutiny, and Hugh of Brienne, his opponent in the earlier dispute, and Maria of Antioch each made points which could well have told against him. Anyone who looked to the speeches made before the High Court rather than to the court's decisions for a justification of Hugh's rights to the throne might not have been convinced. On the other hand, owing to the paucity of independent evidence for these disputes, it is difficult to evaluate the degree to which the narrative parts of the collection give an accurate and unbiased account.

1264/6: Hugh of Antioch-Lusignan (Hugh III) versus Hugh of Brienne

The dispute between Hugh of Antioch-Lusignan and Hugh of Brienne was over who should be regent of Jerusalem on behalf of the young Hugh II of Cyprus who in turn was regent for the titular king, Conradin of Hohenstaufen. Since 1243 legal opinion in Jerusalem had maintained that the regent should be the titular king's nearest heir in the East to claim the regency, the *plus droit heir aparant*. In that year the Hohenstaufen lieutenant had been ejected and Alice of Champagne declared regent. The regency passed to her son, King Henry I of Cyprus, and eventually to his son, Hugh II. Hugh was a minor and so needed a regent to exercise his authority in both Cyprus and Jerusalem. Between 1253, the date of Henry's death, and her own death in 1261, the regent of Cyprus was Hugh's mother, Plaisance of Antioch, and it was Plaisance who in 1258 successfully claimed the regency of Jerusalem on Hugh's behalf. In 1263 Isabella of Lusignan, Hugh's aunt and heir presumptive, acquired the regency of Jerusalem, but in Cyprus, where she had waived her claim, the regent was her son, Hugh of Antioch-Lusignan. In the intervening periods, 1253–58 and 1261–63, the vassals in Jerusalem had chosen one of their own number to act as regent.[14]

[14] For a full discussion, see Riley-Smith, *Feudal Nobility*, pp. 185–98, 209–17, 318–20.

On Isabella's death in 1264[15] Hugh II's next of kin were his two cousins, the sons of his father's sisters. Hugh of Brienne, the son of Maria, the elder sister, was younger than Isabella's son, Hugh of Antioch-Lusignan, and the central issue in their dispute was which of the two was to be regarded as the senior and thus as the *plus droit heir* of Hugh II.

Hugh II would have come of age at about the beginning of 1268.[16] So ostensibly all that was at stake in this dispute was the right to administer the kingdom of Jerusalem for a few years. But what is not known is whether the young king was thought likely to live long enough to be succeeded by children of his own. Had his death been anticipated at the time of the dispute, the outcome would have been all the more important, since whoever was declared to be his closest heir could expect to succeed to the kingdom of Cyprus and be regent of Jerusalem for the absentee Hohenstaufen for an indefinite period. There is no direct evidence, other than the fact of his premature death, to suggest that Hugh was delicate; indeed, despite his youth—he can only have been thirteen at the time— plans for him to marry a daughter of the lord of Beirut were in progress by May 1265,[17] and so presumably his death was not then regarded as imminent. On the other hand, his family seems to have had a record of ill health: both his mother and his grandfather, Hugh I, had died young, and his father had been afflicted with obesity.[18]

Historians have assumed that the dispute between the two cousins followed close on Isabella's death, and so have dated it to 1264. It is possible, however, that this assumption is unfounded. There had been a considerable delay before either Plaisance or Isabella had

---

[15] 'L'estoire de Eracles empereur et la conqueste de la Terre d'Outremer', *RHC. Historiens Occidentaux*, ii, p. 448.

[16] Hugh would have reached his majority on his fifteenth birthday. Both Hugh of Antioch-Lusignan and Maria of Antioch (see below, chaps. 11, 12) stated that he was not of age at the time of his death in November or December 1267. (See below, note 19; also 'Les Lignages d'Outremer', *RHC. Lois*, ii, p. 444.) His birth cannot therefore have been before November/December 1252, but, as his father died on 18 January 1253, it cannot have been later than mid-1253, even allowing for the unsupported possibility that it was posthumous.

[17] Clement IV, *Registre*, ed. E. Jordan (Paris, 1893–1945), no. 882. For the only near-contemporary statement that the marriage actually took place, see 'Lignages', p. 444.

[18] Plaisance of Antioch's parents were married in 1234 ('Annales de Terre Sainte', ed. R. Röhricht and G. Raynaud, *Archives de l'Orient latin*, ii (1884), pt 2, p. 439), and so presumably she cannot have been aged more than about twenty-five at the time of her death in 1261. Hugh I died aged twenty-three. See Hill, *History of Cyprus*, ii, p. 82. For Henry I as Henry 'Gras', see 'Documents relatifs à la successibilité', p. 420; 'Les Gestes des Chiprois', *RHC. Documents Arméniens*, ii, pp. 670, 741, 756, 769.

claimed the regency, and there may have been a similar delay after the death of Isabella. The earliest, and indeed the only, reference before Hugh II's death late in 1267[19] to Hugh of Antioch-Lusignan as regent of both Cyprus and Jerusalem is in a letter of May 1267,[20] but in a papal letter of February 1266 and in the narrative accounts of the events of 1265 and 1266 he is described solely as regent of Cyprus.[21] The letter of May 1267 mentioned the dispute in a manner which suggests that it had not arisen recently and, in fact, could be construed as meaning that the dispute had taken place three years earlier, but in the absence of more conclusive evidence the possibility that the dispute belongs to 1265 or 1266 must remain.

Whatever the merits of Hugh of Antioch-Lusignan's legal claim to be regent, there can be little doubt that from a purely political point of view he was the more attractive candidate. At the time of the dispute he was already regent of Cyprus and he proved himself ready to use Cypriot military resources in the defence of Latin Syria: in 1265 he brought 130 knights as well as mounted sergeants and squires to Acre, and in the following year he was accompanied by a 'mout belle compaignie de gens d'armes, chevaliers et autres'.[22] Furthermore, he was closely allied by ties of blood to influential figures. His father, Henry of Antioch, was uncle of the then prince of Antioch and in 1263–4 had been associated with his wife in the regency of Jerusalem;[23] Hugh's own wife, to whom he had been married or at least betrothed since 1255,[24] was a member of the Ibelin family and so was closely related to several of the leading nobles in the Latin Kingdom. Hugh of Brienne, on the other hand, had no near relatives in the East to whom he might look for support,[25] and although he is said to have given what military help he

---

[19] The sources vary as to the exact date: November 1267 ('Eracles', p. 456; 'Gestes', p. 769; Marino Sanudo, 'Liber secretorum fidelium crucis', ed. J. Bongars, *Gesta Dei per Francos* (Hanover, 1611), ii, p. 223) and 5 December 1267 ('Annales', p. 453 (wrongly naming him Henry); 'Chronique d'Amadi', ed. R. de Mas Latrie, *Chroniques d'Amadi et de Strambaldi* (Paris, 1891–3), i, p. 209).

[20] *Thesaurus novus anecdotorum*, ed. E. Martène and U. Durand (Paris, 1717), i, cols. 1013–14.

[21] Clement IV, no. 838; 'Annales', p. 452; 'Eracles', pp. 450, 455; 'Gestes', pp. 759, 766; Marino Sanudo, p. 222; 'Amadi', p. 207. See Hill, *History of Cyprus*, ii, p. 154.

[22] 'Gestes', pp. 759, 766. See also 'Eracles', pp. 450, 455.

[23] See Riley-Smith, *Feudal Nobility*, p. 217.

[24] Alexander IV, *Registre*, ed. C. Bourel de la Roncière *et al.* (Paris, 1895–1959), no. 71.

[25] His mother's relations were all equally closely related to Hugh of Antioch-Lusignan. On his father's side his nearest relative in the East seems to have been his second cousin, Julian of Sidon. See W. H. Rüdt-Collenberg, *The Rupenides*,

The royal house of Jerusalem to illustrate the disputes of the 1260s

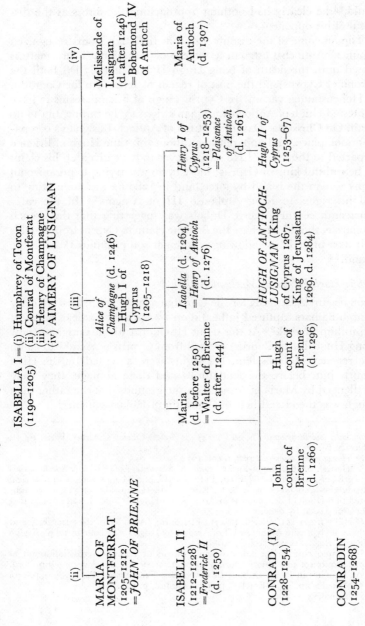

Note: names in capitals—kings and queens of Jerusalem.
names in italics—regents of Jerusalem.

could,[26] he clearly had nothing approaching the forces at the disposal of his opponent.

The outcome of the dispute was that the High Court recognized Hugh of Antioch-Lusignan as regent of Jerusalem. There matters rested until the death of King Hugh II late in 1267 left both the throne of Cyprus and the post of regent of Jerusalem for Conradin of Hohenstaufen vacant. In Cyprus Hugh of Brienne seems to have contested Hugh of Antioch-Lusignan's right to the throne, but to no avail. On Christmas Day 1267 Hugh of Antioch-Lusignan's coronation took place, and apparently at about this time Hugh of Brienne departed to the West.[27] He seems never to have given up his claim to be rightful king of Cyprus; in 1275 he was trying to organize an army to win the island by force, and in 1289 he was attempting to sell his rights to King Alphonso III of Aragon.[28] In the early fourteenth century, Pierre Dubois was suggesting that the French monarchy should purchase the Brienne claim to Cyprus from Hugh's heir as a prelude to endowing a younger son of Philip IV with the island.[29]

1268: Hugh III versus Maria of Antioch

1268 began disastrously for the Christians in the Latin East: in early March Baibars captured Jaffa and on 15 April the castle of Beaufort fell to him as well.[30] At this point Hugh of Antioch-Lusignan (now King Hugh III of Cyprus) crossed from Cyprus to Acre[31] to claim the regency of Jerusalem. His rights were accepted by the High Court, but, before the feudatories had done homage, they were challenged by Maria of Antioch on the grounds that she rather than Hugh was the closest heir of Conradin of Hohenstaufen.

Hethumides and Lusignans. The Structure of the Armeno-Cilician Dynasties (Paris, 1963), table IX(B).

[26] Thesaurus novus anecdotorum, i, col. 1014.

[27] 'Gestes', p. 769. Ibn al-Furāt (Ayyubids, Mamlukes and Crusaders: Selections from the Tārīkh al-Duwal wa'l Mulūk, ed. and trans. U. and M. C. Lyons, with historical introduction and notes by J. S. C. Riley-Smith (Cambridge, 1971), ii, p. 129) stated that Hugh of Brienne was in Armenia on Hugh II's death and implied that his claim passed by default.

[28] Hill, History of Cyprus, ii, p. 171; E. Lourie, 'An offer of the suzerainty and escheat of Cyprus to Alphonso III of Aragon by Hugh de Brienne in 1289', English Historical Review, lxxxiv (1969), 101–8.

[29] 'Opinio cujusdam suadentis regi Francie ut regnum Jerosolimitanum et Cipri acquireret pro altero filiorum suorum, ac de invasione regni Egipti', ed. C.-V. Langlois in Pierre Dubois, De recuperatione Terre Sancte, (Paris, 1891), p. 140.

[30] 'Annales', p. 453; 'Eracles', p. 456; 'Gestes', p. 771.

[31] 'Annales', p. 453.

Most historians have ascribed the pleading as recorded in our documents to the period following Conradin's death in October 1268 and have assumed that it concerned not the regency of Jerusalem but the throne.[32] The internal evidence of the pleading, however, proves that this view is erroneous: at the end of chapter nine it is stated that Maria of Antioch was claiming the regency (*bailliage*) in her subsequent speech (chapter twelve); in his reply to Maria (chapter thirteen) Hugh also referred to the *bailliage* and spoke of Conradin as if he were still alive, while in chapter eleven he had made it clear that it was the death of Hugh II that had precipitated the claim. Furthermore, Hugh's remarks at the beginning of chapter eleven concerning his arrival in Acre in response to messages about the perilous state of the kingdom would belong more naturally to 1268 than to 1269, an uneventful year, and the fact that Geoffrey of Sergines was still prominent may also suggest that our account of the dispute pre-dated the arrival of the news of Conradin's execution. Geoffrey died on 11 April 1269; if the pleading had been for the throne, the problem then arises as to why, if Hugh were accepted as king before that date, his coronation should have been delayed until 24 September.[33] It is not hard to see why historians have been misled: we know from other sources that following Conradin's death Maria claimed the throne,[34] and the recorded pleading has been seen as a transcript of the proceedings at that time. In fact it is now clear that Maria claimed first the regency and then the throne. Our documents themselves are misleading in places. The rubric to chapter ten speaks of Hugh's coronation as king of Jerusalem, but it is clear from the context of the chapter that it ought properly to refer to his coronation as king of Cyprus. The only other place where Hugh's coronation is referred to is in the last chapter, and there the context does not necessarily indicate that it followed directly on the pleading. It is true that both Hugh and Maria spoke of claiming the kingdom, but both were concerned with lordship over Jerusalem rather than with the crown. Thus Hugh asked to be received as the 'seignor de ce royaume' (chapter eleven) while

[32] See La Monte, *Feudal Monarchy*, p. 77. Mas Latrie (*Histoire de Chypre*, i, p. 424 and n. 4) thought that the pleading pre-dated Conradin's death but was for the throne of Jerusalem. Riley-Smith (pp. 220–1 and nn. 173, 177–8) has interpreted chapter 11 as relating to the regency of Jerusalem and belonging to the period before Conradin's death and chapters 12–15 as relating to the throne and belonging to the period after Conradin's death.
[33] 'Annales', p. 454; 'Eracles', p. 457. Hugh III may have been crowned king of Cyprus as little as three weeks after the death of Hugh II.
[34] See below, p. 11 and n. 41.

Maria asked for the 'seignorie de Jerusalem' (chapter twelve). As has recently been demonstrated, this terminology was characteristic of regency for an absentee and uncrowned king who had reached his majority,[35] and so, far from indicating that the parties were disputing the accession to the throne, it is perhaps further evidence that they were claiming the regency.

As in his dispute with Hugh of Brienne, there is little doubt that in 1268 Hugh III was regarded as being the more suitable candidate. We have seen that he could provide military assistance from Cyprus, and this consideration alone would have weighed heavily in a year which had already seen the loss of Jaffa and Beaufort and which was to see the collapse of the principality of Antioch. Hugh was already experienced in government and capable of providing what had been lacking for so long: strong rule and, in all likelihood, a stable dynasty. Maria on the other hand was over forty and unmarried.[36] It is not known whether she already intended to sell her rights to Charles of Anjou,[37] but the prospect of her rule cannot have been attractive. There can be no questioning Hugh's popularity in 1268. Even the two main groups which were later to give their backing to Charles, the Templars and the French garrison at Acre, were behind him at this stage. The Templars do not seem to have broken with him decisively until after William of Beaujeu, a relative of the French royal house and former Templar commander of Sicily, had been elected master of the Order in 1273.[38] The commander of the French garrison in 1268 was Geoffrey of Sergines, who, as seneschal of Jerusalem, apparently presided over the hearing and was the first to do homage. After Geoffrey's death Hugh evidently remained on good terms with the French, appointing as seneschal Robert of Crésèques and as marshal William of Canet, the nephew of Geoffrey's successor as commander of the garrison.[39]

---

[35] See Riley-Smith, *Feudal Nobility*, p. 188.   [36] 'Gestes', p. 773.

[37] Hugh was said to be in fear of Charles as early as 1268 (Ibn al-Furāt, ii, p. 130).

[38] See J. Richard, *Le royaume latin de Jérusalem* (Paris, 1953), p. 327; M. L. Bulst-Thiele, *Sacrae Domus Militiae Templi Hierosolymitani Magistri: Untersuchungen zur Geschichte des Templerordens 1118/19–1314* (Göttingen, 1974), pp. 259–60, 263–5. See also 'Gestes', p. 779. There is some evidence that the Templars gave Maria support earlier ('Gestes', p. 773), but as late as June 1271, Thomas Berard, master of the Temple, witnessed a document in which Hugh III was described as king of both Jerusalem and Cyprus (*Cartulaire général de l'ordre des Hospitaliers de S. Jean de Jérusalem (1100–1310)*, ed. J. Delaville Le Roulx (Paris, 1894–1906), no. 3422).

[39] For Geoffrey of Sergines and the French garrison, see Richard, *Le royaume latin*, pp. 297–8. For Robert of Crésèques and William of Canet, see *Cartulaire général*, nos. 3323, 3326; 'Eracles', pp. 458, 463; 'Gestes', p. 767.

With the execution of Conradin of Hohenstaufen by Charles of Anjou on 29 October 1268, the legitimate descent from Frederick II and Queen Isabella II of Jerusalem came to an end. Hugh was accepted as the rightful king of Jerusalem and was crowned in Tyre on 24 September 1269.[40] Whether Maria challenged his rights to the throne in the High Court is unclear, but she certainly asked the patriarch of Jerusalem for coronation, had a clerk interrupt Hugh's coronation with a protest on her behalf, and appealed to Rome.[41] Although the accounts of the regency disputes may have been assembled by Hugh III in combating her case at the papal curia and the subsequent sale of her rights to Charles of Anjou,[42] these later developments fall outside their scope.

Pleading and legality

However much Hugh of Antioch-Lusignan may have struck his contemporaries as the more suitable candidate for the regency and ultimately the throne of Jerusalem than either Hugh of Brienne or Maria of Antioch, it was important that his rule should be seen to be legitimate. In both 1264/6 and 1268 due legal process was followed. The High Court was convened and on each occasion the vassals were joined by representatives of the clergy, military orders, Italian communes and burgess confraternities. Although in 1264/6 and perhaps in 1268 the other groups were allowed some part in the discussion, the operative decision was made by the vassals in private. In 1268 and presumably in 1264/6 Hugh then swore the customary oath for a regent on taking up his appointment[43] and the vassals did homage. Before any decision could be reached there had to be the formal pleading in which the claims and counter-claims were stated. In 1264/6 the protagonists each spoke four times and their speeches are, so far as the Latin East is concerned, a unique example of legal dialectic. In 1268 the pleading was less formalized, with Maria's speech apparently following Hugh's initial claim after some delay and Hugh's second speech terminating the public debate. Just as the procedures for recognizing the regent had to be correct for the regent's power to be regarded as legitimate, so what was said in the pleading mattered since it was on that that legally the decision recognizing his rights to the regency rested. Much of the interest of

[40] 'Annales', p. 454; 'Eracles', p. 457.
[41] Gregory X, *Registre*, ed. J. Guiraud and L. Cadier (Paris, 1892–1960), no. 103; 'Gestes', p. 773; 'Amadi', p. 211. See Riley-Smith, *Feudal Nobility*, p. 222.
[42] See above, p. 4. See Riley-Smith, *Feudal Nobility*, pp. 222–8.
[43] For a description of this oath, see John of Ibelin, p. 312.

these materials for the disputes of the 1260s lies in the way in which they reveal the grounds on which the claimants based their cases and, following from this, the extent to which the pleas and the eventual outcome on each occasion conformed with existing precedents and legal theory.

In 1264/6 three contradictory legal principles, backed up by subsidiary arguments based on precedents, were adduced by the contenders. Hugh of Antioch-Lusignan argued that he was the *plus droit heir* because he was the elder of the two claimants in the same degree of relationship to Hugh II; he also argued that he should be regent because he was descended from the previous regent. Hugh of Brienne's case was based on the assertion that he was Hugh II's *plus droit heir* because his branch of the family was senior to that of his opponent. Only the first of these arguments was upheld by the court, but all three deserve examination, if only to draw attention to the extent to which the two cousins were confused in their own thinking and in their use of precedents.

In the thirteenth century the feudal jurists of the Latin East were agreed that fiefs were to be inherited by the closest heir of the last in seisin and the *bailliage* of fiefs of a minor heir was to be held, if both parents were dead, by the closest adult heir.[44] Despite precedents which pointed to the contrary,[45] both Hugh of Antioch-Lusignan, in his principal argument, and Hugh of Brienne accepted the premiss that the regency was to be settled in accordance with these rules. The difference of opinion arose over the question of how who was the closest heir should be determined. Hugh of Antioch-Lusignan argued that for male heirs in the same relationship to the last in seisin the eldest inherited; just as an elder brother would inherit in preference to a younger brother, so he, as the elder cousin, should inherit in preference to the younger cousin.[46] In support of this contention he asserted that there were numerous precedents, but he only referred to three specifically: two, a case involving a certain Hugh of Masaire at Sidon and another in which Walter of Floury was given the hereditary marshalcy of Tiberias in preference to Elias Charles, were not discussed in detail,[47] but the third, the

[44] See Riley-Smith, *Feudal Nobility*, pp. 14–16, 38.

[45] See below, pp. 16–17.

[46] These views were repeated by John of Ibelin (pp. 224–5) and Geoffrey Le Tor ('Livre', *RHC. Lois*, i, pp. 435–6). See Riley-Smith, *Feudal Nobility*, p. 219.

[47] A Hugh of 'Mazelria' witnessed a charter issued by Balian of Sidon in 1228 (*Regesta Regni Hierosolymitani* (*MXCVII–MCCXCI*), compiled by R. Röhricht (Innsbruck, 1893, 1904), no. 986). He was probably the Hugh of 'Mazarea' who was a vassal of the lord of Beirut in 1223 (ibid., no. 963). Walter of Floury is known

succession to the lordship of Tiberias, seems to have been of considerable importance for him. In 1241 Richard of Cornwall had secured the return of Tiberias which had been held by the Muslims since 1187.[48] In keeping with the normal rules of inheritance in such cases,[49] the heir was the closest relative of the last in seisin, Eschiva of Bures. She and her four sons, Hugh, William, Otto and Ralph of Tiberias, had all died before 1241, and so the question was which of Eschiva's grandchildren should inherit. Two contenders emerged: Eschiva, the daughter of Otto of Tiberias, and her cousin, also named Eschiva, the daughter of Ralph. Ralph had been younger than Otto, but his daughter was the elder of the two women,[50] and, largely on the advice of Philip of Montfort, it was to Ralph's daughter that Tiberias passed. Thus Hugh of Antioch-Lusignan could argue that the principle had been established that an elder cousin should inherit even when a member of a more junior branch of the family. Hugh of Brienne could only reply that this case did not constitute a true judicial precedent, since the point at issue had not been settled by *esgart* of court; apparently Eschiva, daughter of Otto, had withdrawn her claim on learning of the body of opinion against her.

Hugh of Brienne claimed that he should hold the regency because his mother was older than his opponent's. In effect he was claiming that when there were two contenders for an inheritance or *bailliage* who were in the same degree of relationship to the last in seisin, the principle of successoral representation should be applied. Had she lived, his mother, Maria, would have been Hugh II's heir; as all members of that generation of the family were now dead, he was the next heir as the representative of the senior line in the female descent. In principle, successoral representation as a custom governing the inheritance to fiefs was rejected in the Latin East, being denied by men as diverse as the author of the 'Livre au Roi' writing *c.* 1200 and the Cypriot ambassadors to the papal court in 1360.[51] Hugh of

---

from a document of 1233, though without the title of Marshal (ibid., no. 1046). A John of Floury, marshal of Tiberias, is known from documents of 1261, 1262 and 1269 (ibid., nos. 1297a, 1322, 1370; and see no. 1259). Elias Charles, a vassal of the lord of Caesarea, is known from documents of 1253 and 1255 (ibid., nos. 1210, 1233, 1238). [48] See Richard, *Le royaume latin*, p. 253.
[49] For the custom when seisin had been interrupted by Moslem occupation, see Riley-Smith, *Feudal Nobility*, pp. 15–16.
[50] For the family's genealogy, see 'Lignages', p. 455.
[51] 'Le Livre au Roi', *RHC. Lois*, i, p. 630; Leontios Makhairas, *Recital concerning the Sweet Land of Cyprus entitled 'Chronicle'*, ed. and trans. R. M. Dawkins (Oxford, 1932), i, para. 106.

Brienne's strongest supporting argument was from a Cypriot precedent involving members of the Beduin family. On this occasion a younger cousin in the senior line had inherited in preference to an elder cousin in the junior line and the validity of the case as a precedent was emphasized by the fact that the defeated party had lost even though his counsel had been the distinguished jurist, Philip of Novara. Hugh of Antioch-Lusignan's riposte was that there had been a miscarriage of justice, and he tried to argue that a more telling precedent from Cyprus was the *conoissance* by which he had been made regent in 1261 and so accepted as Hugh II's heir. In turn, Hugh of Brienne stated that he had deliberately allowed his rights to pass by default in 1261 and so the *conoissance* was irrelevant to the present debate. Of perhaps greater interest is another supporting argument employed by Hugh of Brienne, this time from French customary law: the Kingdom of Jerusalem had been conquered by Frenchmen who had brought with them their own institutions; Jerusalemite institutions should therefore accord with those in France; in France the dispute would be settled by the principles described by Hugh, and in consequence he should have the regency. Specious though this argument may seem, a similar interpretation of the origins and nature of Jerusalemite law seems to have been shared by at least one contemporary, James of Ibelin, and so perhaps it was widely held at that time.[52] In support of his contention, Hugh of Brienne had cited the twelfth-century example of the count of Sancerre's advice being accepted in a case involving the division of a fief among heiresses. The case may have been a *cause célèbre*—it was also referred to by Philip of Novara[53]—but, as Hugh of Antioch-Lusignan pointed out, it did not prove the superiority of French law over that of Jerusalem, only that in the absence of a suitable precedent the High Court could seek advice from elsewhere—advice which anyway would not be binding.

Hugh of Antioch-Lusignan's other argument, that he should have the regency because his immediate ancestor, his mother, had held it, is of interest because, as will be seen, it raised problems concerning the precedents for the succession to the regency during the previous quarter of a century, and was to reappear in a slightly different form in his dispute with Maria of Antioch. Hugh of Brienne pointed out that this argument was incorrect as *bailliage* was not

[52] 'Document relatif au service militaire', *RHC. Lois*, ii, p. 431. See Riley-Smith, *Feudal Nobility*, p. 140.
[53] Philip of Novara, 'Livre', *RHC. Lois*, i, p. 542.

heritable, and, given the premiss that the rules for determining who should hold the *bailliage* of fiefs and who should have the regency of the kingdom were identical, he was right.[54] Hugh of Antioch-Lusignan seems to have conceded this point, since he did not use the argument in his later speeches, but he then appears to have assumed that Hugh of Brienne based his claim upon it. Instead of recognizing that he was thinking in terms of successoral representation, he evidently thought that Hugh of Brienne was arguing that as his mother would have had the regency had she lived, he should have it by inheritance from her. Because of this confusion, Hugh of Antioch-Lusignan's counter-arguments lacked the force they might otherwise have had.

Turning now to the 1268 dispute, we find that Maria of Antioch too based her arguments on the premiss that right to the regency should be determined on the same principles as right to the *bailliage* of the fiefs of a minor heir. Her claim rested squarely on the fact that she was Conradin's *plus droit heir*: her relationship to him was one degree closer than Hugh's, and, indeed, she was the only surviving descendant of Queen Isabella I of Jerusalem of her generation. Quite rightly she also pointed out that she was the closest relative in the East of Isabella II, the wife of Frederick II, who was the last queen of Jerusalem to have had seisin of the kingdom. The genealogical information on which her case rested was stated accurately, and her speech, which had evidently been carefully prepared, is a model of lucidity. By contrast, Hugh III's two speeches were loosely worded and obscure in their argumentation. His first speech is that of a man who was not anticipating any contradiction, and his second is clearly a spontaneous reply delivered immediately after Maria's speech had been read. In both it is clear that he based his claim on his relationship to Hugh II; he had been recognized as Hugh's heir, had held the regency for him in his minority, and now that he had died should have it in his own right. This argument explains both the relevance of the earlier dispute to that of 1268, for it was then that Hugh III was accepted as his cousin's heir, and why the account of the earlier dispute should later have been used together with the account of the 1268 dispute in justification of Hugh's position as king of Jerusalem. As for Maria's claim, it was brushed aside as misconceived; either Hugh had not understood it, or, more likely, he deliberately distorted it; he wrongly asserted that Maria was claiming that Conradin was the last in seisin of the kingdom and

[54] See Geoffrey Le Tor, p. 436.

then poured scorn on the whole idea of claiming by inheritance from the Hohenstaufen.

It is at once clear that the legal arguments which determined the outcome of these two disputes were incompatible. In 1264/6 the High Court accepted Hugh of Antioch-Lusignan as regent 'pource quil estoit ainsnes dou conte de Braine'.[55] In other words it had upheld the plea that he, the elder of the cousins of Hugh II, was the young king's *plus droit heir* and so should be regent; the ideas that he should be regent as his mother's heir, or that Hugh of Brienne should be regent as the representative heir, through his mother, of Hugh II were rejected; the premiss that the right to be regent was determined in the same way as the right to hold the *bailliage* of fiefs had been vindicated. In 1268, however, the court passed over a plea argued on the basis of the successful premiss of a few years earlier: instead of allowing a claim on the grounds of closeness of relationship to the person for whom the regency was to be held, it appears to have allowed a claim on the basis of relationship to the previous regent. Exactly what happened at the hearing in 1268 is not clear. After Maria had had her deposition read for her and had heard Hugh's reply, she withdrew. When the vassals came to announce their decision, she would not return to the court, and, in delivering their verdict, their spokesman, James Vidal, perhaps implied that the vassals were awarding the regency to Hugh because Maria had thereby not presented her case properly. This could indicate that the vassals recognized the justice of Maria's claim but had seized on this as a legal loophole to circumvent it.[56]

Before we jump to the conclusion that whereas the 1264/6 dispute was resolved by a fair decision, the 1268 dispute ended in a travesty of justice, it is necessary to examine the precedents. There had been two occasions before 1264, in 1246 and in 1253, when a regent other than a parent had died while exercising the office. In 1243 when Conrad of Hohenstaufen came of age and the vassals decided to use his majority as an excuse for setting aside the regency of his father, Frederick II, Conrad's closest relative in the East was his great-aunt, Alice of Champagne, the eldest surviving half-sister of his grandmother, Maria of Montferrat. Alice was declared regent, and she held the regency until her death three years later.[57] At the time of her death Conrad's closest relative in the East was her half-sister, Melissende of Lusignan, the widow of Bohemond IV, but, although

---

[55] See below, p. 41.
[56] See Riley-Smith, *Feudal Nobility*, p. 222.   [57] Ibid., pp. 210–12.

Melissende tried to put in a claim,[58] the regency passed to Alice's son, King Henry I of Cyprus. Henry died in 1253, but the regency was not awarded to any member of the Jerusalemite royal family until 1258 when it was given to Henry's son, the infant Hugh II. We do not know the date of Melissende's death, but even assuming she were already dead there were several people in the East in 1258 who, though they may not have appeared in the High Court to claim the regency, were more closely related to the Hohenstaufen. Henry I's surviving sister, Isabella, and his cousin, Maria of Antioch, the daughter of Melissende, were one degree closer than Hugh II, and if the principle expressed by Hugh of Antioch-Lusignan in 1264/6 that the eldest cousin in the same degree of relationship should be recognized as the closer relative had been followed, then both he and the sons of his aunt Maria would have taken precedence over the young king.[59] Thus in 1246 and 1258 the new regent was not the closest relative of the titular king, but, so it would seem, the closest relative of the previous regent. And so when in 1264/6 Hugh of Antioch-Lusignan asserted that he should have the regency from his mother, the previous regent, and when in 1268 he claimed the regency as the heir of Hugh II, his thinking could well have been influenced by these earlier cases. Although theory and precedent may have pointed in different directions, precedent, it might be argued, was on his side.

The most telling objection to this hypothesis is the fact that at no point did Hugh of Antioch-Lusignan make any explicit reference to the precedents of 1246 or 1258. His reasons can only be surmised. In 1264/6 he probably realized that, irrespective of precedents, the doctrine that the regency was to be settled by the *bailliage* rules, including the provision that the *bailliage* was not heritable, was strongly held, and he was content to accept this principle since its logical outcome was that he would win. On the other hand, there may have been good reasons for not arguing from these precedents if in fact the thinking behind the 1246 and 1258 decisions was more sophisticated than I have hitherto suggested. Unfortunately we have no direct evidence for the arguments actually used on these occasions, and political considerations may have been more persuasive than legal principles: Henry's acceptance in 1246 seems to have been

---

[58] Innocent IV, *Registre*, ed. E. Berger (Paris, 1881–1919), no. 4427. See Riley-Smith, *Feudal Nobility*, p. 212.

[59] Maria's elder son, John, was evidently in the West at this period ('Catalogue d'actes des comtes de Brienne, 950–1356', compiled by H. d'Arbois de Jubainville, *Bibliothèque de l'École des Chartes*, xxxiii (1872), nos. 174–82).

accompanied by lavish bribes, and Hugh's can be seen as the result of a political manœuvre inspired by his mother, Plaisance of Antioch, and her lover, John count of Jaffa, and should be understood in the context of the war of St Sabas.[60] Instead of making what at first sight seems to be the simplest assumption, that Henry I and Hugh II, like Hugh of Antioch-Lusignan in 1268, claimed the regency as the heirs of the previous regents, let us suppose that the principle of successoral representation was applied on these occasions: the descendants of Alice of Champagne would thus have taken precedence over the more junior line of Melissende and her daughter, and the son of Henry I, the descendant in the male line, would have taken precedence over Henry's sisters and their children. By applying this principle, Henry I would rightly have become regent in 1246 and Hugh II would have been next in line. Had these arguments been used in 1246 or 1258, Hugh of Antioch-Lusignan would have hesitated to refer to these earlier events in 1264/6 since his opponent, Hugh of Brienne, was the representative heir of Hugh II at that time. As has been seen, Hugh of Brienne did argue with reference to successoral representation. Admittedly he made no use of these instances as precedents, but the fact that he thought that representation could be applied to the succession to the regency suggests that the principle may have had some currency. Whatever the truth, the decision of 1264/6 ruled out any further appeal to this principle, and so when in 1268 Hugh of Antioch-Lusignan found the arguments which had turned to his advantage in the previous dispute used against him, there was no possibility of his posing as Conradin's representative heir in the East. Instead he resorted to the crude and distinctly dubious claim that he should be regent because he was the heir of the previous regent; presumably he was relying on his political backing to overcome the legal obstacles.

The problem of trying to reconstruct the arguments which may have been considered or rejected by the protagonists and their advisers is that we can never be sure how widely a particular legal principle was accepted or how heavily an individual precedent may have weighed. Close examination increases the apparent complexity of these disputes and we do not know how much contemporaries were aware of some of the finer points. If we accept the validity of the arguments upheld in 1264/6, 1268 saw the triumph of expediency over legality. But how far the outcome of the 1264/6 dispute ac-

[60] See Riley-Smith, *Feudal Nobility*, pp. 214–17.

corded with the earlier precedents and the arguments which may have determined their consequences is another matter. While an outward semblance of legal propriety was maintained, constitutional considerations could be manipulated to ensure that on each occasion the more suitable candidate emerged victorious.

The text of the account of the regency disputes of 1264/6 and 1268 occupies fos. ccxliiij^r–cclxij^v of Vaticanus latinus 4789. It has not been thought necessary to collate this manuscript with any of the seventeenth-century copies since, as has already been remarked, they are all derived from it. But because so many historians have discussed these disputes using Beugnot's edition, the 'Documents relatifs', his page and chapter numbers and the more important of the missing phrases and longer passages have been noted. Editorial emendations to the text have been kept to a minimum, but capitalization and punctuation have been modernized.

I am most grateful to Mgr Charles Burns, *archivista* at the Archivio Segreto Vaticano, for his kindness in obtaining microfilm of Vaticanus latinus 4789 and for securing permission to print this section from it. Thanks are also due to Dr L. H. Butler, Dr R. C. Smail, and Mr A. B. Hunt for their advice and assistance, and, above all, to Professor J. S. C. Riley-Smith. It was he who first introduced me to the disputes of the 1260s and his help and encouragement have been of enormous value in undertaking this publication.

[1]* Ces sont les erremens dou roi Huge[1] et dou conte de Braine[2] sur le fait dou bailliage dou royaume de Jerusalem, et tout premier ce est le dit dou roy Hugue.[a]

'Seignors, il est chose certaine que la royne Aalis,[3] mayole, fu dame de ce royaume, et lot et tint et en usa come dame, et morut saisie et tenant come de son droit. Et quant Dieu ot fait son comandement de li, ce royaume eschei a mon oncle, le roy Henri,[4] qui fu son fis, si lot et tint et usa come seignor, et morut saisi et tenant come de son droit. Et quant Dieu ot fait son comandement de lui, ce royaume eschei a mon seignor Hugue,[5] son fis, nostre petit seignor, que Dieu creisse en bien, et ce mon dit oncle neust heu heir de sa feme espouse lors qui[l] morut, fust escheu ce royaume a madame ma mere[6] com a son droit heir. Mais pource que il eschei au dit Hugue, la royne Plaisance,[7] sa mere, pour ce quil estoit merme daage, ot le bailliage de ce royaume par lusage doudit royame pour le droit de son dit fis. Et quant Dieu fist son comandement de la dite royne Plaisance, le dit bailliage vint a ma dame ma mere, qui fu fille de la royne Aalis et seur dou roy Henri et ante doudit Hugue, [b]come a celle a qui ce royaume fust escheu com a plus droit heir doudit Hugue cil[b] fust mesavenu de lui. Et la raison en est clere, car il est us ou costume ou assise en ce royaume, (fo. ccxliiij[v]) quant heir merme daage na pere ou mere qui puisse tenir son bailliage, que le plus droit heir et le plus prochain de ces parens, qui sont en vie, a qui cescheete doie escheir, a la garde et le bailliage de ces biens devant tous autres gens quant il les requiert, et avoir les doit, car il auroit leritage ce il escheoit. Et pource madame ma mere, qui estoit le plus droit heir

---

[a] MS. chap. ccxcij (Beugnot, chap. iii, pp. 401–2).
[b] The words come a celle . . . doudit Huge c[il] omitted by Beugnot.

---

* Archivio Segreto Vaticano, Codex Vaticanus latinus 4789, fo. ccxliiij[r].
[1] Hugh of Antioch-Lusignan, regent of Cyprus (1261–7), regent of Jerusalem (1264/6–9), king of Cyprus (as Hugh III, 1267–84), king of Jerusalem (1269–84).
[2] Hugh, count of Brienne (1261–96), count of Lecce (1271–96).
[3] Alice of Champagne, wife of King Hugh I of Cyprus, regent of Jerusalem (1243–6).
[4] Henry I, king of Cyprus (1218–53), regent of Jerusalem (1246–53).
[5] Hugh II, king of Cyprus (1253–67), titular regent of Jerusalem (1258–67).
[6] Isabella of Lusignan, daughter of Hugh I of Cyprus and Alice of Champagne, regent of Jerusalem (1263–4).
[7] Plaisance, daughter of Bohemond V of Antioch, third wife of Henry I, regent of Cyprus (1253–61), regent of Jerusalem (on behalf of her son, 1258–61); died 1261.

et la plus prochaine de parente doudit Hugue a avoir [le]scheete
de ce royaume, requist li et monseignor mon pere[8] le bailliage de ce
royaume, et lorent et tindrent et en userent tant come elle vesqui
com de leur droit. Et puis que Dieu ot fait son comandement de li,
je, qui sui son fis et son droit heir et cousin germain doudit Hugue,
sui venus en ce royame com en mon droit. Et vous fais assavoir que
je sui le plus droit heir et le plus prochain parent dou monseignor
Huge, mon cousin, a avoir et tenir le bailliage de ce royaume, qui
est sien, jusques a son parfait aage, et di coment: car je entens que
il est us ou coustume ou raison en ce royaume que, quant aucune
escheete deritage ou de bailliage [eschiet][a] a plusors parens, qui sont
en un degre de parente a celui ou a celle de par cui lescheete leur
vient, de celle part dont elle muet, que lainsne de ceaus qui sont en
vie la pardevant les mainsnes, ce il la requiert. Et ce est clere chose,
que enci doie estre, car par lassise ne lusage de ce royaume fie ne
seignorie qui eschee ne se part entre freres ne entre autres parens
masles ains le doit tout avoir lun deaus, cest assavoir, lainsne de
ceaus qui sont en vie devant tous les autres parens, se il le requiert;
que trop seroit fort chose et estrange, que de ceaus qui sont en un
degre de parente le mainsne heritast devant lainsne (fo. ccxlv[r]) la
ou lainsne le requeist, ne onques navint en ce royaume, ne i avendra,
se Dieu plaist, que seroit contre lassise et lusage de ce royaume et
tort apert. Et je di que je sui lainsne de tous les parens qui sont en
vie de monseignor Hugue, mondit cousin, a qui lescheete de ce
royaume peut escheir, qui soient desendus a nostre dite ayole, et
pource est il clere chose selonc raison ou lusage de ce royaume, que
je sui son plus prochain parent et son plus droit heir, si com je ai
devant dit, a avoir son bailliage de ce royaume. Que fis ou fille
demore en saisine ou en teneure de ce dont son pere ou sa mere
meurt saisi et tenant com de son droit. Et puis que enci est,
dont est il clere chose a conoistre a chascun, que ce bailliage est
mon droit par les raisons que je ai dites: que aces est clere chose et
seue que ma dame mamere morut saisie et tenant de ce bailliage
com de son droit, et que je sui lainsne des parents dou mon cousin
si com je ai dit. Pour quoi je doi avoir le bailliage de ce royaume
devant tous autres, com celui qui sui le plus droit heir dou dit
Hugue a avoir cescheete, si le veulle avoir, et pour toutes les raisons

---

[a] *Suggested by Beugnot.*

---

[8] Henry of Antioch, a younger son of Bohemond IV, died 1276.

que je ais dites, ou pour aucunes delles, ^ase vous conoisses que je
avoir le doie; et^a ce vous conoisses que je le doie avoir, je en euffre a
faire ce que je doi com baill, faisant lon a moi ce que lon doit com a
baill.'

[2]   Ce est le dit dou conte de Braine apres ce que le baill[9] a fait
sa requeste.^b

'A ce que vous dites que la royne Aalis fu vostre ayole et le roy Henri
vostre oncle et monseignor Hugue son fis, que Dieu face preudome,
vostre cousin germain, et que vous estes le plus droit heir doudit
Hugue a avoir le bailliage de ce royaume par les (fo. ccxlv^v) raisons
que vous aves dites, je di que non estes ains le sui je; quausi fu la
royne Aalis mayole et le dit roi mon oncle, com il furent vos, et le
dit Hugue mon cousin come vostre. Et quant la royne Aalis, nostre
dite ayole, morut et la seignorie de ce royaume eschei a ces enfans,
ma mere[10] et la vostre et le roy Henri, nostre oncle, mamere,^c qui
estoit ainsnee de ces enfans, eust heu lescheete devant ces autres
enfans, pource quelle estoit lainsnee, ce ne fust quen cest royaume
heritent les fis devant les filles; et pource ot le dit roi, nostre oncle,
leritage par devant ma mere. Et il est usage en ce royaume que le
fis et la fille demore el point de son pere et de sa mere, quant il
meurt, a avoir leur drois et leur escheetes mais que de bailliage. Et
puis que enci est, je, qui sui fis de la contesse Marie qui fu ainsnee
de vostre mere, doi avoir le baillage de ce royaume devant vous
auci com mamere leust devant la vostre, ce elles vesquissent, come
celui qui sui demores el point de ma mere avoir ces drois et ces
escheetes si come je ai devant dit. Et quil soit voir, que fis ne fille
ne demore en tel saisine ne en tel teneure come vous dites dou
bailliage, il est chose seue que bailliage ne[s]chiet, ne ne peut escheir,
au fis ne a la fille de celui qui a tenu le bailliage, sil y a plus prochain
parens ou plus droit heir de lui a leir de par qui lon tient le bailliage
de celle part dont leritage meut; que ce le roi, nostre oncle, et nos
meres eussent eu une seur mainsnee de vostre mere, il nest pas

^a *The words* se vous conoisses . . . le doie; et *omitted by Beugnot.*
^b *MS. chap.* ccxciij (Beugnot, chap. iv, pp. 403–4).
^c *MS.* et mamere.

[9] i.e. Hugh of Antioch-Lusignan, so-called because he was already regent (*bailli*)
of Cyprus.
[10] Maria of Lusignan, wife of Walter of Brienne.

doute que elle neust eu le bailliage de nostre dit cousin devant nous come selle qui seroit plus prochain de lui que vous estes. Dont je di que vous ne deves pas avoir (fo. ccxlvj^r) ce bailliage par ce que vous dites que vous demores en tel saisine et en tel teneure come vostre mere avoit doudit bailliage. Et a ce que vous dites que il est us ou costume ou assise en ce royaume, que, quant il y a plusors parens qui apartienent a home ne a feme en un degre et il meurt, que cescheete eschiet et vient a lainsnee de ces plus prochains parens ^aqui sont en vie qui li apartienent en un degre de celle part dont leritage meut, et que vous estes lainsne des plus prochains parens^a dou monseignor Hugue, qui fu fis dou roy Henri, qui soient desendus de nostre dite ayole, et que, par lassise ou lusage de ce royaume ou par raison, vendroit a vous lescheete de ce royaume, se Dieu faisoit son comandement doudit Hugue sans heir que il eust de sa feme espouse, et que vous, par les raisons que vous aves dites, deves avoir le dit bailliage, je di que non deves et di coment: car vostre ainsneesce en ce cas ne vous doit valoir contre moi, pource que^b il est chose seue que madame mamere fu ainsnee de la vostre, et fu heir de la royne Aalis a avoir lescheete de ce royaume devant vostre mere, et la premiere ainsneesce doit avant aler et doit estre premiere contee, et a celle se doit on prendre et tenir. Et puis que enci est, je di que je doi avoir le bailliage des biens de nostre dit cousin par ainsneesce de madame mamere com celui qui sui son heir et demores en son point a avoir ces raisons et ces escheetes. Et a ce que vous voles que lassise ou lusage de ce royaume vous vaille a avoir le bailliage pour ce que vous estes ainsne de moi, je di que ce ne vous ne doit valoir que assise ou usage y a de ce peut estre que ce est des freres et des seurs, ne, je nentens, (fo. ccxlvj^v) que, par us ou costume ou assise^c de ce royaume, gens qui sont en tel cas com nous soumes, que lainsne le puisse ne doie avoir devant le mainsne, ne que esgart ne conoissance de court en fu onques fait en ce royaume que il leust ou deust avoir ^dpar lassise ou lusage de ce royaume;^d mais el royaume de Chipre, ou lon a jure a tenir les us et les costumes et les assises de ce royaume, avint le contraire de ce que vous dites. Que par celle haute court fu esgarde que sire Oste Beduin, qui estoit mainsne de sire Thomas de Malandre qui estoit son cousin germain si com nous soumes, eust le fie de sire Thomas Beduin, leur ayol, devant le dit Thomas de Malandre qui estoit

---

^a The words qui sont en vie . . . plus prochains parens *repeated by Beugnot.*
^b MS. que *repeated.*   ^c MS. assisise.
^d The words par lassise . . . ce royaume *omitted by Beugnot.*

ainsne de lui, pour ce que le dit Oste fu fis de lainsne des enfans de
sire Thomas Beduin, ne ne demora quil ne leust, pource que le dit
Thomas de Malandre estoit ainsne de lui.[11] Ne nul ne doit entendre
que la dite court, ou il a tant de preudes homes et de sages, eust ce
esgarde quelle esgarda, cel[l]e entendist que lesgart quelle fist fust
contre lassise ou lusage dou ce royaume; ne par defaute de bieu
plaidoier ne doit nul entendre que le dit Thomas de Malandre le
perdist, puis que il lot a son conseill sire Phelipe de Nevaire,[12] que
lon tient au meillour plaideour de sa mer. Et fort chose est a croire,
que il ait usage en ce royaume qui soit contraire a lusage de France;
que ceaus qui les y establirent ou conquest de la tere furent franceis,
et au royame de France est usage que le fis de lainsne ou de lainsnee
a leritage devant le fis dou mainsne ou de la mainsnee soit ainsne
dou fis dou lainsne ou de lainsnee. Et a ce que vous dites que fie ne
seignorie ne separt en ce (fo. ccxlvij^r) royaume entre freres ne entre
autres parens masles, et que lainsne le doit avoir devant le mainsne,
par celle raison ne deves vous avoir le bailliage de ce royaume
devant moy, ains le doi je avoir devant vous, que il est chose certaine
que mamere fu ainsnee de la vostre et plus droit heir de la royne
Aalis sa mere que la vostre. Et puis que elle fu ainsnee, et puis que
a la premiere ainsneece se doit on prendre, si come je ai devant dit,
il est bien clere chose que je sui plus prochain parent de vostre dit
cousin et le plus droit heir de vous a avoir le bailliage de ces biens,
et que la raison est moie et non vostre. Et pour toutes les raisons
que je ai dites, ou pour aucunes delles, di je que le bailliage de ce
royaume et que la raison en est moie et non vostre, et que cest mon
droit, et le doi avoir devant vous; [a]si le veull avoir, se les homes de
la haute court de ce royaume conoissent que je avoir le doie, et se
il conoissent que je avoir le doie, je euffre a faire ce que je doi com
baill, faisant lon a moi ce que lon doit com a baill.'[a]

[a] *Beugnot concludes* se la court de ce royaume conoist que avoir le doie.

---

[11] The Beduins were a Cypriot feudal family which attained some prominence
in the fourteenth century. The earliest known members of the family are Arnulf
and Thomas Beduin (presumably the man of that name mentioned here) who both
witnessed the treaty between the Cypriots and Genoese of 1232 (*Regesta Regni
Hierosolymitani,* no. 1049 (wrongly dated 1233)). Neither Otto Beduin nor Thomas
of Malandre are otherwise known.

[12] Philip of Novara, the Cypriot jurist and politician. The fact that the present
tense (tient) is used of him here has been understood to mean that he was still alive
at the time this speech was made. If so, this is the last known reference to him and
establishes the date of his death as falling during or after 1264. See G. Paris, 'Les
Mémoires de Philippe de Novaire', *Revue de l'Orient latin,* ix (1902), 166–7.

[3]   Ce est le segont dit dou baill a premiere dit dou conte.[a]

'A ce que vos dites que le bailliage de ce royaume est vostre droit et
non le mien, pource que quant la royne Aalis, nostre ayole, morut
ce royaume eschei a ces enfans, vostre mere et la moie et le roy Henri
nostre oncle, et que vostre mere, qui estoit lainsne de la dite royne,
eust eu cescheete devant ces autres enfans pour ce que elle estoit
lainsnee, se ne fust ce que en ce royaume heritent les fis devant les
fille, voirs est que[b] ce royaume eschei au roy Henri, nostre oncle,
par la mort de nostre dite ayole com a celui qui son droit heir estoit,
et il (fo. ccxlvij[v]) vint en ce royaume, et lot et tint et usa come
seignor jusques a sa mort com de son drot. Mais a vostre mere
neschei riens qui valoir vous doie de chose qui escheir li peust de
par sa mere, com celle qui not onques saisine ne teneure ne avoir
ne la peust davant le dit roy, et cest aparant. Car puis que le dit
roy, nostre oncle, en fu saisi et tenant, si com est desus dit, se vostre
mere peust demander aucune raison en ce royaume par lescheete que
vous dites qui li eschei de par sa mere, elle le perdi par la teneure
doudit roi, et que ce soit voirs, il est cler a conoistre que ce elle le
hust survescu, ce que elle ne fist mie, et il fust mort sans heirs de sa
feme espouse, et elle vosist requere la seignorie de ce royaume et
avoir, il convenist que elle la requeist de par le dit roi, son frere, et
non pas par la dite royne, sa mere, pour ce que il en morut derainement saisi et tenant come de son droit. Car il est us ou coustume ou
assise en ce royaume que lon doit requere escheete de par le derain
saisi et tenant, et non de par autre qui valoir li doie; que ce il la
requiert de par autre lon ne li est tenus de respondre. Ne a vostre
mere neschei riens, ne ne peut escheir, de ce royaume de par le roy,
nostre oncle, pour ce quelle morut avant de lui; qua mort na morte
ne peut riens escheir, pour quoi vostre mere not, ne ne pot avoir
droit en lescheete dou roi, nostre oncle. Et puis que elle ne ot ne ne
pot avoir droit, vous ne le poes ne le deves avoir de par lui, et puis
que vous ne laves ne poies avoir de par lui, donc di je que ainsneesce
ne vous peut ne ne doit riens valoir a avoir le bailliage ne lescheete
de ce (fo. ccxlviij[r]) royaume devant moi, qui sui devant vous. Et a
ce que vous dites que vous voles que lassise ne lusage de ce royaume
[ne] me doie valoir a avoir le dit bailliage, pour ce que je sui
ainsnes de vous, je di que si doie et veull que lassise ou lusage de ce
royaume ou raison me vaille et doie valoir a avoir le dit bailliage.

[a] *MS. chap.* ccxciiij (Beugnot, chap. v, pp. 405–6).
[b] *This word is followed by* en, *struck out.*

Car il est clere chose et aperte que ce royaume est escheu par la mort de nostre dit oncle a son dit fis, Hugue nostre dit cousin, et que aucun doit avor par assise ou par usage de ce royaume ou par raison le bailliage de ces biens, donc le doit avoir celui qui plus grant raison y a devant les autres, se il le requiert. Et je ai plus grant raison et plus grant droit que les autres qui aucune maniere de droit et de raison y pevent demander, come celui qui sui lainsne de tous les parens de nostre dit oncle qui derainement morut saisi et tenant et de nostre dit cousin a qui ce royaume est escheu, si com je ai dit, que de nostre dit ayole sont desendus. Car par lassise ou lusage de ce royaume, fie ne signorie ne separt ne ne doit partir entre heirs masles, ains le doit avoir lun deaus, donc est il cler a conoistre que ensi doie estre com je ai dit; que trop seroit fort chose et estrange et tort apert, que de ceaus qui sont en un degre de parente le mainsne heritast devant lainsne la ou lainsne le requist, ne onques navint ne ya ne vendra, ce Dieu plaist, que ce seroit contre lusage et lassise de ce royaume *a*et tort apert. Car en ce royaume ne fit onques use,*a* ne raison ne le done, que le mainsne des parens qui sont en un degre eust heritage ne le bailliage devant lainsne, quant il le requiert, auci des autres parens com des freres, (fo. ccxlviij*v*) ne il ne se trovera ja que le mainsne heritast devant lainsne la ou lainsne le requeist, donc est il clere chose que je [qui] sui ainsne de vous doi avoir le bailliage de ce royaume devant vous. Et a ce que vous dites que esgart ne conoissance de court ne fu onques fait en ce royaume, que lainsne de ceaus qui sont en tel cas come nous soumes eust leritage ne le bailliage devant les mainsne, se enci est com vous dites, il nest demore que porce que debat de tel cas ne vint onques en court; et de choses si cleres et si usees com cest est, nest mestier de metre sen sur court a faire ent esgart ne conoissance, que ce seroit uiseuce et tenu abusion auci com se lon le faisoit des freres. Et a se que vous dites que le contraire de ce fu fait en Chipre, ou lon a jure de tenir les us et coustumes et les assises dou royaume de Jerusalem, et esgarde par la haute court dou fait de sire Oste Beduin et de sire Thomas de Malandre, esgart nest pas assise ne ne doit estre tenus com assise; que court ne peut faire esgart que de paroles de quoi lon se met en esgart, et plaideer peut faillir et faut souvent, que mout meillour plaideour de sire Phelippe de Nevaire a lon veu souvent faillir a dire ce que mestier li estoit en plait, et il est chose certaine que mesire Phelipe de Nevaire failli lors a bien plaideer, et que ce qui lors en fu fait par esgart fu par la defaute de

a The words et tort apert ... onques use *omitted by Beugnot.*

ce que lon ne dist pas tout ce que mestier y fu si com il a este aparant. Que la ou les homes de la haute court de Chipre furent assembles plus esforceement que[a] lon ne lesvit piesa et messire Phelippe aveuc eaus, jos le bailliage dou royaume de Chipre par leur conoissance, com le plus droit heir dou fis dou roi, nostre dit oncle, a avoir son bail(fo. ccxlix[r])liage sauve madame mamere se elle le requeist; et ce fu fait vostre oyant et vostre veyant, qui esties en vostre parfait aage, sans droit que vous y demandicies ne sans chalonge ne debat que nous y meyssiens. Pour quoi je dis que ledit esgart ne vous doit valoir, mais a moi doit valoir la dite conoissance quelle fu fait par toute la coumunaute des houmes de la dite court de Chipre, vostre oyant[b] et vostre veyant; ne le fait de sire Oste Beduin ne de sire Thomas de Malandre ne fu pas en tel cas com le nostre, ne le dit esgart qui en fu fait ne vous doit valoir. Et a ce que vous dites que les usages de ce pais furent pris et estrais des usages dou royaume de France, et que par lusage de France le fis de lainsne encor soit il mainsne emporte leritage quant il eschiet devant lainsne quant il sont en tel cas com nos soumus, je ne sai que il soit ensi com vous dites, et tout le fust il, ne requier je riens par lusage dou France, mais par lusage de ce royaume le requier je, [c]les quels doivent estre tenus et maintenus en ce royaume;[c] ne en ce royaume nest pas lusage tel com vous dites quil est en France, ains est tout le contraire. Et bien est aparant par les raisons que je ais dit, et pour ce que la dame de Thabarie et de madame Eschive de Thabarie, qui sont en tel degre de parente come nos soumes et leur fait semblant au nostre, fu que la dame de Thabarie ot la seignorie de Thabarie devant madame Eschive, pource que elle estoit ainsnee de li, ne ne demora que elle ne leust, pource que elle fu fille dou mainsne, et ce fu pource quelles ne puissent riens requerre ne avoir de par leur peres, qui onques ne furent saissis ne tenans, ains (fo. ccxlix[v]) lot de par madame Eschive, leur ayole, qui derainement fu saisie et tenant.[13] De par celle meysme maniere ot sire Gautier de Flouri[d] la mareschaucie de Thabarie devant sire Helies Charles, et a Sayete avint il auci dou fait qui fu de sire Hugue de Masaire.[14] Ne onques le contraire de

---

[a] *This word is followed by* que, *struck out.*
[b] *MS.* voyant.
[c] *The words* les quels doivent . . . en ce royaume *omitted by Beugnot.*
[d] *In margin* ci dit de le marschal de Flury *in a fifteenth-century hand.*

---

[13] For the succession to Tiberias, see above, p. 13.
[14] For Walter of Floury, Elias Charles and Hugh of Masaire, see above, p. 12 note 47.

ce navint en ce royaume pour quoi il est clere chose que lusage de
ce royaume nest pas tel com vos dites que celui de France est. Et
pour toutes les raisons que je ai ore et autre fois dit, ou por aucune
delles, di je que le bailliage de ce royaume est mon droit et non le
vostre, si le veull avoir, se les homes de la haute court de ce royaume
conoissent que je avoir le doie, et *se il conoissent que je avoir le
doie,* je euffre a faire ce que je doie come baill, faisant lon a moi
ce que lon doit com a baill.'

[4] Ce est le segont dit dou conte au segont dit dou baill.[b]

'Vous aves entendu coment jai dit que mamere fu ainsnee de la
vostre et coment elle fu droit heir de nostre dit ayole, la royne Aalis,
et de nostre dit oncle, le roy Henri, devant vostre mere come celle
qui estoit ainsnee de vostre mere, et par quel raison [c]vostre ainsneesce ne doit valoir contre moi, et coment lainsneesce [de] mamere
doit valoir contre vos, et coment la premiere[c] ainsneesce doit avant[d]
aler, et que celle ce doit on prendre et tenir, et coment je sui demoures el point de mamere a avoir ces raisons et ces escheetes, et
par quel raison la teneure de vostre mere dou bailliage, que elle
tient, de ce royaume ne vos doit valoir, et par quel raison je sui plus
droit heir de vous a avoir le bailliage de ce royame par devant vous.
Et a ce que vous dites que il ne me (fo. ccl[r]) doit valoir, ce que ma
mere fu droit heir devant la vostre de la royne Aalis, nostre ayole,
et de nostre oncle, le roy Henri, ne que lainsneesce de mamere ne
me doit valoir, ne qua celle ne se doit lon tenir, je dis que si fait par
les raisons que jais autre fois dites. Et se il estoit enci com vous dites
ce ne me doit pas ennuire par raison, car la en vie de vostre mere ne
li eschei riens de madite ayole ne par mon dit oncle qui valoir vos
doie, com celle qui riens ne tint ne ot en ce royaume de heiritage
qui escheu li fust de par eaus, si com il est aparant que mon seignor
Hugue, qui est desendus de nostre ayole, est en vie, a qui ce royaume
eschei par la mort de nostre dit oncle; et puis que enci est que [a]
vostre mere, tant come elle vesqui, neschei riens deritage de par
nostre dite ayole ne de nostre oncle quelle tenist ne heust come le
sien, donc di je que tout auci com mamere heust eu la seignorie de
ce royaume devant la vostre, se il fust mesavenu de nostre dit oncle

---

[a] The words se il conoissent . . . le doie omitted by Beugnot.
[b] MS. chap. ccxcv (Beugnot, chap. vi, pp. 407–9).
[c] The words vostre ainsneesce . . . la premiere omitted by Beugnot.
[d] MS. avoir.

B

sans heir de cespouse, la doi je avoir, se il mesavenoit de nostre dit cousin sans heir que il eust de sa feme espouse; et puis que enci est, il est cler a conoistre que je doi avoir le bailliage de ce royaume devant vous. Et a ce que vous dites que bailliage de ce royaume est esc[h]eu, et que aucun le doit avoir, et que celui qui plus grant raison y a *a*le doit avoir, ce est voirs, et je, qui plus grant raison y a*a* de vous par les raisons que je ai dites ores et autrefoit, le doi avoir devant vous, ne vostre ainsneesce ne vos doit valoir en ce cas; mais celle de mamere me doit valoir *b*par les raisons que je ai avant dites, ne*b* ne doit demourer que elle ne me vaille (fo. cclv) pour chose que vous aies dite, *c*qui soit assise ou usage en ce royaume ou raison que fie ne seignorie ne se part.*c* Et a ce que vous dites *d*quil ne fu onques use en ce royame, ne raison ne le done, que le mainsne heritast devant lainsne qui sont en un degre auci bien dautres com de freres, se il estoit si com vous dites, ce que je nentens pas, ne fu il onques use en ce royaume que lainsne des parens qui sont en un degre, autres que freres ou seurs, eust heritage ne bailliage devant le mainsne de lainsne par esgart ne par conoissance de court. Et*d* se la dame de Thabarie ou sire Gautir de Flouri*e* ou autres lont eu, si com vous dites, ce ne este par droit ne par esgart ne par conoissance de court, ains a este parce que ceaus qui raison y avoient se sont soufeis de venir en court et de demander leur raison; pour quoi di je que ce ne vous vaut, ne valoir ne vous doit, *f*na moi ennuire, que je naie par devant vous le bailliage de ce royaume com celui qui suis plus droit heir de vous a avoir le par devant vous par les raisons que je ai dit.*f* Et a ce que vous dites que esgart, qui fu fait en Chipre de sire Oste Beduin et de sire Thomas de Malandre, [ne] me vaille, et que vous voles que la conoissance qui fu faite en Chipre dou bailliage, que vous eustes, vous vaille a avoir cestui bailliage, je di que le dit esgart me doit valoir, mais a vous ne doit valoir la dite conoissance, et di raison pour quoi; car le fait de sire Oste Beduin et de sire Thomas de Malandre, qui requeroient lescheete de leur ayole, fu debatue en court par les parties longuement, et apres fu esgarde que la raison estoit de sire Oste Bed(fo. cclj*r*)uin, et encor fust il mainsne doudit Thomas, pource que il estoit fis de lainsne des enfans de son ayol. Et quant vous requeistes le bailliage de Chipre,

---

a The words le doit avoir . . . raison y a *omitted by Beugnot.*
b The words par les raisons . . . avant dites, ne *omitted by Beugnot.*
c The words qui soit assise . . . ne se part *omitted by Beugnot.*
d The words quil ne fu . . . conoissance de court. Et *omitted by Beugnot.*
e Cross in margin.
f The words na moi ennuire . . . je ai dit *omitted by Beugnot.*

il est chose seue que je ne le debati ne en court, ne mits pour debatre,
le que je men souffri que lonour de madame mante, vostre mere,
qui nouri mavoit, que je doutai quelle ne me seust maugre; ne celle
conoissance, qui adonc fu faite, ne vous doit valoir *ne a moi
ennuire, et ce la court connut ce que vous dites, celle conoissance
ne vos doit valoir contre moi* a avoir le bailliage de ce royaume par
les raisons que je ai dites; ains doit valoir a moi lesgart qui fu de
sire Oste Beduin et de sire Thomas de Malandre, si come je ai
devant dit. Et a ce que vous dites que vous voles requere le bailliage
par lusage de ce royaume et non pas par celui de France, vous aves
entendu que je ai dit autrefois, quil ne fu onques esgarde ne coneu
en ce royaume que lainsne de ceaus qui sont en un degre autres que
freres, fis de la mainsnee,*b* heust heritage ou bailliage devant le
mainsne fis de lainsnee, et que les usages de ce pais furent pris et
etrais de ceaus de France au conquest de ce roiaume. Et puis que
vous dites que dou mainsne fis de lainsne ne fu onques fait esgart
ne conoissance en court, et je di que lainsne fis de la mainsnee*c* ne fu
onques fait esgart ne conoissance de court en ce royaume, dont je
di com se doit prendre as usages de France; et je ai dit autre fois
que lusage de France est, et encor je di; et que il soit voirs, ce que
je di autrefois est avenu en ce royaume, qui navoit este debatu ne
coneu par esgart ne par conoissance de court, (fo. cclj*v*) de quoi lon
estoit ensere que lon se travailloit de savoir la verite de lusage de
France et*d* par sel usage lon deliveroit le fait en ce royaume, et se
est chose aperte et seue. Car quant messire Henri le Bufle fu mort
et ces filles furent en debat de lescheete de leur pere, lon sen acerteni
par lusage de France et atendi lon plus dun an le conte de Sansuerre
pour savoir quel usage estoit en France de tel cas, *e*et par lusage qui
fu delivree celle quarele si com est aparant que encor court en ce
royaume.[15] *e* Pour quoi par ceste raison, et por toutes les autres que
je ai dites ores et autres fois ou par aucune delles, je veull avoir le
bailliage de ce royaume par devant vous, com celui qui sui le plus

---

a The words ne a moi ennuire . . . contre moi *omitted by Beugnot.*
b MS. mainsneece.   *c MS.* lainsnee.   *d MS.* et *repeated.*
e The syntax of these lines is obscure as some words are evidently missing. The meaning,
however, seems clear enough.

---

[15] Henry Le Bufle (fl. 1155–65) is last known from a document of March 1165
(*Regesta Regni Hierosolymitani*, no. 412). Stephen, count of Sancerre (1152–91) was
in the East in 1171 (William of Tyre, 'Historia Rerum in Partibus Transmarinis
Gestarum', *RHC. Historiens Occidentaux*, i, p. 988; see Robert of Torigny, 'Chro-
nica', ed. R. Howlett, *Chronicles of the Reigns of Stephen, Henry II and Richard I* (Rolls
Series, 4 vols, 1884–9), iv, p. 249).

droit heir de nostre dit cousin a avoir cescheete, se les homes de la
haute court, ^aqui si sont assembles, conoissent que je le doi avoir. Et
ce il^a connoissent que je avoir le doie, je euffre a faire ce que je doie
com baill, faisant lon a moi ce que lon doit com a baill.'

[5] Ce est le tiers dit dou baill au segont [dit]^b dou cont.^c

'Vous aves entendu coument jais autrefois dit, et encor di, que riens
neschei a vostre mere de par nostre dite ayole, la royne Aalis, qui
valoir vous doie, ne ne par nostre dit oncle, le roi Henri, neschei
riens a vostre mere nescheu ne pot que elle morut avant de lui, na
mort na morte ne peut riens escheir, et par quel raison lainsneesce
de vostre mere ne vous doit valoir a avoir le bailliage de ce royaume
pour nostre dit cousin. Et a ce que vous dites que vous nentendes
que ce que je ais dit fust onques use en ce royaume, ne raison ne
done, que le fis dou mainsne, quant il est ainsne, heritast devant
(fo. cclij^r) le fis de lainsne ce il est mainsne de lui, ausi bien des
parens qui sont en un degre taignans a celui de qui lescheete leur
est venue de la ou elle meut com des freres, se vous ne le[n]tendes,
pour ce ne remaint il mie quil ne soit et doie estre si com je ais dit,
et di pourquoi. Car il est chose manifeste, que quant on meurt et il
y a ij fis que autant li ataint lun de parente com lautre, et que auci
devroit avoir part el fie et en la seignorie le mainsne com lainsne, se
lusage de ce royaume ne li toloit, qui est tel^d que lainsne la tout. Et
par celle meisme maniere et par tel raison il est clere chose et aperte,
que se un home a deus fis et il meurent ains de lui sans avoir aucune
teneure des biens de lor pere et chascun de ceaus ait fis, que son fie
et sa seignorie eschiet as fis des fis, et puis que il eschiet a ceaus, donc
le doit avoir lainsne devant le mainsne; car auci bien sont il en un cas
lun devers lautre a avoir leritage de leur ayol com leur peres, cil
eussent survescu leur pere, car lusage de ce royaume est que lon doit
requerre sescheete de par le derain saisi et tenant, dou di je que les dis
cousins de par leur pere ne pevent riens requerre, qui onques nen orent
teneure ne raison quil avoir puissent, ce il eussent survescu leur pere,
[et] a leur enfans ne leur doit riens valoir. Pour quoi je di que lainsneesce de vostre mere ne vous doit valoir, con celle qui morut ains
nostre dit oncle, son frere; et puis com ne doit requere escheete

^a The words qui si sont . . . Et ce il omitted by Beugnot.
^b Supplied from table of rubrics, fo. 16^v.
^c MS. chap. ccxcvj (Beugnot, chap. vii, pp. 409–10).
^d This word is followed by que lains, struck out.

fors de par le derain saisi, et que fie ne seignorie ne se doit partir, si com jais autrefois dit, il convient que lun des ij qui sont en un degre lait, et puis quil convient que lun lait, il est bien droit et raison que lainsne lait devant (fo. cclij^v) le mainsne; et enci a tous jours este use ne onques en ce royaume navint le contraire, pourquoi je di qui est clere chose, que je qui sui ainsnes de vous doi avoir ce bailliage devant vous, qui estes le mainsne. ^{a}Et a ce que vous dites que il ne fu onques use par esgart ne par conoissance de court, qui lainsne fis dou mainsne ou de la mainsnee heritast devant le mainsne fis de lainsne ou de lainsnee,^{b} je di que ce il na este fait par esguart ne par conoissance de court ce ne me doit nuire, qui nest demoure que parce que tel cas ne vint onques en court. Que quant tel cas sont avenus, ceaus qui estoient certains que il ni avoient droit, et que ce il venoient en court quil le perderoient par esgart de court, si nauroient honour ne profit et venir ysi sen soit soufers. Que fort chose est a croire, que, ce il cuidassent desrainier par court, que ces que je ais nomes se fussent soufert devenir en court requere leur raison et de si grans fais come ceaus estoient, ce le contraire de ce que je ais dit ne fu onques en ce royaume esgarde ne coneu ne fait en court ne dehors court. Ne le fait de la dame de Thabarie et de madame Eschive, sa cousine, ne fu pas par souffrance ains fu acertaine par les plus sages homes qui de sa mere fussent au jour, et il en y avoit plus lors quil na ore que ceaus qui ores sont y estoient et plusors autres qui sont puis mors, et par tous fu dit et conseille au seignor de Sur, leur oncle,^{16} sur qui elles cestoient mises que droit et la raison en estoit de la dame de Thabarie, pour ce que elle estoit ainsnee de madame Eschive qui estoit fille de lainsne. Et par les raisons que je ai dites di je que raison et ce, qui a este fait et use en ce royaume (fo. ccliij^r) de tel cas com le nostre est, me doit valoir a avoir le bailliage de ce royaume devant vous, car chose acertenee par tant de gens doit porter plus grant force et estre meaus tenue que esgart et conoissance que lon pert souvent par ce que le plait est mal plaidee. Et encor di je que la conoissance, qui fu faite en Chipre de mon bailliage, me doit meaus valoir qua vous lesgart qui fu faite

---

^{a} *The passage beginning at this point and ending with the words* je ais dites (p. 34, n. *a*) *omitted by Beugnot.*
^{b} *MS.* de la mainsne ou de la mainsnee.

---

^{16} Philip of Montfort, lord of Tyre (Sur) (*c.* 1246–70). The two Eschivas were the children of two brothers (Otto and Ralph of Tiberias) married to two sisters, the daughters of Helvis of Ibelin and Raynald of Sidon. Philip was the son of Helvis by her later marriage to Guy of Montfort. See 'Lignages', pp. 455, 461.

de sire Oste Beduin et de sire Thomas de Malandre, par les raisons
que je ais dites.[a] Et a ce que vous dites que vous voles come se preigne
a lusage de France pour aucunes raisons que vous aves dites, et
pource meismes que vous dites que lon atendi le conte de Sanseure
un an et plus pour acertener le fait de messire Henri le Bufle, de
quoi lon se trovoit ensere, et quencor court en ce royaume ce que
adonc fu establi tout fust il ensi com vous dites, di je que ce cas nest
pas semblant a celui, car tel cas com celui des seurs fu adonc nestoit
onques avenu en ce royaume, ne de cestui cas en quoi vous et moi
soumes ne peut lon dire quil ne soit avenu en ce royaume plusors
fois ne que lon se soit onques trove enserre. Quant il avint que lon a
veu tousjours user en ce royaume que lainsne fis dou mainsne ou de
la mainsnee a leritage devant le mainsne fis de lainsne ou de lainsnee,
se il le requiert, quant il sont en un degre de parente de celle part
dont lescheete meut, [b]si com il a este aparant de plusors si com je[c]
lai autre fois dit.[b] Et aucune fois est avenu que court estoit enseree
daucunes choses, et que lune court mandoit demander conseill a
lautre [d]court, ne celle qui demandoit conseill[d] nestoit pas pource
tenue de tenir le conseill ne lusages des autres cours a qui elle
demandoit conseill, se il ne li sembloit bon; et (fo. ccliij[v]) mout de
fois est avenu que la court de ce royaume a mande requere conseill
en Chipre, en Antioche, a Triple et en autres leucs de quels le plus
nont pas tel usage com il y a en ce royaume, que lon fust tenus de
tenir les usages de celui pais de toutes les autres choses qui en ce
royaume avendroient, et tout soit ce com ait aucune fois demande
conseill as autres cours nest lon pas tenus de croire leur conseill ne[e]
tenir leur usage se il ne leur semble bon. Et pour toutes les raisons,
que je ai dites ore et autre fois, ou par aucunes delles, di je que je
doi avoir le bailliage de ce royaume et avoir le veull devant vous
com le plus droit heir de nostre cousin a avoir cescheete, [f]ne pour
chose que vous aies dite ore et autre fois, je ne veull quil demeure
que je naie le dit bailliage, se les homes de ceste court conoissent
que je avoir le doie, et se il conoissent que je le doi avoir, je en euffre
a faire ce que jen doi com baill, faisant lon a moi ce que lon doit com
a baill.'[f]

[a] End of passage omitted by Beugnot.
[b] The words si com il . . . autre fois dit omitted by Beugnot.
[c] MS. le.
[d] The words court, ne celle qui demandoit conseill omitted by Beugnot.
[e] MS. de.
[f] Beugnot concludes se la court conoist que je avoir le doie.

[6] Ce est le tiers dit dou conte au tiers dit dou baill.[a]

'Vous aves entendu coment jai plusors fois dit, et encor di que [de par] la royne Aalis, nostre dite ayole, eschei ce royaume a ces enfans, et que mamere fu lainsnee de ces enfans et fu plus droit heir de lui, que vostre mere ne fu, a avoir lescheete de ce royaume, et coment je sui par les raisons que je ais dites demores el point de ma mere a avoir ces drois et ces escheetes, et coment et pour quel raison je sui plus droit heir de vous a avoir le bailliage de ce royaume. Et a ce que vous dites que quant un home meurt qui a ij fis, que autant li taint de parente lun com lautre, et que auci devroit part avoir el fie, (fo. ccliiij[r]) et en la seignorie le mainsne ne con lainsne, se lusage de ce royaume ne li tolloit, qui est tel que lainsne la tout; et que, par celle meisme raison, se un hom a ij fis et il meurt sans avoir aucune teneure de ces biens, et chascun deaus a fis, que lescheete dou pere des ij freres eschiet as fis des fis; et que puis qui leur eschei lainsne le doit avoir devant le mainsne, je di que ce est voirs ce il est fis de lainsne, mais ce il est fis dou mainsne, je di que il ne le doit pas avoir. Et a ce que vous dites que il est husage en ce royaume con doit requere cescheete de par le derain saisi et tenant, je nentens que lusage de ce soit tel com vos dites, que la court de ce royaume en fist onques esgart ne conoissance que lusage fust tel com vous aves dit, ne en tel cas com nos somes ce ne vous doit valoir; car trop est clere chose et manifeste, que mamere fu plus droit heir que la vostre de nostre dite ayole et de nostre dit oncle, et ce vostre mere survesqui la moie et ot le bailliage de ce royaume, ce ne me doit nuire, que jai autre fois dit et encor di, que bailliage neschiet pas de baill a baill quant il y a plus prochein parent ou plus droit heir de celui ou de celle por cui lon tient le bailliage; ne vostre [mere] en sa vie naquist riens des biens de nostre dite ayole ne de nostre dit oncle a heritage qui valoir vous doie. Et bien est clere chose, que puis que ensi fu que vostre mere morut sans avoir teneure daucune chose qui escheir li peust a heritage de nostre dite ayole ne de nostre dit oncle, que tout auci com ma mere fu leur droit heir devant la vostre, que je le doi estre et sui devant vous, pour ce que je sui son fis, quelle estoit ainsnee de vostre mere, et que je sui demores par lusage de ce royaume el point ou ma mere estoit (fo. ccliiij[v]) quant elle morut a avoir ces raison et ces escheetes; pour quoi je di que encor fust ce que gent, qui fussent en tel cas com nos somes, covenist a requerre de par le derain saisi et tenant, ce que je nentent pas, suis je et doi

[a] *MS. chap.* ccxcvij (Beugnot, chap. viii, pp. 410–12).

estre droit heir de nostre dit oncle et de son dit fis par devant vous, pour ce que ma mere fu droit heir devant la vostre de nostre dit oncle, qui estoit ainsnee de la vostre. Et trop seroit estrange chose et contre toutes manieres des drois et des raisons, que vous, qui estes fis de celle de la quel mamere estoit plus droit heir doudit roy, nostre oncle, par devant vostre mere, deucies avoir le bailliage ne leritage de chose, qui fust escheue de nostre dit oncle [a]et qui est de nostre dit cousin, par devant moi, qui suis fis de celle qui de nostre dit oncle estoit plus droit heir par devant la vostre, et le fust de nostre dit cousin celles vesquissent.[a] Et a ce que plusors gens en ce royaume, qui estoient ainsnes et fis de mainsnes, ont herite et [eu] leur escheetes devant les mainsnes fis des ainsnes qui estoient en tel cas com nous somes, vous aves entendu, coment jai dit autre fois, par quels ce ne me doit nuire na vous valoir, car se aucune personne se veaut souffrir de requerre et davoir sa raison, celle soffrance ne doit pas tolir la raison de celui ou de celle qui la veaut avoir et la requiert. [b]Et de ce que vous dites que le fait de la dame de Thabarie et de madame Eschive, sa cousine, fu mis sur le seignor de Sur a acertenir de cui la raison estoit et quil fu acertene par les plus sages gens de ce pais, ce nen sais je, et tout fust il enci ce ne me doit mie ennuire ne a vous ayder. Car mout de fois avient que lon quiert aucune chose a aucune gens, que ceaus a qui lon le re(fo. cclv[r])quiert ne sont mie bien voyans cler de la raison, et mout de fois semble as gens cune chose soit raison que a ceaus meismes semble puis le contraire quant il oient la raison dune part et dautre; ne tel maniere denqueste nest pas esgart ne conoissance ne ne la doit on tenir a usage ne a assise; et parmi tout ce est il chose seue et certaine, que ce que le seignor de Sur fist de celui fait, quil le fist par lassent des parties, ne null peut meaus laisser sa raison, que celui de qui elle est. Ne se que ma dame Eschive, ne les autres que vous dites qui en tel cas furent, se laisserent de requere et davoir leur raison, me doie tourner a damage, ains vell avoir le bailliage de ce royaume par devant vous, com selui qui sui le plus droit heir de nostre dit cousin, que vous nestes, a avoir cescheete par devant vous, selle escheoit par les raisons que je ai dite.[c] Et a ce que vous maves porte une maniere dexample, que sune court demande[d] conseill a autre des choses dont elle se treut enserree, et que porce nest mie celle court qui demande conseill

---

[a] *The words* et qui est . . . celles vesquissent *omitted by Beugnot.*
    [b] *The passage beginning at this point and ending with the words* je ai dite (*below, n. c*) *omitted by Beugnot.*
    [c] *End of passage omitted by Beugnot.*   [d] *MS.* devant.

tenue de croire le conseill ne tenir lusage de lautre, cil ne li semble
bon, et que la court de ce royaume a plusors fois requis conseill a
plusors cours, ne que porce nest elle pas tenue de tenir les usages
de celles cours, je di que ceste comparison nest pas conminan et di
coment: que chose est seue, quant Anthioche fu conquise par
crestiens, que Boemont[17] en fu seignor que jentens qui fu de Puille,
et peut estre quant il en fu seignor quil y mist les usages tels com il
vost, et auci le conte de Toulouse, qui fu seignor de Triple,[18] et auci
firent les autres qui furent seignors[a] des autres [seignories] quant
elles furent conquises; et le royaume de Jerusalem soit lon bien
que fran(fo. cclv[v])sois conquisterent, et quil pristerent et traisterent
les usages de ce royaume de ceaus de France, pour quoi je di que
de cestui cas se doit lon prendre a lusage de France, ne quil doit
demourer por chose que vous aies dite, com ne si preigne. Et por
toutes les raisons, que je ai dites ore et autre fois, ou pour aucunes
delles, veull je avoir li dit bailliage, se les homes de la haute
court de ce royaume conoissent que je avoir le doie; et cil conoissent
que je le doi avoir, je en euffre a faire ce que je doi come baill,
faisant lon a moi ce que lon doit come a baill.'

[7] Ce est le quart dit dou bail au tiers dit dou conte.[b]

'Jais mout de paroles dites et plusors raisons monstrees les quelles
vous et les homes de la court aves entendues quil nest mestier que
je redie, et pour le fait abergier je mostre brefement par vive raison,
coment je sui plus droit heir de vous a avoir ce bailliage et leritage
de ce royaume, cil mesavenoit de nostre dit cousin a qui Dieu doint
bone vie. Il est certaine chose quil nos convient a requerre ce
bailliage, se nous le volons avoir, de par celui a qui leritage de ce
royaume est escheu com a droit heir, ce est mon seignor Hugue, le
fis de nostre dit oncle, [c]a qui ce royaume eschei de par nostre dit
oncle[c] qui derainement morut saisi et tenant com de son droit. Et
pour ce devons nous requerre cest bailliage de par nostre dit cousin,
quil est assise ou lusage en ce royaume, que, quant fie ou seignorie
eschiet a enfant merme daage et il na pere ne mere, que celui ou

---

[a] *MS.* seignorns.
[b] *MS. chap.* ccxcviij (Beugnot, chap. ix, pp. 412–13).
[c] *The words* a qui ce royaume ... dit oncle *omitted by Beugnot.*

---

[17] Bohemond of Taranto, prince of Antioch (1098–1104); died 1111.
[18] Raymond of St Gilles, count (as Raymond IV) of Toulouse (1088–1105),
first count of Tripoli.

celle qui est son plus drot heir a avoir celle escheete devant tous
(fo. cclvj^r) autres se lenfant merme daage moroit doit avoir le
bailliage doudit fie ou de la devant dit seignorie devant tous ces
autres parens, et la si la requiert; et il est voirs que la seignorie de ce
royaume eschei a nostre dit cousin par la mort de nostre dit oncle,
et que madame mamere ot et tint le bailliage de ce^a royaume et en
morut saisie et tenant com le plus droit heir de nostre dit cousin a
avoir cescheete. Et il est certaine chose et veraie, qua vostre mere
neschei heritage ne bailliage de ce royaume ne aucun autre chose
de par nostre dit oncle nescheir ne li pot, pour ce que elle morut
lonc tens avant de lui, qua mort na morte ne peut riens escheir, si
com jais autre fois dit; ne de par nostre dit cousin ne li poroit riens
escheir, com a celle qui ne fu onques heir doudit Huge nestre ne le
pot, pource quelle morut lonc tens ains quil fust nes ne engendres,
ne que son pere eust espousee la royne Plaisance, sa mere. Et puis
que de par nostre dit oncle ne li eschei aucune chose ne escheir ne
li pot, pour les raisons que je ai dites, ne quelle ne fu onques heir de
nostre dit cousin si com jais avant dit, donc est il clere chose quelle
not ne pot avoir aucun droit en ce royaume, et puis quelle ne lot ne
avoir ne le post, vous de par lui ne laves ne avoir ne poes. Et puis que
de par li ne laves ne ne poes avoir, sa[i]nsneesce ne vous vaut ne ne
peut valoir a avoir lescheete ne le bailliage de ce royaume devant
moi; et ce je, de par ma mere, qui survesqui la vostre et nostre dit
oncle et qui ot le bailliage de ce royaume si com jais autre fois dit,
ne puis requerre ne avoir droit el dit bailliage par les raisons que
vous dites, donc est il certaine chose que vous ne le (fo. cclvj^v)
poies requerre ne avoir de par vostre mere par les raisons que je ai
dites; et ce nous de par nos meres ne le poons requerre navoir, donc
covient il, se nos le volons avoir, que nous le requerons de par nostre
dit cousin si com jai autre fois dit. Et puis que de par lui le nous
covient a requerre, je die que je le doi meaus avoir de vous que je
suis ainsnes de vous; que par raison que vous dites que vostre mere
heust eu leritage et le bailliage de ce royaume devant la moie, se
elles vesquissent et il leur fust escheu por ce que vostre mere fu
ainsnee de la moie, di je que par celle meisme raison le doi je avoir
devant vous, puis que il nos est escheu, que je sui ainsne de vous. Et
je vous ais autre fois dit et di encor, que je ne sai que les usages de
France sont, et tout fust lusage de France tel com vous aves dit, ce
que je nentens mie, je ne requier ne ne doi requere le bailliage de ce
royaume par autre usage que par celui de ce royaume; par les quels

---

^{a} MS. ce *repeated.*

usages je le doi avoir pour toutes les raisons que je ais dites, ne ne
veull quil demore pour chose que vous aies dit ne dies, que je ne
laie devant vous. [a]Pour toutes les [raisons] que jai dites ores et autre
fois, ou par aucun delles,[a] ce les homes de la haute court de ce
royaume, qui si sont, conoissent que je le doi avoir, et de ce me met
je en leur counoissances, et cil conoissent que je le doi avoir, je en
euffre a faire ce que je doi com baill, faisant lon a moi ce que lon
doit com a baill.'

[8]   Ce est le quart dit dou conte au quart dit dou baill.[b]

'Ja soit ce que je aie plusors fois dit et mostre clerement par quels
raisons je sui le (fo. cclvij[r]) plus droit heir de vous a avoir le bailliage
de ce royaume, com celui qui sui le plus droit heir de vous de nostre
dit oncle, a qui ce royaume est escheu par la mort de nostre dit
oncle, qui derainement en morut saisi et tenant, por aberger le fait
[et] eschiver riote, je dirai as plus courtes paroles que je porai ce
que besoign mest a avoir ce bailliage par devant vous qui est mon
droit. Il est chose certaine que ce royaume eschei de par la royne
Aalis, nostre ayole, a ces enfans, et que ma mere fu lainsne de ces
enfans et son plus droit heir devant la vostre, et puis que ce royaume
eschei de par nostre dite ayole a ces enfans et que mamere fu son
plus droit heir devant la vostre, je sui plus droit heir de vous a avoir
ce bailliage. Car par forme de droit et de raison nous nous devons
prendre a nostre dite ayole, dont leritage nous est escheu, par droit
ligne desendant; et ce nos devons requerre ne avoir le bailliage de
ce royaume par la droite ligne desendant de nostre dite ayole par
les raisons que je ai dites, et il le nous convient a requere de par
nostre dit cousin, a qui ce royaume est escheu par la mort de nostre
dit oncle qui derainement morut saisi et tenant, je di que je sui plus
droit heir de nostre dit cousin, que vous nestes, a avoir cescheete de
ce royaume, cil estoit mesavenu de lui, dont Dieu len gart, pour quoi
je doi avoir le bailliage de ce royaume par devant vous. Et clere chose
est et certaine, que nous ne poons avoir raison que par nos meres,
qui furent seurs germaines de nostre dit oncle et antes de nostre dit
cousin, et puis que nous ni avons raison ne ne poons a (fo. cclvij[v])
avoir que par nos meres, et ma mere fu ainsne de la vostre et plus
droit heir de nostre dit oncle et de nostre dit cousin que la vostre,
se elles vesquissent, dont sui je plus droit heir de vous a avoir ce

---

[a] *The words* Pour toutes les . . . par aucun delles *omitted by Beugnot.*
[b] *MS. chap.* ccxcix (Beugnot, chap. x, pp. 413–14).

bailliage, com celui qui sui fis de celle qui leust eu devant la vostre.
Et a ce que vous aves dit et dites que mamere morut ains la vostre,
et que pource a vostre mere vint ou pot venir la raison davoir
lescheete de nostre dit oncle a heritage, cil fust mesavenu de lui sans
heir de cespouse, ce ne vous vaut ne ne doit valoir ne a moi ennuire,
que a vostre mere en sa vie neschei riens de nostre dit oncle a
heritage. Et puis quelle en sa vie naquist la raison qui li vint ou pot
venir, pource quelle survesqui mamere com celle a qui neschei riens
de nostre dit oncle a heritage, si com jais dit, ne riens nen ot ne tint
qui valoir vous doie, di je que par celle meisme raison lescheete de
nostre dit oncle est revenue a moi par devant vous tout auci com elle
estoit de mamere par devant la vostre. Car nos soumes demoures el
point de nos meres a avoir tel raison chascun lun devant lautre, com
nos meres eussent, celle[a] vesquissent, lune devant lautre, ne il nest
pas doute que ma mere ne leust devant la vostre, dont la doi je
avoir devant vous; que estrange chose seroit et tort manifest ce
vous, qui estes fis de celle de la quel mamere estoit plus droit heir a
avoir lescheete de nostre dit ayole et de nostre dit oncle et de nostre
cousin, si com jai dit, [deucies lavoir par devant moi];[b] ne je nentens
que de gens, qui soient en tel cas com nos somes, il avenist onques
par esgart ne par conoissances de court ne par raison ce que (fo.
cclviij[r]) vous aves dit qui est plusors fois avenu et fait en ce royaume,
ne il navendra ja, se Dieu plaist, car se seroit contre toutes manieres
de drois et de raisons et tort manifest et apert. Et pour ces raisons
et pour toutes les autres que je ai dites ores et autre fois, je di que
vous ne deves avoir le bailliage de ce royaume par devant moy, ains
le doi avoir par devant vous come celui qui sui plus droit heir de
vous dou fis dou roy nostre dit oncle a avoir cescheete, cil mesavenoit
de lui sans heir de cespouse dont Dieu len gart, ne ne veull [c]pour
chose que vous aies dites ore et autre fois, quil demeure que je naie[d]
le dit bailliage par devant vous, si le veull[c] avoir se les homes de la
haute court conoissent que je avoir le doie. Ne pource que vous dites
que vous nentendes que lusage de Franche est tel com jais dit, et
que tout fust il tel que vous ne requeres que par lusage de ce royaume,
je ai dit et encor di, que il est chose certaine que lusage de France
est tel com jai dit, et que il fu mis et establi au conquest de la terre
en ce royaume; et je nentens que puis que cest usage fu establi, quil

---

[a] *MS.* de celle.
[b] *There is clearly a phrase missing here. The reconstruction is based on the wording of the parallel passage, above p.* 36.
[c] *The words* pour chose que . . . si le veull *omitted by Beugnot.*
[d] *MS.* nage.

eust autre establi ^aau conquest de la terre en ce royaume, et je ne
croi que il eust autre establi^a par le seignor ne par les homes, quil le
cassast ne qui contraire li fust; por qui je veull que cel usage me
vaille et doit valoir pour les raisons que jai dites ores et autre fois,
se la court conoist que valoir me doie. Si vell avoir le bailliage de ce
royaume par devant vous pour toutes les raisons que je ai dite ores
et autre fois ou par aucunes delles, se les homes de la haute court de
ce royaume conoissent que je avoir le doie, si me met (fo. cclviij^v)
je en leur conoissance; et cil conoissent que je le doi avoir, je en
euffre a faire ce que je doi com a baill, faisant lon a moi se que lon
doit com a bail.'

[9]   Ce est la maniere coment la haute cour dou royaume de
Jerusalem connut par lassise dou dit royaume que le bailliage
de Jerusalem montoit au baill, por ce que il estoit ainsne dou
son cousin, le conte dou Braine, et^b coument li firent les
homages.^c

Apres cest aleguacion la court dou royaume et messire Joffre de
Sargines[19] et le legat[20] et les maistres[21] et les comunes[22] et les
frairies[23] sacorderent que le baill eust le bailliage dou royaume avant
que le conte de Braine, et tous les chevaliers homes liges furent dune
part et conurent par lassise dou royame de Jerusalem que le bailliage
montoit au dit baill pource quil estoit ainsnes dou conte de Braine.
Et lors messire Goffroi de Sargines se despoula et ala premiers et
fist homage au baill, et puis tous les homes et bourgois et fraires. Et
ensi ot le roy Hugue le baillage dou royaume de Chipre et puis^d
celui de Jerusalem, et tint le bailliage tant que le petit roy trespassa
de ce ciecle, et puis se fist coroner dou royaume de Chipre. Mais

---

^a *The words* au conquest . . . eust autre establi *omitted by Beugnot.*
^b *MS.* et *repeated.*
^c *MS. chap.* ccc (Beugnot, chap. xi, pp. 414–15).
^d *This word followed by* de *struck out.*

---

[19] Geoffrey of Sergines had accompanied St Louis to the East in 1248. He was
regent of Jerusalem from 1259 until 1263, and seneschal of Jerusalem and commander of the French garrison at Acre from 1254. He died 11 April 1269.
[20] William, former bishop of Agen (1247–62), papal legate, patriarch of Jerusalem and bishop of Acre (1262/3–70).
[21] The masters of the Military Orders.
[22] The Italian mercantile communes.
[23] The burgess confraternities.

entre ces faites vint damoisele Marie,[24] et requist le bailliage dou royaume de Jerusalem, et dist aucunes choses que vous ores ci apres.

[10]   Ce est la maniere coment les homes de la haute court de Jerusalem[25] resurent au seignor le sus dit baill, et fu corone doudit royaume apres la mort dou roy Huge, qui estoit mermeaus, qui tenoit son bailliage.[a]

Quant Dieu fist son comandement de Hugue, le petit roy qui fu fis dou roy Henri et de royne Plaisance, le roy (fo. cclix[r]) Hugue, qui tenoit son bailliage adonc pource que elle estoit mermeaus, ala avant et requist as houmes de la seignorie, et les homes le resurent a seignor et fu corones. Et apres avint en Acre a requere le royaume de Jerusalem as homes et a la gent Dacre, le legat et les gens de religion et le maistre dou temple[26] et de lospital[27] et des alemans[28] et le consle de Pise[29] et le baill de Veneise[30] et les frairies et tous les homes Dacre que la se troverent, et [le] desus nome roy dist as homes de la haute court de Jerusalem qui la estoient assembles en la presence des dessus nomes:

[11]   Ce est la maniere coment le sus dit baill asembla la haute court dou royaume de Jerusalem et leur requist le dit royame com droit heir, et coument la dite court conut que il estoit le droit heir, et li offrirent leur homages.[b]

'Seignors, vous saves bien si com nos vous le deymes autre fois en la presence dou patriarche, qui adonc estoit, si a le plus de vous autres qui si estes asembles, que, quant vous nos feistes assavoir le pereillous estat ou le royame estoit, nous en alames a plus tost que nos poemes. Et nostre venue fu pour ij choses: lune pour le grant besoign de ce royaume, et lautre pour entrer raison de ce royaume qui escheu

---

[a] *MS. chap.* cccj (Beugnot, chap. xii, p. 415).
[b] *MS. chap.* cccij (Beugnot, chap. xiii, pp. 415–16).

---

[24] Maria of Antioch, daughter of Melissende of Lusignan and Bohemond IV of Antioch, died 1307.
[25] *lege* Chipre.
[26] Thomas Berard (1256–73).
[27] Hugh Revel (1258–77).
[28] Anno of Sangerhausen (1257–74).
[29] Unknown.
[30] Michele Doro.

nous estoit. Et nous deymes adonc que nos aviens aucunes autres
choses a dire et requerre, *que nous ne voliens lors dire ne requerre,*
jusques atant que le leuc et point fust. Et or nous semble quel soit
leuc et tens de dire. Car le seignor de Sur et dou Thouron[31] sont
ores ci, qui nestoient adonc, pour qui nous vous faissons assavoir
quil ne nous convient pas ores a retraire, que nous soumes (fo.
cclix^v) ne dou soumes venus ne de quel gens estrais, car nos entendons
bien que asses est seu et coneu a entre vous. Et si saves coment ce
royaume, dou quel nous tenons le bailliage, nous est [es]cheus a
heritage par la mort dou monseignor Huguet, mon cousin, que
Dieus pardoint, qui merme daage estoit. Et quel royaume, puis que
nous venimes, nous soumes entres et avons use et usons com de
nostre droit, pourqui vous nous faites le homages et les redevances
et les servises si com lon doit a faire a seignor de ce royaume, et nous
somes prest de faire vers vous se que nous devons.' Et quant le roy
ot ce retrait, les devant dis homes de royaume alerent dune part et
au chief dune piesse se retournerent et firent dire par la coumunaute
et par lotroi deaus tous par un deaus, cest assavoir par sire Jaque
Vidan,[32] que selon clere requeste, que le roy lor avoit fait, il estoient
tout aparailles de faire li leur homages et leur redevances et servises,
si com lon estoit use de faire au seignors dou dit royaume.

[12] Ce est coment damoissele Marie, fille de messire Beamont,[33]
fist lire une charte par un clerc en la presence de la haute
court de Jerusalem, faissant lor assavoir que elle estoit plus
droit heir [a]^b avoir le dit royaume que le baill nestoit, pour
ce que elle estoit desendue de lainsne[e]^c seur de la mere de
sus dit baill.[34] ^d

'Par devant vous, monseignor Hugue de Leisegniau par la grace de
Dieu roy de Chipre, je, damoissele Marie, sui venue par devant

---

^a *The words* que nous ne . . . dire ne requerre *omitted by Beugnot.*
^b *Supplied from table of rubrics, fo.* 17^r.
^c *Supplied from table of rubrics, fo.* 17^r.
^d *MS. chap.* ccciij (Beugnot, chap. xiv, pp. 416–17).

---

[31] John of Montfort, son of Philip, lord of Tyre (1270–83). He had inherited the
lordship of Toron from his mother.
[32] James Vidal (fl. 1249–77). For his career, see Riley-Smith, *Feudal Nobility*,
p. 37.
[33] Bohemond IV, prince of Antioch (1201–33).
[34] The final statement in the rubric is erroneous; the genealogical details given
in the body of this chapter, however, are correct.

vous, seignors, par les religions et homes liges de la haute court dou royame de Jerusalem, et vous fais assavoir com de fu chose que la (fo. cclx[r]) royne Yzabeau[35] fu dame et droit heir dou royaume de Jerusalem; si ot plusors filles: lune des filles fu la royne Marie,[36] qui fu filles dou marques,[37] et espouse le roy Johan;[38] de ceste Marie fu nee Yzabel,[39] espouse de lempereor Fedric;[40] de ceste Yzabel fu nes le roy Conras,[41] pere de Conradin;[42] lautre de[s] avant dites filles fu la royne Aalis, que la devant dite Yzabeau ot dou conte Henri de Champaigne;[43] de la devant dite Aalis fu nes ly rois Henri de Chipre, et dou roy Henri de Chipre fu nes Huguet qui morut avant son aage; lautre fille de la royne fu madame Melissent,[44] princesse Dantioche, fille dou roy Heimeri de Lesignau,[45] qui fu mamere, si com chascun set. Por la quel chose je vous pri et requier et conjuir, si com vos estes tenus de garder et sauver et maintenir chascun en son drot, par les us ou coustume dou royaume de Jerusalem, com cele qui sui le plus prochain heir dou royaume et le plus aparant et fille de la fille de la royne Yzabel [a]et la plus prochaine de la royne Yzabel,[a] mere dou roy Conras, la deraine saisie dou royaume de Jerusalem, a qui vous estes tenus de sauver ces heirs par vous fois, et com celle, que madame mamere survesqui toutes ces seurs, que vous en saisine et en teneure me metes de la seignorie de Jerusalem, et me faites homage et redevance come a dame et a plus aparant heir qui soit ores en ce royame de Jerusalem. Et je sui aparaille et bien le vous euffre tout se que les seignors et les dames doivent faire a leur homes, selonc se que les autres seignors dou dit royaume ont fait et use de faire.' Quant le clerc ot leu la charte, le desus nome roy demanda a la damoysele ce que le clerc ot leu et dit lavoit dit pour elle, et elle respondi que oil. Tantost le desus nome (fo. cclx[v]) roy dist:

[a] *The words* et la plus . . . la royne Yzabel *omitted by Beugnot.*

---

[35] Isabella I, queen of Jerusalem (1190–1205).
[36] Maria of Montferrat, queen of Jerusalem (1205–12).
[37] Conrad of Montferrat, king-elect of Jerusalem, died 1192.
[38] John of Brienne, king of Jerusalem (1210–25), co-ruler of the Latin Empire of Constantinople (1231–7).
[39] Isabella II, queen of Jerusalem (1212–28).
[40] Frederick II of Hohenstaufen, died 1250.
[41] Conrad IV of Hohenstaufen, king of the Romans, died 1254.
[42] Conradin (Conrad V) of Hohenstaufen, executed 1268.
[43] Henry, count of Champagne (1181–97), ruler of Jerusalem (1192–7).
[44] Melissende of Lusignan, wife of Bohemond IV.
[45] Aimery of Lusignan, king of Cyprus (1196–1205), king of Jerusalem (1197–1205).

[**13**] Ce est le respons que le sus dit baill fist contre la request[e]*a* de la sus dite damoisele Marie.*b*

'Dame, nos vous responderons, pour ce que aucunes choses atouchent a nous de ce que vous aves fait dire, et les homes vous feront tel respons, com il lor semblera que a eaus apartient. Saches, dame, que nous vodriens que vous eussies bien et honor, pource que vous mapartenes de si pres com chascun seit, et se qui seroit de vostre raison, Dieus le seit, que vodriens que vous leussies, et quil vous fust garde par tens. Et pour ce que nous vodriens que chascun seust coment lon vous forsconseille, nos esclersirons devant toute ceste gent aucune chose que vous nous deymes arseres devant le maistre dou temple et le sire de Sur [et] devant plusors autres gens. Tout, soit ce que nos avons, yroient a plaidoier a vous, ne vous nestes en point que vous le puissies faire par plusors raisons. Et ce nous ne fuissiens au pais, et il ne eust nul autre heir, et vous feyssies as homes tel requeste com vous leur faites, si sen passeroient il legierement; toutes voies se que nos dirons sera pour esclersir les gens se que vos nous deymes.'

'Saches,*c* dame, que nos volons que chascun sache que, selonc lusage de ce royame, qui veaut requerre escheete ou heritage, il convient quil le requiert de par celui ou de par celle qui en a eu la deraine saisine, cil est de celui lignage, et asses est seu et debatu qui est ensi, et si autrement seroit grant tort seroit et grant perill en par (fo. cclxj*r*) plusors manieres, car nulle saisine ne teneure ne vaudroit riens, et les heirs costiers deseriteroient souvent les drois heirs desendans de la souche, et autres maus a ces se poroient faire; et puis que requere convient, par raison et par usage, de par ceaus qui ont este derainement saisi. Car si fu mon oncle, le roy Henri, et son fis de tel maniere de teneure et de saisine come heir merme peut estre saisi, et que je ne soie lor plus prochain et lor plus droit heir nul ne le peut contredire ne debatre; et se vos voles requerre de par le roy Conrat, nos vous disons que le roy Conrat est en son aage,[46] et lon seit bien que le bailliage ne se peut requerre que par soi meymes de par le derain saisi. Et vous entendes a requerre de par le roy Conrat, que on seit bien, que onques ne fu saisi, et que se il fust present il li convendroit requerre de par le derain saisi et non mie de par lui.

---

a Supplied from table of rubrics, fo. 17r.
b MS. chap. ccciiij (Beugnot, chap. xv, pp. 417–18).
c MS. initial S decorated.

---

[46] i.e., Conradin. Maria was in fact claiming from Isabella II.

Et celui meismes li covendroit requerre de par autrui, cest assavoir de par le derain saisi, donc est il bien clere chose que vous, ne autre, ne poies requerre de par lui, et ne pour quant ces choses ne disons nous mie pour fourme de plait, car elles ne nous ont besoign. Et saches, nos volons bien que chascun sache, que, se les homes de ce royaume entendent que vous naves nulle raison, que il la vous sauvent se vous laves, et tenes en sont par droit et selonc lusage de ce royaume, et bien lont fait tout jours des heirs que il entendent que avoient raison, tout sans ce que il fussent present, ne que nul ne requist de par eaus, si com est aparant de Conrat et de ces heirs; et ce il entendissent que vous ou vostre mere ou autre eusies (fo. cclxjᵛ) droit, il leussent sauve com il firent a eaus.' Et quant le desus nome roy ot ce dit, les homes liges dou royaume alerent ensemble pour faire respons a la desus nomee damoisele des choses que elle avoit dites, et sur ce la dite damoysele sen parti sans oyr respons.

[14] Ce est la maniere coment les homes de la haute court vindrent en presence dou dit roy, et li firent savoir coment il estoient venus faire respons a la sus dite damoysele Marie sur la requeste que elle lor fist, et troverent que elle estoit partie de la, et li manderent par iij homes que ce elle voloit atendre li feroient respons de ce que elle a requis.ᵃ

Adonc les homes liges revindrent devant le roy, et parla par la comunate de tous sire Jaque Vidan, et dist au desus dit roy en tel maniere: 'Sire, les houmes liges de ce royaume qui si sont estoient a uno part pour faire respons a damoyselle Marie daucunes paroles que elle avoit dites et fait dire na pas granment en la presence de vous [et] de ces seignors qui si sont; de qui il voloient faire respons de ce que a ceaus montoit, et sur ce il entendirent quelle sen aloit hors de se gens; siᵇ manderent par iij homes se elle voloit atendre qui li feroient respons a ce que elle avoit requis et dit, et elle ne vost riens atendre, ains sen ala; dont les homes de la seignorie qui si sont vous dient, que pour chose que il aient oye jusques, il ne se beent riens a retraire de ce faire quil vous ont offert a faire, faisant vous a eaus de quil vos ont requis, se vous de vostre volente ne vous en voles arester.'

[15] Ce est le repons que le sus (fo. cclxijʳ) dit roy fist as homes de la sus dite court, que nulle chose nestoit dite ou faite que il

---

ᵃ MS. *chap.* cccv (Beugnot, chap. xvi, p. 418).　　　　ᵇ MS. si *repeated.*

deust arester de non faire en vers eaus ce que il doit, et que il
feissent vers lui se que eaus faire devoient.[a]

Si que le desus nome roy lor respondi et dist que chose nestoit dite
ne faite dont il deust arester, et quil estoit prest et aparaille de faire
ce que il lor avoit autre fois dit a faire vers eaus se que il devroit, [b]et
que il feissent vers lui se que il faire devroient,[b] si com il avoient dit;
si que le desus nome Jaque Vidan li paroffri un escrit en qui se
contenoit la tenour dou serement que il disoient que les seignors
doudit royaume estoient use de faire et devreent faire. Et il tout ensi
le jura, com il contenoit en celle escrit, et tantost com il ot se fait les
homes liges, qui la estoient dou dit royaume de Jerusalem, li firent
homage et tout premierement messire Goffrei et le sire de Sur et le
sire dou Thouron et tout le remenant de homes qui la se troverent; et
puis apres resut les homages des autres qui li estoient tenus a faire;
et apres ressut le serement des frairies et de tous les autres que
serement li devoient; et tint le royaume de Jerusalem quites et en[c]
pais, et fu corones a Sur, la ou les roys de royaumes se coronent; et
fist tant par son sens que temple et ospitau et sire Goffrey de Sargines
et toutes manieres des gens lobeyssoient et servoient come au seignor.
Et tant pourchassa et fist vers le legat et vers tote la gent de religion,
qui[l] li firent une lettre ouverte, seelees de leurs seaus, de trestous
leur eremens qui sont desus escris, et coment le royaume li eschut
par lusage, et coment il le requist as homes come son droit, et il li
firent homage com a droit heir, et que plus (fo. cclxij[v]) droit heir ne
avoit, ne le conte de Braine ne damoisele Marie, et en tel maniere
ot et tint le dit roy les ij royaumes quites et en pais, com de son droit
et sa raison, par lassise et lusage dou royaume de Jerusalem et de
Chipre.

[a] MS. chap. cccvj (Beugnot, chap. xvii, pp. 418–19).
[b] The words et que il . . . il faire devroient omitted by Beugnot.
[c] MS. em.

II
GEORGE RAINSFORD'S
'RITRATTO D'INGLITERRA'
(1556)

edited by

P. S. DONALDSON, M.A., Ph.D.

George Rainsford's *Ritratto d'Ingliterra* appears, in the two manuscripts in which it has come down to us, as an appendix to Stephen
Gardiner's *Ragionamento dell'advenimento delli inglesi et normanni in
Britannia*. Apart from catalogue references and one brief note in
J. A. Muller's introduction to *The Letters of Stephen Gardiner* (Cambridge, 1933), neither the Gardiner work nor that by Rainsford has
been mentioned by scholars. Professors Paul Oskar Kristeller and
William Nelson directed my attention to these texts some years ago,
and suggested the project which has resulted in the publication of
Gardiner's treatise under the title *A Machiavellian Treatise by Stephen
Gardiner* (Cambridge, 1975) and in the edition of Rainsford's appendix presented here. Though it has proved necessary to publish
the two texts separately, they are very closely connected works, and
should be studied together. Rainsford was Gardiner's translator; it
was he who was responsible for the Italian version in which Gardiner's last work survives, and to which his own composition was
appended. The Rainsford text was, therefore, explicitly offered as
a supplement to what Gardiner had done. In his dedication of the
composite volume to Philip II he gave this as the reason for his own
work:

> So that nothing might be lacking in this little book that might
> contribute to an understanding of the laws, procedures, customs,
> nature and humour of the people of Britain, I have composed and
> here appended a portrait of the realm. (fo. IVr)

Thus his own work was composed expressly to supplement what
Gardiner had written.

Gardiner's treatise is a political dialogue whose subject is dynastic
transition: it deals with the changes of dynasty in England's past, and

does so with an eye on present application. The shaping question, which remains however for the most part implicit, is how can a new prince, who is also a foreigner but who has come into power by friendly means rather than by conquest, rule England effectively and establish a lasting dynasty. The answers offered are complex, and their treatment would take us beyond the scope of this introduction: the reader may refer to *A Machiavellian Treatise* and its introduction. It will suffice here to say that Gardiner has Philip in mind, that his book appears to have been prepared as a manual of advice for that king, and that Gardiner uses Machiavelli continually, applying Machiavelli's ideas to contemporary issues and naturalizing his lengthy quotations from *The Prince* and *The Discourses* by providing examples and amplification drawn from English history. The study of this treatise puts Gardiner's political thought as a whole in a new light, and requires a reappraisal of Gardiner's career in his last years, when he was Mary's chancellor, for in the *Ragionamento* he counsels the foreign prince how best to stay in power, and this calls into question the common view that Gardiner opposed Spanish rule and was narrowly nationalistic in his aims. The work is in fact so pro-Spanish that one must suppose that it was never intended for an English audience, but was meant as a private book of counsel for Philip and his advisers. No trace of the English original has survived, and the fact that the two extant manuscripts of the Italian version come from Hapsburg collections—Philip's own library and the library of Antoine Perrenot de Granvelle—tends to confirm the hypothesis that this was a private or secret text. It is therefore to a work of the greatest political sensitivity that Rainsford offers to make additions, and I shall argue that the kind of information Rainsford adds was selected with the changing political situation in mind.

George Rainsford[1] himself is otherwise unknown as a translator or author and, in order to reconstruct the story of the composition and transmission of these texts, it has been necessary to gather the scattered and meagre evidence about his life from county records, heraldic visitations and the like. From these sources we learn something about his connections (particularly with Gardiner) though nothing that helps us get to know the man himself—we have no letters and no references to him in the letters of others. He was the third son of an Oxfordshire gentleman and married Katherine

---

[1] For documentation on Rainsford, see *A Machiavellian Treatise*, pp. 4–15. These pages also provide more extended discussion of the transmission of the text.

Taverner, daughter of a prosperous Essex yeoman. In 1552 he was involved in a legal dispute concerning the administration of his father-in-law's farm. In 1559 he died, and left a total of £90 'in money and money worth', and the lease of a farm in North Weald Bassett to his six children and son-in-law. Fortunately, rather more can be discovered about his family, and the trail leads to a strong presumption that he must have known Gardiner personally. His eldest brother, William, was a gentleman-usher to Henry VIII. He served the king for most of the reign, was knighted and was considerably enriched by grants and leases at the time of the Dissolution. George Rainsford's next eldest brother, John, was also a gentleman-usher for a time, and before that he and his son Thomas had both been in the service of Honour Grenville, Lady Lisle. Lady Lisle was a close ally of Gardiner's in the cause of conservative religion. She was his hostess during his frequent visits to Calais during his diplomatic missions to France in Henry's reign. Her son, James Basset, entered Gardiner's household in the late 1530s, went to the Tower with him under Edward VI, attended him at his death bed in 1555, and became his executor (one of several) when he died. On Gardiner's death, Basset became Mary's chamberlain, and a favourite of Philip II. When, in the spring of 1556 (Rainsford's treatise is dated March 16), Mary began a concerted diplomatic effort to convince Philip, then absent from England at Brussels, to return to England, her arguments centred upon the feasibility of Philip ruling England. She commissioned Lord Paget to make her case, and it was Basset who corresponded with Paget in the Queen's name during these negotiations. Thus, the likeliest reconstruction of events seems to be that Basset either knew of Gardiner's work before he died, or, as executor, came into possession of it at Gardiner's death on 12 November 1555. As Mary's chamberlain, he knew that the Queen's intention was to convince Philip of exactly what Gardiner had wished to demonstrate in the treatise: namely that a Hapsburg monarch could not only rule England, but pass it on to his heirs, if English history and Italian political thought guided his policy. Thus, if the treatise were translated and sent to Philip, it would make an impressive addition to the other persuasions Paget brought to Brussels, especially as Gardiner had been thought one of the privy councillors least favourable to Spanish rule. The project called for some discretion as well as some haste, and therefore Basset (I suggest) selected the brother of trusted family retainers for the job of translating it. We do not know whose idea it was to add a

Description of England to Gardiner's work—but whether it was done at the suggestion of Paget or Basset or another, or was Rainsford's own idea, it is clear that the *Ritratto* provides political balance to Gardiner's work. It was useful to have Gardiner's support on the main point, that Philip could rule in England, but on several other matters the late chancellor's work ran counter to the policies (now dominant) of Paget's faction. Gardiner stresses peace in his treatise, urging the king to mend the rift between Hapsburg and Valois, and ignore the warlike persuasions of his Italian suitors. Rainsford's *Ritratto*, on the other hand, celebrates the military might of England, and recounts the litany of victories over France and Scotland. Gardiner warns, both explicitly and implicitly, against the factiousness and rebelliousness of the nobility, and says that a wise king will ally with the poor. Rainsford, in keeping with Paget's politics, praises the wealth of the nobility and gentry, and is critical of the lower classes and insensitive to the sufferings of the poor.

Rainsford's work, then, was a description of England with a diplomatic purpose and a political slant—'politic history' in the practical and immediate sense: his intention was to provide certain very basic information about England, and to make several significant political distinctions between himself and the author to whose work his own was appended. Thus he is not to be compared with the greater describers of England—Harrison, Leland, Norden—but rather with the Venetian ambassadors and other foreign residents who described the country with an eye to political utility rather than scholarly accuracy. His work is of that genre; he selects many of the same topics to discuss, allots them the same kind of brief treatment, and may well have been acquainted with some contemporary accounts of England written by foreigners. He certainly uses Machiavelli's *Ritratto delle cose della Francia*, adapting French examples to his own task, and he quotes at length from Polydore Vergil's *Anglica Historia* (also used by Gardiner in the *Ragionamento*). He may have used other authors as well—there are, for example some parallels between the *Ritratti* and an anonymous Italian work on England written in Mary's reign, probably before his own work was done.

His discussion of the English economy, particularly his discussion of the causes and effects of the notorious price rise, deserves comment. His analysis fails, like all contemporary accounts, the standards of modern economic history. He holds nothing constant, so that prices, wages, supply and demand circle interminably, one being used to explain another as the argument requires. But though we can place no confidence in his 'proof' that three of the four classes in the realm profited by the price rise, we can take his argument as evidence in the area of social history, as a reflection of class attitudes. Rainsford is unusually callous in his attitude towards the poor, unusually (for his period at any rate) naïve in his celebration of English wealth, especially when contrasted with the nearly contemporary (1549) *Discourse of the Commonweal* and other works of the period.

This edition has been prepared in conformity with the editor's text of Rainsford's translation of Gardiner's work. The Escorial manuscript (E) has been chosen as the basic text even though it has a greater number of grammatical errors than the Besançon manuscript (B), since E was the presentation copy for Philip and because study of the variants suggests that it was the earlier text, of which B may be a corrected copy.

Manuscripts and transmission of the text

The manuscripts are Besançon 1169 and Escorial I–III–17, described fully in the introduction to *A Machiavellian Treatise*. Although E contains a greater number of grammatical errors, it was the presentation copy prepared for Philip of Spain. B appears to be a corrected text, based on E or on a closely related manuscript. B is a less formal text—the hand is less careful, the spacing far less even and generous, and the illumination and other formalities of presentation in E are lacking in B—though it should be pointed out that the italic hand of B, though less careful, appears to be more practised. Castan[1] conjectured that B was the work of an Italian copyist, and while it is not necessary to suppose this, since competent italic scribes were available in England at the time,[2] it is none the less true that the scribe of B is more at home in the hand, and in the language as well. But whatever the faults of scribe E, the fact that the copy sent to Philip contains the greater number of errors suggests haste and/or a less than perfect command of Italian by Rainsford himself, whose language is quite fluid, but occasionally awkward and often incorrect. The Rainsford text occupies fos. 141–189 in the E manuscript, and fos. 70–93 in B.

The E manuscript is clearly the dedication copy, destined for Philip II. It was included in a 1574 catalogue of Philip's books, so

[1] *Catalogue général des manuscrits des bibliothèques publiques de France: Départements*, vol. 32, *Besançon*, ed. A. Castan (Paris, 1897), I, 823.
[2] H. Jenkinson, *The Later Court Hands in England* (Cambridge, 1927), p. 63; A. Fairbank and B. Dickins, *The Italic Hand in Tudor Cambridge* (London, 1962), *passim*.

it was actually owned by him before becoming part of the Escorial collection. The B manuscript was probably intended for Antoine Perrenot de Granvelle, for it appears in early catalogues of his library, which became the basis for the collection founded by the Abbé Boisot, now the Bibliothèque Publique de Besançon.

As I have argued in *A Machiavellian Treatise*, it is likely that the manuscript of Gardiner's original treatise in English, now lost, was transmitted to Rainsford by James Basset for translation, quite possibly with Paget's advice and knowledge, and that the addition of a description of England was thought advisable on several likely grounds—to increase Rainsford's chance of reward, to fill in some of the gaps in Philip's knowledge of England left untouched by Gardiner's contribution, and to moderate the effect of the whole volume in several key areas so as to bring the late chancellor's work more into harmony with the views of the Paget faction.[1] Rainsford, whose voice is very like that of Paget, had the last word.

If the hypothesis concerning Basset's role in transmitting the text of Gardiner's work is correct, then Rainsford would have started on the *Ritratto* some time after Gardiner's death on 12 November 1555, and finished presumably by 16 March 1556, when the dedication is dated. If, on the other hand, Rainsford, perhaps at Gardiner's own request, had started a translation of Gardiner's work during Gardiner's own lifetime, then he could also have started work on his own composition earlier as well. Since the earliest date at which Gardiner could have begun his own work was August 1553, we have a safe set of dates for Rainford's composition of the *Ritratto*—August 1553 to March 1556—and a strong likelihood that the entire work was done after Gardiner's death, November 1555 to March 1556.

Sources, analogues and influences

1. Polydore Vergil. Rainsford used Polydore's *Anglica Historia*, available in editions of 1534, 1546, and 1555: it is not clear which edition he used, especially as he quotes in Italian, not Latin. It is Polydore (imitating Julius Caesar) from whom Rainsford derives his quadripartite division of England, and his echo of the opening words of the *Anglica Historia* ('Britannia omnis . . . dividitur in partes quatuor') announces that work as his model for literary imitation (on a much smaller scale). Rainsford goes out of his way to retain this well-known phrase. Polydore had divided Britain into four parts—Rainsford's 'England' includes Cornwall and Wales, but not

[1] See also below, pp. 58–64.

Scotland, and yet, rather than lose the echo, he provided four parts by dividing England itself into Kent and the curiously awkward 'Northland'. It is interesting that, having made this division, he proceeds to borrow part of Polydore's description of Scotland for his own account of 'Northland' (fos. 142r, 143r, 144r: *Angl. Hist.* (1534), pp. 7–8).[1] He borrows some of the description of Wales (fo. 144r: p. 8) and of Cornwall (fos. 145v–146v: p. 9) but seems to misunderstand Polydore's remark about the Cornish language being similar to the Welsh. The description of 'Kentish' people and geography (fos. 148r–156r: pp. 13, 14) is based on Polydore's description of England proper, but Rainsford elaborates a good deal, and, particularly where Polydore Vergil had minor criticisms to make of the English character or climate, even engages in selective, biased omission or in explanation or apology for what the Italian historian found amiss. Thus Rainsford has nothing but praise for English hospitality, while Polydore, though duly impressed, points out that there is a certain servility in dining at another man's cost. When Polydore criticizes the English lower classes for their vices and for their unfriendliness to foreigners, Rainsford accepts the verdict, but is quick to interpolate a phrase to the effect that plebeians in other lands are similarly churlish, and offers several excuses for their behaviour—they have never travelled, and so are naturally suspicious of foreigners, and they are also wary because in the times of the struggle between Lancaster and York both sides were guilty of bringing foreigners into the realm, who did injury to the common people. The *Anglica Historia* is used for Rainsford's account of the claim of England to the crown of France (fos. 174r–177r: pp. 355–6, 449) and for bits and pieces of Rainsford's version of the various military victories of the English over the French and the Scots (fos. 179r ff: pp. 185–7; 180r: 226; 180v: 246; 182r: 371; 182r–183r: 371–2); and for the description of Ireland (fos. 186v–188v: pp. 217–19). The parallels to Polydore, which are often word for word, are given in the notes, as are those to other sources. Polydore was of course a standard authority in the mid-century, so that Rainsford may well have known him independently of Gardiner's use of the same author in the *Ragionamento*: but since Polydore is Gardiner's regular source for English history, and Gardiner quotes him on occasion in Latin, it seems likely that Rainsford was influenced in his choice of source material by the Gardiner treatise he had in hand to translate.

[1] *Polydoris Vergilii Urbinatis Anglicae Historiae Libri XXVI* (Basel, 1534).

2. Machiavelli.   Gardiner had quoted extensively in his work from *The Prince* and the *Discourses*, and it is apparent (cf. *Machiavellian Treatise*, esp. pp. 156–8, 166) that Rainsford had before him a copy of these works while translating Gardiner from English to Italian, and that, when he came to a Machiavelli quotation, he referred, with more or less care, to the original. In the *Ritratto*, neither of the major works of Machiavelli is cited or paraphrased, but use is made of Machiavelli's *Ritratti delle cose della Francia*.

The identification of this work of Machiavelli's as a source rests on choice of subject matter and on verbal parallels. Among the subjects which Rainsford and Machiavelli have in common (Machiavelli on France, Rainsford on England) are an interest in why the respective realms are richer than they have been in the past, the character of the people, the quality of the soil, the income of the crown, the historical enemies of the countries, the claims each has to the throne of other countries, etc. The similar choice of subjects is not decisive, however, without consideration of verbal parallels, since we have to do in this case with a rather well-defined literary and diplomatic genre—as an examination of various 'descriptions' of European countries[1] in the sixteenth century will show, there was a great deal of coincidence in the chosen topics—a coincidence partly dictated by the practical purposes to which such treatises were put, and partly by the evolution of literary norms for such efforts. Thus an author might include a list of the laws peculiar to the country about which he wrote because the king or minister for whom he wrote needed to know them, or because he found such a list in his literary model—in Tacitus or Polydore or Machiavelli. When allowance for the standardization of the genre has been made, the similarities between Machiavelli and Rainsford remain suggestive of direct influence, and this suggestion is confirmed by direct borrowing. Rainsford echoes Machiavelli in his description of the

---

[1] For descriptions of England, see the reports of the Venetian ambassadors, beginning with Trevisano, in the *Calendar of State Papers, Venetian*. Also *A Relation . . . of the Island of England (1500)*, ed. C. A. Sneyd, Camden Soc. (London, 1847); *Two Italian Accounts of Tudor England: A Journey to London in 1497; A Picture of English Life under Queen Mary*, trans. C. V. Malfatti (Barcelona, 1953); *The Second Book of the Travels of Nicander Nucius of Corcyra*, ed. J. A. Cramer, Camden Soc. (London, 1841). Other sources are listed in Joan Thirsk, *The Agrarian History of England, Vol. IV: 1500–1640* (London, 1967). The availability of such works for Rainsford's use is doubtful in some cases (the diplomatic material especially) but we know that the Italian *Relation* was available, and Polydore Vergil appears to have used it in his own work (see J. D. Mackie, *The Earlier Tudors 1485–1558* (Oxford, 1952), p. 28). Rainsford may have known the *Picture of English Life under Queen Mary* (see below, pp. 57–8).

chancellor's responsibilities, in his numbering of the bishoprics, archbishoprics and parishes of England (for reasons still obscure, Machiavelli included this information in his description of France), and in his description of the law of primogeniture. The quotation is not word for word, but rather Rainsford adapts Machiavelli's remarks, particularly when the fact that one author is writing about France and the other about England makes this necessary. Thus, in the case of the law of primogeniture, we may compare the two versions:

li stati de' baroni di Francia non si dividono tra li heredi come si fa et nella Alamagna et in piu parti d'Italia: anzi pervengano sempre nelli primi geniti; et quelli sono li veri heredi; et li altri fratelli stanno patienti: et aiutati dal primogenito, et fratello loro; si danno tutti all'arme: et si ingegnano in quel mestieri di pervenire à grado, et à conditione di potersi comperare uno stato: et con questa speranza si nutriscano. (1532 Giunta ed., p. 59)

Non dividono i stati et patrimonii tra gli figlioli, come si fa in Alemagna et in Italia, anzi il primogenito solo é herede; li altri fratelli stanno pacienti, et à la cortesia del primogenito. Pero si danno tutti à l'armi, et di servire nella corte, accioche per quel mezo vengino à gradi di comperarsi un stato di vivere à pari di lor fratelli. (fo. 156r–v)

Rainsford has simply trimmed Machiavelli a bit, and has added the necessary addition of service in court. Machiavelli's context leads him to ignore this, since his interest is in showing why the French have such good soldiers, whereas Rainsford's purpose, in context, is the wider one of describing the custom of primogeniture itself.

3. *Ritratti del Regno de Inghilterra.* This work, first printed, with a translation, by C. V. Malfatti in *Two Italian Accounts of Tudor England* (Barcelona, 1953), is an anonymous work, bound in the manuscript version with the *Successi d'Inghilterra* of Francesco Commendone (Escorial X–III–8). Since Commendone had been sent to England in 1553, and since the author of the *Ritratti* seems, on internal evidence, to have been a papal subject, Malfatti felt confident in assuming that the *Ritratti* was written by someone in Commendone's retinue. Thus it would be most significant indeed if a direct relation between Rainsford's work and that of a member of the Papal diplomatic party in England could be shown. However, such a relationship, though quite possible on the basis of several passages, cannot be considered firmly established. The several parallels in subject matter, the law of patrimony (see above for

Rainsford's borrowing from Machiavelli on this), the account of
the various offices of the land, etc., are not nearly so close as the
parallels between Machiavelli and Rainsford, and can be accounted
for by reference to the logic of the task itself, or to generic require-
ments. None the less, there is one passage considerably closer than
the others, namely the account of the jury system in England, and
I have included the parallels in the notes.

The Ragionamento,   It is not surprising that in several instances one
can hear an echo of the *Ragionamento,* on which Rainsford must have
been working concurrently, in the *Ritratto.* To my ear, there is such
an echo in Rainsford's passage on the parliaments, which begins
'Il re che circa gloria per via de giustitia non puole publicare nuove
leggi ne rompere le vecchi, fare guerra, conchiudere pace, commandare tributo ò essattioni del popolo senza consentimento del
commune consiglio detto il parliamento.' (fo. 171r–v).
      This strikes one as related to the Machiavellian–Gardinerian
attitude towards law. Gardiner, influenced in this by Machiavelli,
places high value on the observance of old law, and the folly of
making new laws or exacting new taxes, while at the same time
curiously relativizing the moral issues—following such laws is the
proper path for 'un re che circa gloria per via de giustitia': but there
are other kings, in other circumstances in which justice is not so
important as security, and therefore, even while recommending just
rule, Gardiner refrains from categorical rule-making, and from
moralizing, as does Rainsford here.
      In another passage, Rainsford seems to recapitulate Gardiner's
argument concerning English history in capsule form. Rainsford is
discussing the reasons for the xenophobia of the English commons:

> There is also another reason why they hate foreigners, and that is
> because in the past they have suffered from the cruelty of the
> Danes, the raids of the Scots, and the harsh rule of the Normans.
> Their possessions have been destroyed, their goods taken, their
> friends and relations killed. These things also happened quite
> often in the period when the factions ruled: first one side, then the
> other, calling foreigners into the country as mercenaries, who in-
> dulged in plundering the poor people like thieves rather than
> serving them as soldiers against the enemy. (fos. 152v–153r)

This recalls Gardiner's account of the several foreign dynasties who
had ruled England, his account of the 'factions' of York and Lan-

caster, and his Machiavellian warnings about mercenaries, all of which form part of an implicit argument, in the Marian political context, against Philip bringing in large numbers of Spaniards, an essential restriction for Philip to observe if he was to rule happily and peacefully in England, a country whose history dictated a minimal Spanish presence.

At this point it is necessary to examine the ways in which Rainsford was *not* influenced by the Gardiner text. It is important to assess differences as well as similarities not only in order to clarify Rainsford's purposes, but also because we possess Gardiner's *Ragionamento* only in Rainsford's translation, and therefore the divergence between what Rainsford wrote under his own name and what he wrote as Gardiner's translator can provide an indication of his reliability. In fact there are several sharp divergences in opinion and in tone on issues which were important ones in 1555 and 1556: Rainsford's attitude towards the dissolution of the monasteries, towards class relations, and towards the question of war with France differs from Gardiner's on these subjects, these differences suggesting that his work as translator was honest, and that he allowed to stand in the Gardiner text opinions which he would not have written himself.

Gardiner's opinion of the dissolution of the monasteries is given in his account of the revolts in Lincoln and York in 1536. Of Henry VIII, Gardiner says 'truly he gave his people great opportunity to conspire against him when he began the rape of the spiritual property and the overthrow of the monasteries' (fo. 127v). The dissolution, then, was a nearly sufficient excuse for revolt, in Gardiner's eyes and, in his political activity as Mary's chancellor, he favoured the return of as much Church land as possible, as did the Queen herself.[1]

Rainsford's attitude is quite different—the emphasis falls upon the profitable use to which the abbey lands had been put. His context is the account he gives of the wealth of England, to which the dissolution greatly contributed:

One reason for their wealth is that the income of the monasteries and other holy places, which made up one fourth of the realm, are at present divided: part free to nobles and part sold and rented to merchants and farmers. So that each of the four classes has succeeded in drawing gain from these properties, which before the

[1] E. H. Harbison, *Rival Ambassadors at the Court of Queen Mary* (Princeton, 1940), p. 216.

time of Henry were so shut within the cloisters that only the king
and a few poor people benefited by them, whereas now everyone
gains by them, and the crown is much enriched, not without,
however, the infamy of the first usurper. (fo. 162v)

And later, cataloguing the wealth of the Crown, Rainford writes 'I
will not mention the goods of the monasteries and other holy places
which Henry added to the crown income. They are inestimable.'
(fo. 173r). Henry was a usurper of Church property, as he must have
been for anyone writing from the point of view of the Catholic
restoration: but the emphasis falls upon the benefits of the dissolution. Rainsford could not have spoken this way had he entertained,
as Gardiner did, the idea of restoring those lands to the Church.

This passage also exemplifies a second difference between Rainsford and Gardiner, a difference in class attitudes. One notes here
Rainsford's customary bias towards the nobility, the merchants and
the wealthy farmers, and his belittling of the extent and significance
of the sufferings of the poor. The tone of dismissal in 'each of the
four classes has succeeded in drawing gain from these properties,
which before the time of Henry were so shut within the cloisters that
only the king and a few poor people benefited by them, whereas now
everyone gains by them'[1] is confirmed by Rainsford's attitude towards the *artisani* (by which he means those classes who earn their
living by the work of their hands) and the poor in his discussion of
the effects of inflation. At first, Rainsford offers to demonstrate that
two classes, the farmers and the gentlemen, have been enriched by
inflation, and that the other two classes, the merchants and artisans,
have not been impoverished ('mostrerò ch'il mercadante et l'artesano non sono per questo modo neanche impoveriti' (fos. 164v–165r)).
But as it turns out, his argument on this point, based upon balance of
trade, can apply only to the merchants, and Rainsford cannot make
good the offer to show that the artisans have held their own, and
concludes 'pero l'alzamento delli commodità in Ingliterra ha
arrichito tre sorti delli detti huomini, et la quarto vive, cioe l'artesano
quantunqe non in quella morbidezza che soleanno' (fos. 166v–167r).
Most of the evidence now available indicates that the price rise of the
mid-century created severe hardships for the wage-earner (see below, pp. 65–8); but even without such evidence one can note that

[1] 'ogni sorti deli predetti quatro si prevaglion, et cavano utile di quelli beni,
iquali dinanzi il tempo di Henrico eran in tal modo inchiuse nelli chlaustri, che
nullo (eccetto il re et pochi poveri) prevalevano di quelli, dove al presente sono
utile generalmente di tutti' (fo. 162v).

the argument is confused and the tone apologetic, for Rainsford is no longer arguing that the artisans have maintained their standard of living, but that it doesn't matter. As for the poor, Rainsford does not include them in his fourfold division of English society, attributes their poverty to old age and large families, and celebrates the system of poor relief as an adequate remedy for their needs:

> For those who are very poor, who, because of age or being bur-
> dened with many children, cannot make a living, there is pro-
> vision made in each parish of the land for them to receive charity
> at public expense, and men are assigned to distribute necessities
> to them once a week. And therefore the poor do not go begging
> in England, but alms are given to them in their own houses. This
> holy work was instituted by Henry, and confirmed in perpetuity
> by Edward his son. (fos. 167r–v)

While it is true that the poor relief legislation of Henry and Edward (especially 27 Henry VIII c. 25 and 5 & 6 Edward VI c. 2) attempted to create a system of parish relief, the system was not an effective one, for it lacked adequate provision for enforcement.[1] One might compare Rainsford's callous dismissal of the problem here with the humane and responsible preamble of the Henrician draft bill for poor relief which Elton discusses in his article.

To this account of Rainsford's bias against the poor and in favour of the upper classes we must add his discussion of the English character (fos. 151v–156r) based on Polydore Vergil, in which it is the life of the gentry which exemplifies the English virtues, the plebeians being discourteous, lazy, insolent, impatient of insults and xenophobic. Rainsford follows Polydore in this, and he adds to his source at this point an explanation of why the English common people hate foreigners. His work as a whole is dedicated to a foreign consort, and the point was a touchy one during the reign of Philip and Mary. It must be said that, though he finds reasons for the vices which Polydore attributes to the English plebeians, he does accept the negative judgment of his source, while at the same time removing Polydore's criticism of the English mode of country hospitality among the gentry. Polydore makes the point that it is always servile to dine at another's cost, and this Rainsford omits (fos. 155r–156r and note).

---

[1] See Sir George Nichols, *A History of the English Poor Law* (London, 1854, rev. ed. 1898, repr. 1967), pp. 94–148; E. M. Leonard, *The Early History of English Poor Relief* (Cambridge, 1900), pp. 53–66, especially p. 61; G. R. Elton, 'An Early Tudor Poor Law', *Economic History Review*, 2nd series, vi (1954), 55–67.

c

Like Rainsford, Gardiner deals in the *Ragionamento* with the question of the poor reputation which the English commons enjoy among foreigners ('licentioso, audace, desiderabile d'innovare, tumultuosa, morbida' (fo. 44r)), but Gardiner's defence of the English common people is far more thorough and committed than is Rainsford's. It is in fact a partisan defence, for Gardiner argues that a citizen army is always better than a mercenary one, that English people should be armed, and that a prince who trusts and allies himself with the poor, and not with the factious and self-serving nobility, will rule securely. For Gardiner it is a princely virtue—'affability'—to take the side of the poor, and to this virtue he gives a central place:

> among all the qualities there is none of greater force in gaining fame and reputation with a people than to listen to the complaints and supplications of the poor and avenge their injuries. (fo. 126v)

It was this virtue which strengthened King Stephen's rule, and it was likewise by listening to the complaints of the poor that Absalom was enabled to challenge Solomon's power in Israel. Solomon himself, and Augustus Caesar, practised this virtue (fos. 126v–127v), and in more recent times, the tradition of affability was carried on by Henry VIII. Here Gardiner offers two grim examples of affability which are significant for our purposes. The first is an incident which took place, according to him, during the uprisings in the North. During the revolts of 1536, the gentlemen who followed the king's party used the rebelliousness of the people as an excuse for illegal confiscations and evictions. When out hunting one day, Henry chanced upon a poor man who was making his way to court to complain of these practices. Henry comforted him and assured him that 'defenderò li mei simplici pecore dalla ingordigia deli lupi et vendicarò le ingiurii d'essi' (fo. 129r). When he inquired into the case, Henry had the offending gentlemen hanged at their own gates, and thus

> he acquired great love and trust among the people who before hated him because he had usurped religious property. They lifted their hands to the heavens, thanking God for giving them such a king who listened to the complaints of the poor and gave them justice. . . . (fos. 129v–130r)

The second example concerns Henry's ordering the execution and mutilation of those who had been allowed to oppress the people during the reign of Henry VII (fos. 130r–132r). Even such savage measures come under the head of affability, and it is true of the treatise as a whole that the prince is advised to make common cause with the 'people', and more particularly the poor, even when their interests are opposed to those of the gentry and nobility. Gardiner's attitude is thus far different from Rainsford's: it is a paternalistic attitude, reinforced by the Machiavellian consideration that the people are a surer foundation on which to build an enduring rule than are the upper classes.

As in the case of the issue of Church property, the difference between Gardiner and Rainsford is one which reflects a factional division in Mary's Council and in her Parliaments, a split between the party of Lord Paget and that of Gardiner.[1] In both cases Rainsford takes the position Paget would have taken, and which was, after Gardiner's death in November 1555, the dominant tendency in Philip and Mary's government. On a third issue as well, Rainsford sounds more like Paget than Gardiner, and that is the issue of war and peace. Gardiner had been the leader of the peace party from the moment the Spanish match became a possibility. He participated in the peace conference at Marck and worked in other ways to mend the rift between Hapsburg and Valois.[2] In the *Ragionamento* he blames the wars in Tuscany on the blandishments of the Italian exiles (fos. 96r–97r) and warns Philip against listening to his own Italian suitors crying for war. The treatise ends with an impassioned plea for peace (fo. 138r–v), and if, as I have argued in my introduction, the *Ragionamento* was meant to influence Philip on a number of important issues of the day, foremost among these would be the issue of peace. Rainsford does not take a position on the subject in the *Ritratto* in the sense that he does not argue for war, but the tendency of the work, given the context of the time and circumstances in which he wrote, is clearly in that direction. Nearly a quarter of the whole treatise is given to military matters (fos. 169r–171r, 176r–185r); Rainsford celebrates the military power of England, gives a firm statement of the claim of England to the Crown of France, and recites the litany of English victories over the Scots and the French. This section can only be taken as the work of a man for whom the prospect of war was acceptable, for in the spring of 1556 the pressures for English entry into the war with France were mounting,

---

[1] See Harbison, *Rival Ambassadors*, pp. 62, 216 ff; *A Machiavellian Treatise,* pp. 12–15, 25–7, 36–7.
[2] *Calendar of State Papers, Spanish*, XI, 347; Harbison, *Rival Ambassadors*, ch. ix; *A Machiavellian Treatise*, pp. 28–30.

and would soon draw the nation into that war, despite the provisions
of the marriage treaty between Philip and Mary, which stipulated,
at Gardiner's request, that England was to remain neutral in such
a case.[1]

Gardiner's *Ragionamento* survives only in Rainsford's Italian
version. We have his word for its authenticity, and his claim may be
supported in several ways. In the first place, the treatise is of a piece
with what Gardiner did as chancellor in Mary's reign, and at the
same time helps to explain details of strategy and intention which
have heretofore been obscure, as I have argued in *A Machiavellian
Treatise*. And, as it is both one with, and helps to explain, Gardiner's
politics, so it is like his earlier writings and yet adds something new to
the picture, of explanatory force.[2] I have also shown that Rainsford
was very likely to have known Gardiner, and that, through his
family connections with James Basset, was in a position to have access
to Gardiner's papers after his death. The *Ritratto*, in so far as the
attitudes and opinions it expresses are different from Gardiner's,
provides further support for the hypothesis that Rainsford worked
from an authentic Gardiner text, and suggests in addition that he
refrained from making intentional changes in that text as he translated. If Gardiner's opinions were somewhat out-of-date in the spring
of 1556, they were allowed to stand nevertheless, and Rainsford's
own views, so like those of Paget, were confined to an appendix.

The price rise

It is in his discussion of the rise in prices (fos. 163v–169r) that Rainsford most clearly reveals his biases, for his contemporaries and
modern commentators are nearly unanimous in the view that the
mid-century inflation caused widespread suffering, whereas Rainsford presents it as a great benefit to the nation as a whole, and denies
that it has caused suffering, admitting only that the artisans no
longer live in that 'morbidezza' to which they had grown accustomed, and blaming such real poverty as there was on old age and
large families (fo. 167r and above, p. 61).

His position is that the English were never richer than at the time
at which he wrote. The causes for their wealth he gives as (1) the
dissolution of the monasteries (fo. 162r–v) which benefited all four

---

[1] Harbison, *Rival Ambassadors*, p. 102.
[2] Arguments concerning the coherence of Gardiner's thought throughout his
career are presented in my Columbia dissertation, 'A Machiavellian Treatise by
Stephen Gardiner' (1972), and have been expanded for future publication.

classes, gentlemen, merchants, farmers and artisans (though, characteristically, he only demonstrates a benefit in the case of the first three): (2) drainage and land-reclamation: (3) inflation (fos. 163v–169r). The gentlemen and farmers benefit by this, as the selling classes. They are nearly self-sufficient, and what they buy (chiefly luxury imports) represents only one per cent of what they sell. Three-quarters of the commodities of the realm are sold outside the kingdom, and when the greater part of the commodities of a nation are exported, it is in the common interest to have high prices. The merchants do not lose because of the high prices, because they buy dear and sell dear. As noted above, Rainsford begins by offering to show that the artisans, or wage-earners, are not injured by high prices either, but he abandons the attempt, and rests content with implying that such a lowering of standard of living as they have undergone has been a matter of exchanging a luxurious for a merely adequate standard; that inflation can have caused real and widespread suffering is denied by implication; what poor there are have old age and large families to thank for it, and are, in any case, well taken care of by poor relief.

In order to gauge the position taken by Rainsford, it is well to remind oneself of the ordinary range of contemporary comment on the phenomenon of the price rise. In 1549, the author of 'Policies to reduce this Realme of Englande unto a Prosperous Wealthe and Estate' unequivocally connected the price rise to the immiserization of the populace:

> [a nation is] not worthie to be cawled a floureshinge realme yf the most parte of the persons and people lyve in extreme pouertie, victuall being alwaies at so hieghe price that in those yeres in which Corne doth mystake in eney thing, or Cattell chaunce never so littell thorrowe morren or other incessions to Die, a great nombre of the people shalbe in dainger of famyne . . . the highe price of all thinges is not only the greateste matter that the people grudge at: and one of the principall oucasion of povertye and faymine: but also the cheyfiste cawse that the kinges maiestie cannot without expence of wonderfull great sommes of money mentaigne his warres againste his eneymies.[1]

The author warns of the danger of insurrection because of the price rise, and finds its causes in the fall of the exchange rate between

---

[1] R. H. Tawney and Eileen Power, *Tudor Economic Documents* (New York, 1963, first pub. 1924), III, 314–15.

England and Flanders, which he in turn attributes to the high price
paid for silver at the mint, and to engrossing.

William Forrest's *Pleasaunt Poesye of Princelie Practise* (1548) takes
a similar view:

> The worlde is chaunged from that it hathe beene
> Not to the bettre but to the warsse farre:
> more for a penye wee haue before seene
> then nowe for fowre pense, whoe liste to compare
> This suethe the game called makinge or marre.
> Vnto the Riche it makethe a great deale,
> but muche it marrethe to the Commune weale.[1]

The author of the *Discourse of the Common Weale* presents several
points of view. The merchant holds that everyone has suffered from
inflation:

> every man finds himself grieved at this time and no man goes clear
> as far as I can perceive: the gentleman that he cannot live on his
> land only as his father did before; the artificer cannot set so many
> awork by reason all manner of victuals is so dear; the husband-
> man by reason his land is dearer rented than before. Then we
> that be merchants pay dearer for everything that comes over the
> sea by the third part well, and, because they of beyond the sea
> will not receive our money for their wares as they were glad in
> times past to do, we are fain to buy English wares for them and
> that does cost us dearer by the third part, almost the one-half
> dearer than did beforetime.[2]

But the doctor in the dialogue holds that the merchants have not
suffered as others have. The knight asks him what loss we have by the
price increases, if we sell our commodities as dearly as do the
foreigners, and the doctor replies that to some it is no loss at all (the
merchants, who buy dear and sell dear); to some, indeed, it is a gain
(to those who hold fixed leases and sell agricultural products 'they
pay for their land good cheap and sell all things growing thereof
dear'); but to others the inflation is 'a greater loss than it is profit
to the other, yea, generally, to the utter impoverishing of the realm'.[3]
In this third category the doctor includes noblemen and gentlemen
who live on rents (he discounts here the effects of rack-renting) and

---

[1] Tawney and Power, *Tudor Economic Documents*, III, p. 40.
[2] *A Discourse of the Commonweal of this Realm of England*, ed. Mary Dewar (Char-
lottesville, 1969), p. 33. [3] Ibid., p. 80.

'yeomen, servingmen and men of war that having but their old stinted wages cannot find themselves therewith as they might beforetime without rapine or spoil'.[1]

One finds an awareness, in contemporary accounts, that the price increase affected different classes differently: but Rainsford is unusual in his insistence that the price increase was good for the nation as a whole and in his denial of the hardship others saw as the consequence of inflation.

Rainsford is extreme also in his view of the effects of foreign trade. He sees the exportation of 'three fourths' of the commodities of the realm as a strength, and claims that the luxury imports consumed by the gentry and farmers are only one per cent of the value of the exports, and that there is therefore a tremendous advantage in maintaining high prices for those exports. This is an unreasonable account of the situation, and it is not surprising that contemporaries did not share Rainsford's view. A letter of William Lane to Cecil of 1551, for example, says that 'we spende and consume with in thys Reme swche sumes and quantytys of forin comodytys that all the wolle, clothe, tyn, lede, lether, and coles, and other mercha[n]dys to be caryyd owte to thys Reme, ys not abyll to contarvayle, paye, or Recompense for the sayde marchandys browghte in to the Reme, note by one quartar parte or lesse.'[2] The author of the *Discourse of the Commonweal* also took a more pessimistic view of foreign trade, and pointed out that while the commodities that left England, such as corn and wool, were necessary to human life, those which returned were luxuries: 'strangers fetch from us our great commodities for very trifles'.[3]

Thus Rainsford's treatise stands nearly alone, both in regard to its overall evaluation of the effects of the price rise, and in regard to the effects of foreign trade. Modern opinion on the subject is scarcely more favourable to Rainsford's analysis. The causes of the phenomenon remain much debated, with population increase, debasement, and the effect of American treasure still, after several generations of debate, among the possible causes.[4] But that there was a price rise in the sixteenth century which was extraordinary and until then unparalleled is not in doubt, and it is to be noted that 1556,

---

[1] *A Discourse*, p. 81.

[2] Tawney and Power, *Tudor Economic Documents*, II, 184.

[3] *A Discourse*, p. 63. On the balance of trade see the remarks of C. E. Challis in P. Ramsey, *The Price Revolution in Sixteenth Century England* (London, 1971), pp. 128 ff.

[4] On this see especially Ramsey, *The Price Revolution*, and R. B. Outhwaite, *Inflation in Tudor and Early Stuart England* (London, 1969).

the year in which Rainsford wrote, is located at an extraordinary peak of the curve. The Phelps Brown–Hopkins price index for consumables (1451–1475 = 100) for the 1550s reads as follows:[1]

1550	262	1555	270
1551	285	1556	370
1552	276	1557	409
1553	259	1558	230
1554	276	1559	255

and the high point reached in 1556–7 is not reached again until 1587. Contemporary accounts must often have been exaggerated, but the preponderance of views contrary to Rainsford's make his difficult to credit, and modern historians, though they disagree on the effects of inflation on various classes, are agreed that it must have meant real misery for the poor. Peter Ramsey summarizes:

> If, as is usually held, the middling ranks of landed society improved their economic position during the sixteenth century, it was not so much at the expense of their betters or of each other as of the poor. The real victims of economic forces in this age were the evicted agrarian smallholder and the landless labourer of both town and country. They lost comfort and status in both real and absolute terms. Their diet deteriorated, with bread bulking significantly larger in their purchases, and it would be two centuries and more before they began to recover the position they had enjoyed in the golden days of the fifteenth century.[2]

The point of the present discussion is not to criticize the shortcomings of Rainsford as an economic theorist, but to assess his biases. That he could write so callously of prosperity at this time is an indication of his bias toward the rich, and his lack of concern for the poor and for human suffering generally. And in this bias, as in other matters, he differed sharply from Gardiner, whose treatise he had in hand to translate.

[1] Ramsey, *The Price Revolution*, p. 39.
[2] Ibid., p. 17.

NOTE ON THE TEXT

The text has been prepared according to the principles followed in the editor's *A Machiavellian Treatise by Stephen Gardiner*. The basic text is E, which, of the two extant manuscripts, has the greater authority: it was the copy presented to Philip II, to whom the translation is dedicated, and, while B may be an emended copy of E, E cannot be a copy of B, for B corrects many of the grammatical errors of E. We cannot imagine the scribe of E systematically introducing errors in gender and agreement for B's legible and correct readings. When the possibility of scribal error in E and the fluidity of Renaissance Italian are accounted for, there remain a great many grammatical errors for which the author himself may have been responsible. The pattern of error is clear enough to suggest that Rainsford's Italian (though quite fluent) was lacking in grammatical precision; even if all the errors were scribal (which is highly unlikely) Rainsford allowed them to stand in the copy destined for the king. The possibility that the E readings preserve linguistic errors of the translator, then, is another reason for its selection as the basic text.

The editorial procedures employed have as their aim the production of an intelligible, rather than grammatically correct text. If Rainsford's Italian is imperfect, his errors and idiosyncrasies are part of the historical evidence and the anomalies of spelling and form of the E manuscript have therefore been retained in the present text, which follows the manuscript exactly except in the case of obvious errors which seriously obscure the meaning, and in graphic matters unlikely to reflect Rainford's knowledge of the language. Thus the word division of the manuscript has been respected as has the use of the accent and apostrophe. Other punctuation has been normalized, as have the use of capital letters and the use of *u* and *v*. The combination *ij* has been rendered *ii*. Paragraph divisions have been made by the editor.

Normalization apart, the E reading has been abandoned only when illegible or clearly in error in a way that seems likely to cause real confusion. In such cases the B reading has been preferred, or, in a very few cases, an emendation has been made. In all such cases rejected readings from the manuscripts are preserved in the apparatus, as are all the B variants except for those of capitalization and punctuation.

Occasionally editorial confirmation of misspellings and other anomalies is indicated in the notes. This has been done in cases of possible confusion: no attempt has been made to direct attention systematically to all of the irregularities of E's usage.

(fo. 141r) RITRATTO D'INGLITERRA[a]
COMPOSTO DA GEORGIO RAINSFORDO

Ingliterra è divisa in quatro regioni principali:[1] Nortlandia, D'ivisione del Realme Wallia, Cornubia, et Cantia, iquali sono tra loro diversi ne'costumi, lingua, et alcuni anche nelle leggi, et ciascaduno di queste quatro contenne in se molte provincie et contadi.

(fo. 141v) Northlandia è la magiore, la qual si stendi da Tamesi Nortlandia fine à Tueda fiume, quale divide Ingliterra da Scotia, et dal mare germanico nel levante, fin ad Herfordia citta posta nelle parti occidentale del regno.

In questa parte havitanno[b] li piu parte deli baroni principali del regno, et è habitata per tutto. Vi non sono ne montagne, ne grand selve, ma fertilissime pianure, le quale (fo. 142r) producono frumenti, orsi,[c] aveni, fave, pise, frutti et herbe per li huomini et altri animali in grand abondantia. Gli popoli verso la Scotia sono L'abondantia buoni soldati, stanno sempre su le armi, lor case sono picolo,[d] et basse, coverte di pallia. Il suo cavallo è ligato sempre à li piedi del letto, et la lanza (per esser lunga) al capo, per mezo de la covertura.

La pace tra i popoli di Scotia et d'Ingliterra nelli confini habita(fo. 142v)ti non è mai ferma et le treuge sono sempre dubiosi. Nulla amicitia ò parentado, nulle[e] patti o conditioni tra L'inimicitia tra gli inglesi et scocesi li regi puole rafrenare questi popoli da li continui scaravinse, scorerie, et robberie quale usano, et hanno usato di lungo tempo uno c'ol altro.

Fanno giustitia tra lor secondo il potere, et non secondo la ragione, perche colui che questa notte havra quaranta[f] capi di bestiame, domane ha(fo. 143r)vra nullo, talche egli sanno per esperientia, meglio che gli altri, che questi sono beni di fortuna, flussi et incerti. Lor cavalli sono buoni, et correno velocissime, manegiano con grand desterità la lanza, talche[g] correndo il cavallo à tutta la forza, piglieranno un facioletto ò guanto[h] dalla terra senza fallire punto. Fanno del panno in grand quantità. Brusano p'el mancamenti del legno (fo. 143v) un certo piere negro Carbone marino durissimo, cavato de la terra, il qual dà un calore vehemente, et lo chiamano carbone marino.[2]

---

[a] DINGLITERRA B   [b] habitanno B   [c] orzi B
[d] picole B   [e] nulli B   [f] guaranta B
[g] tal che B   [h] guante B

Yorcka[b] La citta principale in questa regione è Yorcka,[a] notabile per la morte di Severo imperatore.[3] La venne nomata Nortlandia da la regione del vento, perche north in quella[c] languagio vuole dire settentrio, et lande, terra: cioe settentrionali parti.

Wallia Wallia è posta à la parte senestra (fo. 144r) semisola, circondata da tre bande dal oceano, et verso l'oriente su'l fiume Sabrina detta, et de l'altra parte la citta di Herfordia.

La terra[4] è fertile neli[d] parti verso il mezo giorno, et la produce frumenti, frutti, et herbe, dove sono le pianure. Ma perche la magiore parte sono aspri monti, verso l'oriente gli popoli vivano Vita dura vita dura, mangiando pane d'avena, et lor bevanda è melle et aqua, cotta insieme simile à quella de (fo. 144v) li turchi, et li chiamono in lor lingua metheglyn. Sono di statura generalmente piu alti, che l'inglesi, feroci nella guerra, hanno in odio la vita quieta, nel passato sono stati mal voluntieri subietti à l'inglese, et Lingua ribellorono spesse volte, ma al presente sono obedientissimi.
britannica Tengono l'antica lingua deli[e] Britanni, hanno lor leggi pecu-
Leggi pecu- liari per li privilegii deli regi concedutili. Sono[f] eccetti d'ogni
liare essattione, et tribu(fo. 145r)to che li altri pagino.[g] Il tributo[5]
Il tributto annuale[h] che la provincia paga al re nella pace, è quarante[i] mila
de' walli scudi; nella guerra li mandan sei milia huomini à cavallo, et quatordeici[j] a piedi, et tengono altri tanti parechiati, per li colpi di fortuna.

Le comodità della provincia sono panni grossi, volgarmente frisi detti, iquali fanno in grand abondanzia. Nel tempo d'inverno tutti si vestino di quelli generalmente per lo regno, et gentil-huo(fo. 145v)mini et plebei. La produce capre et vacche, et buoni Molti cavalli per la guerra. In questa provincia le sono molti castelli castelle et fortressi, de iquali[k] alcuni ne sono bene muniti et guardati.
Il Carmerdena è la citta principale.
primogenito Il primogenito del re d'Ingliterra per l'antichità del popolo,
del re e[l] grand nomero di buoni soldati, et accioche si mantengino in fede
chiamato è publicato principe di Wallia, et habità[n] tra loro. Non lontano
principe di (fo. 146r) di Carmerdena sono le mine d'oro.
Wallia[m]
Cornugallia La tertia parte è Cornugallia detta, perche si estendi al sembianza d'un corno in longessa verso l'Espagna per nonanta Sterile mila.[o] La terra è sterile, quello che la produce è piu per la grand

[a] Yorcha B   [b] Yorcha B   [c] quello B
[d] ne li B   [e] de li B   [f] Sone E
[g] pagano B   [h] Word interlined in E   [i] quaranta B
[j] quatordeci B   [k] dei quali B   [l] è B
[m] Wal: E; Walli B   [n] habita B   [o] a cancelling e in E

faticha*a* et industria deli*b* huomini, che di sua bontade. D'indi
vengono il piombo, bronzo, et stagno, et altri metalli quali sono Abondante*c*
portati per tutta Europa. Per queste mine i popoli vivanno in de metalli
(fo. 146v) grand richessa.⁶ *d* Gli popoli sono agili et gagliardi nel Gli
saltare, correre, gittare il ferro co'l pie ò co'll'e*e* brachia,⁷ nel popoli
lottare, et in tutti li altri essercitii del corpo son valentissimi, et non gagliardi
cedono à nulla altra persona di quale provincia o regno che sia.
Hanno un peculiare linguagio differenti dalli walli, et similmente
dali*f* inglesi.⁸ Excestria è la citta principale, dove fanno le caresie Excestria
per le calze, piu fini che (fo. 147r) in qualche altra provincia che
si fa.

La Cantia è la minima parte dele*g* detti quatro, ma per la Cantia
quantità piu nobili, piu richi, et piu abundante. La aera è
temperata. La terrena fertile, quale produce fromenti, frutti, Fertilita
herbe, et ogni altro sorti di grano, pecore, et altri bestiame in
grand abondanza. Qui se fanno di panni alti, li piu fini e megliori
che in qualche altra provincia. Gli popoli alcuni sono morbidi, I popoli
obstina(fo. 147v)ti, impatienti, non comportino ingiuria senza
vendetta. Cantorburia è il capo, ornata di molte belle terre, di
grand fiume,*h* di alti selve, et piacevoli collini, sopra quali ogni
tempo del anno nascono i suavi et varii fiori. D'indi nasce il Proverbio
proverbio delli forestieri, che la terra e buona, ma genti cattivi. di forestieri
Laera*i* in ogni luogo è temperata, il cielo nel estate sereno, et li
notti chiari, li giorni hanno hore diece(fo. 148r)otto di longezza,
li caldi del estate causati della lungezza*j* del giorno, sono con i
piacevoli venti iquali continuamente soflianno, mitigati. Nel
inverno spesse pioge, senza tempestati, senza grand grandine o
nevi.

Ingliterra e abondantissima⁹ dogni*k* cosa necessaria per la vita La bonta
humana per se. L'ha ogni sorte d'bestie eccetto elephanti, camili, della*l*
muli et asini. La non produce animal alcuno velenoso ò rapace [terra?]
eccetto il (fo. 148v) volpe, per la quale dono le mandrie di pecore,
et altri animali vanno sicuro senza castode*m* tutti li notti nelle
pasture pastorando. Ha di buoni cavalli, gentili et miti: sono la Cavalli
magiore parti castrati, et vanno portanti. Li megliore*n* per la
guerra sono nella parte di Northlandia appresso la Scotia, et nella
parte*o* orientali di Wallia. L'ha di pecore et altre bestiame in

a a *cancelling* i *in* E	*b* de li B	*c* Abondantie B
d richezza B	*e* Sic B and E	*f* da li B
g de le B	*h* fiumi B, i *cancelling* e	*i* L'aera B
j longezza B	*k* d'ogni B	*l* Sic B and E
m custode B	*n* megliori B	*o* nelle parti B

grandissima quantità, perche la quarta parte (fo. 149r) del realme è pasture per nodrire questi animali, et altri cervi, dami[a] et conili. Trovono magiore utile nelle pasture, che nel coltivare la terra. La carne di mangi,[b] et di motoni e grassa, et molto piu saporita in questo regno, che in qualche altro. Produce ogni sorti d'uccelli, si salvatichi, come domestichi, galline, caponi, ocche, anati, galli d'India, fagiani, pernici, bitturi, et altri di quella sorte à quatice.[c] (fo. 149v) Qui non manchi sorte alcuno di pesci, ne del

Mine mare, ne delli fiumari. Nela terra son mine d'oro, argento, piombo, bronzo, stagno, et ferro, ma di questo poco.[10]

In Ingliterra sono molte città grande et ricche, ma non si belle et con tal magnificentia fabricate come si vede nelle altre provintie et la cagione e, che i gentilhuomini[d] non si delettono habitare

Le citta nella citta, et li marcadanti dopo hanno gua(fo. 150r)dagnato di vivere honestamente si contentino, et lassino similmente la città comprandosi possessioni nelle[e] villagi, dove vivonno lietamente con ogni cosa che è richiesta per la necessità, et anche à li piaceri.

Londra   Londra è la citta principale, sede regia, ornata con molti belle
Ponte sopra   palazzi, con un ponte di maravigliosa fabrica sopra il qual si vede
Tamese   di bellissime case d'ogni sorti di marcantie piene,[11] governata
per (fo. 150v) ottime leggi, et bagnata del famoso Tamesi, in ogni tempo et in ogni luoco p'el grand fundo ch'el ha navagibile, il qual mena i navi (quantunque grandissimi) de lontani provintie, con varii sorti di mercantie cargati, dal occeano nel quale entra[f] per sesanta mila sicuramente fin a Londra. Le margini del quale d'ogni banda sono con li viridi prati, et con le belle[g] vilaggi, grasse pasture piene delle vagabonde pecore, non senza grand piaceri (fo. 151r) delli naviganti, ornati. Poi si vede Bristolia, Caventria, Norvicia, Yorcka,[h] Hulla, Cestria, Oxfordia, Excestria, Southantona, Canterburia con molte altre, ma questi sono le principale.

Li studii   Duoi studii celeberimi,[i] Oxfordia et Cambrigia, nelli quali ne sono piu che quaranta amplissimi coleggii di petri vivi fabricati, con grand intrade (al' uso della republica) per pagare i lettori, et infiniti altri scolari, i quali (fo. 151v) erano fondati, parti delli regi et delli vescovi, li intradi delli quali sono amplissimi in

---

[a] danni B   [b] recte manzi   [c] aquatice B
[d] First five letters added later in E   [e] nelli B
[f] entrà B   [g] li belli B   [h] Yorcha B
[i] celeberrimi B

Ingliterra et per li altri homini^a virtuosi per mantenere le litere et buoni scientie, senza le quale ogni regno et provincia roina.

Gli popoli sono di statura alti,[12] ben formati et di volto candido, di natura pieni d'humanità, modesti, et benigni et massime li gentilhuomini iquali^c amano la virtu et accarezzono li huomini virtuosi, invitano volon(fo. 152r)tiere li forestieri a festigiare à lor case et li accettino con grata accoglienza. I plebei, per esser altramente educati, son di altra natura, come li sono nelle altre provincie: alcuni sono discortesi, morbidi, insolenti, impatienti d'ingiurii et molti che odino li forestieri d'ogni altre natione, et questo procede per non esser stato egli mai fuora del realme. Pensino ch'il sole non^e spandi suoi raggi in altro luogo, che in Ingliterra, et che non sia provincia al mondo che puole stare (fo. 152v) al paragone di quella. Egli e una altra ragione che li forestieri sono in odio appresso di lor: perche nelli passati tempi per la crudeltà delli daci, le scorrerie delli scocesi, et pe'l^g duro imperio deli normanni, lor possessioni sono stati guasti, i beni tolti, lor amici et parenti amazzati. Il che anche interveniva spesse volte in quel tempo che li fattioni dominorno, perche alhora una parte o altra chiamava dentro il regno i forestieri (fo. 153r) come mercinari,^h[13] in adiuto, i quali si dettero à spogliare i poveri huomini piu presto come ladri, che di servire contra l'inimici come soldati. Queste ingiurii quantunque li sono passati, la memoria tamen de quelli rimangono anchora a presso di lor, et li non possono dismentigare, et per non haver piu discorsi che tal non possono riformare la natura, ne dissimulare la invidia.

Le donne generalmente sono belle, cortese, et non mancano ne anche dela (fo. 153v) gratia secondo il costume del paese. Nel parlare et conversare con gli huomini sono famigliare, et senza suspetto alcuno di male dalⁱ mariti, perche gli hanno tal confidenza nella honestà delle donne, che non temano. Et elle similmente [hanno] tante^j amore ali mariti, et alla honestà, che non danno causa di pensare male de fati lor.

Gli gentilhuomini non habitano nelle città, ma di fuora, dove hanno lor case fornite^k d'intorno d'ogni co(fo. 154r)sa non solo

Side notes:
Statura delli popole^b

Humanita delli gentil-huomini

Natura dei plebei^d

La causa perche non amanno^f li forestieri

L'honesta delle donne

Gli gentil-huomo habitano fuora delle citta

---

^a huomini B
^b popoli B
^c i quali B
^d Natura plebei B and E
^e Word interlined in E
^f amano B
^g p'el B
^h mercinarii B
ⁱ dalli B
^j tanto B
^k Possibly in another hand in E

di quelli, che li recca honore, ma donde anche puole nascere piaceri (con honore) alcuno. Ciascaduno d'essi[a] ha, del suo proprio
delli barchi dove tengono cervi, dami, conili et levori p'el essercitio della caccia, con un grand nomero di cani d'ogni sorti,[b] si per li cervi, levori, volpi, come p'el orsi, tori, et cavalli nella caccia, di quali si dilettono grandemente, per veder con quanta furore et contumacia gli detti animali (fo. 154v) (per esser continuamente usati) conbattino con quelli grand mastivi di maravigliosa forza. Le gentildonne anche vanno a[c] cavalli a la caccia deli cervi et levori. Non prendono piaceri nelli ricchi tapiserie, ne nelli vestimenti di veluto, di seda, ma lor godio è d'aver[d] un nomero di buoni cavalli nella stalla, di vedere cento pari d'arnature[e] pendenti ne le grand sale, (fo. 155r) de tenere a lor servigii chi quaranta, chi cento, chi ducento (et piu ò meno secondo la facultà) valenti giovani in una liverea continuamente in lor case à mangiare[f] et dormire, oltra il salario anche che li danno, la quale è[g] honorevole. L'invitan l'un l'altro continuamente à festigiare.[14] Egli e cosa stupenda di considerare le viande che si consuma nell'anno in un di quelle case. Tutti li vasi che si usano per lor (fo. 155v) tavole sono d'argento. Vengono rare volte à la corte, non circanno[h] ne officii, honori, ne dignitade (eccetti i fratelli minori i quali non hereditanno in Ingliterra): stimano piu preciose d'aver l'amicitia et cori deli popoli di quella provincia dove habita,[i] et quella sua domestica libertà che tutte l'honori, che la corte li puole dare, et con questi liberalitade et magnificentia spendono lor intrade. (fo. 156r) Venga chi voglia troverà sempre in case lor abundantia di varii sorti di viande, senza d'esser domandato al'tro.[k] Da ricevere li huomini lietamente à lor tavole è tenuto per somma humanità appresso l'inglesi.

Usano le legi detti municipales.

Non dividono i stati et patrimonii tra gli figlioli,[15] come si fa in Alemagna et in Italia, anzi il primogenito solo è herede; li altri fratelli stanno pacienti, et à la cortesia del primogenito. (fo. 156v) Pero si danno tutti à l'armi et di servire nella corte, accioche per quel mezo vengino[l] à gradi di comperarsi un stato di vivere à pari di lor fratelli.

Nel giudicare le cause, si criminali come civile, usano questo

Side notes:
Lessercitio de gentilhuomini
Magnificentia
Stimano la liberta domestica piu che l'honori dela[j] corte
Leggi

[a] *Possibly in another hand in E* [b] sorte B
[c] à B [d] d'haver B [e] d'armature B
[f] mágiare B; magiare E [g] i E [h] cercanno B
[i] habità B [j] della B [k] *Sic B and E*
[l] venghino B

modo:[16] eleggono dodeci huomini discreti da diversi parochii, ma tutti di quel[a] medesima provincia et contado dove egli habita, che ha d'esser giudicato. I quali (sendo bene informati del caso, d'el'un et del altra parte) sono giurati per li divini misterii, di giudicare retta(fo. 157r)mente, et giuste senza favore ò invidia d'alcuna parte, et cosi partino tutti insieme in un'altra case[b] dove sono serati che nessuno[c] li parla infin che sono d'accordo della sententia (accioche non sono corrotti) et poi presentandosi innanzi il giudice, egli domanderà si colui che ha d'esser giudicato e reo nelle cose imputatoli ò non, et si li dodeci responderanno negative, il giudice lo pronontia, et lo liberò[d] innocente, ma se li troveranno reo, il giu(fo. 157v)dice de la bocca lor condamni tal persona, et publica la pena ordinata nella[e] legi per tal colpa.

La pena del furto per la legge è morto s'el detto furto passa il valore di sette piacchi. Similmente d'amazzare un huomo. Nondimeno, se colui che ha robbato o fatto homicidio, ò commesso qualche altra sceleratessa[f] (pure che non ha assasinato li huomini per la strada, rotto le porte di alcuno, commesso sacreleggio o machinati contra la maiesta regia) (fo. 158r) s'el sa legere, l'hara la vita perdonata per la virtu di quello la prima volte,[g] et cosi sera liberato di quel prigione regio, et messo in quello del vescovo (perche ciascaduno vescovo ha il suo prigione) et indi (se l'inimici suoi non proccacciono) sera anche liberato dopo pochi giorni per questo ordine. Il detto condemnato sera di nuovo giudicato da dodeci scolari, clerici detti, i quali domandando che male tal persona ha fatto, et non trovando (fo. 158v) alcuno che lo accusase egli, come innocente, per la medesima authorità liberaranno per la qual era innanzi per li altri dodeci condemnato. Ma questa giudicio deli[h] scolari ha forza sopra coloro solamente i quali sono condemnati ali prigioni delli vescovi, et non ad altri. Ma se gia questi liberati per virtu del libro, sono un altra volte[i] in simili maleficio presi, il legere non l'adiutarà piu, et accioche ponno esser (fo. 159r) cognoscuti,[j] l'interior parte della man sinestra è brusata con un ferro ardente, nel qual ferro e una litera la quale manifesterà s'el era condemnato per ladro, o per homicidio.

L'adulterio[17] è punita con grand severita in Ingliterra, perche essendo presi sono ferate tutte duoi, et l'huomo et la donna, in

Modo di giudicare le cause

La pena del furto

Privilegii delli literati

Prigione deli evescovi

L'ignominiosa[k] pena delli adulteri

---

[a] quela B, *last letter added later*   [b] casa B
[c] nissuno B   [d] libera B   [e] nelli B
[f] sceleratezza B   [g] volta B   [h] de li B
[i] volta B   [j] cognosciuti B   [k] L'ignominisa E

una grand gabia di legno posta nel mezo della strada, nel*a* quale poi che hanno cantato tre giorni et tre notti peccavimus et (fo. 159v) mea colpa, con presenti vituperio, et perpetua ignominia, sono menati fuora di quella, et fatti montare su un carro vilissimo (un di quelli che li portino l'ordure et sporchezza fuora della citta), et in quello menati al conspetto del popolo con*b* dolore estremo di tutti li parenti, et amici d'essi, et poi l'huomo fuoro di quella terra dove l'ha in questo modo su'l carro triomphato, bandito, et la donna sforzata (sendo chiusa dentro le muraglie dove (fo. 160r) non vene huomo) d'esser honesta, et vivere vita casta. Il luogo nel quale le sono serate era gia monastieri di francescani, nel' una parte del quale sono ottocento orphani et poveri infanti. Nell'altra parte sono le dette femine separate dal consortio et compagnia delli huomini.

Gli orphani sono ensegnati, chi un mestiero, chi un altro, chi imparanno le littere secondo l'ingenio et capacità dessi. Le femine che sanno fare nullo mestie(fo. 160v)ro lodevole sono similmente ensegnati a cusire, filare, lavorare la seta. Le hanno matrone da governarle. Per questo modo le femine meno pudiche sono divente gia figlie, et heredi (fuora del pensiero del testador) delli padri santi. Talche scrizzando*c* elle hanno trovato un habitatione senza fito, et quella*d* anche al tempo della vita, perche s'el non venne qualche uno per domandarle dalla citta per mogliere, ò vero (fo. 161r) prometter, et esser ubligato in una grand somma di danari (da quel tempo indrio per lor honestà et pudicitia) non usciranno mai. Ma perche pochi le voglianno per mogliere, et nulli quasi che si lascino intrigare, et mettere lor piedi nelli lacci per le honestà di quelle, quale elle stesse stimano poco, le poverette vi rimangino*e* gabbate,*f* facendo lunga penitentia per un picolo piacere. Et vi sono al presente un nomero (fo. 161v) di giovane, belle, gratiose, et ornate d'ogni qualità donescha, eccetto la pudicitia. Gli altri vitii, egli puniscono come si fanno nello*g* altre provintie, secondo le legge civile.

Gli inglesi sono piu ricchi al presente, che non furon*h* mai dinanzi, et accioche posso*i* piu chiaramente mostrare cio, diverò il popolo in quatro sorti d'huomini. La prima e di gentilhuomini che vivano di lor intrade et possessioni. La seconda

La ragione perche li inglesi sono al presente piu richi*j* che non eranno mai innanzi

a nella B
b Word interlined in E
c Possibly for strizzando (stringendo)
d guella B
e rimagino E; rimàgino B
f Recte gabbiate
g nelle B
h Word repeated in B
i possa B
j ricchi B

contadini, p'el coltivare la terra, (fo. 162r) marcadanti per la traffica, et artisani per li stenti delle mani. Di questi quatro sorti, i gentilhuomini et i contadini sono il basso et fondamento che tenghino in tal riputatione quel regno, apresso tutte le nationi forestieri, si per la virtu nella guerra come per le commodità del paese. Una ragione è perche l'intradi delli monastieri et delli altri luogi sacri (iquali sono una quarto del realme) sono al presente distribuite, parte (fo. 162v) gratis à i^a nobili, et parte venduti et affitati a li mercadanti, et ai contadini. Talche ogni sorti deli predetti quatro si prevaglion, et cavano utile di quelli beni, iquali dinanzi il tempo di Henrico eran in tal modo inchiuse^b nelli chlaustri,^{c} che nullo (eccetto il re et pochi poveri) prevalevano di quelli,^{d} dove al presente sono utile generalmente di tutti, et la corona molto arrichita (quantunque non senza l'infamia (fo. 163r) del primo usurpatore.)

Un' altra ragione che molti luogi spatiosissimi, quali nel tempo passato eran paludosi et somersi nell'aqua^e (insieme con altri diserti, pieni de cervi, conili, et altri animali disutili) sono per industria dell'huomini^f al presenti ridotti in buona terrena[18] di seminare et pascere altri animal piu utile, donde nasce magiore copia di fromento, magiore quantità di bestiame, et per consequente magior (fo. 163v) abondanza di lana, et ogni sorti di vetovaglia. La seconda

Le commodità del regno sono lana, panni alti, caresea, cotoni,[19] wolstadi, piombo, et brunso.^{g} Commodita del realme

La tertia ragione è che le dette commodità sono in magior pregio, et stima al presente, che non eranno in qualche altro tempo passato.[20] Qui alcuno mi dirà peradventura,^{h} che queste non sarebbe p'el utile commune, che le commodità d'una provintia sarebbero cara^i et di^j grand pregio, (fo. 164r) rispondo, che tal ragione havrebbe luogo, si le dette comodità fusserò nelle mani di pochi. Ma sendo che la piu parti et la principale parte del realme vendono tal comodità (cioe^k i nobili et gli contadini) e necessario che li sono arrichiti. Perche la lana, che se vendevano innanzi per cento scudi,^{l} hora vendono per ducento. Voi mi dirette^m se questi duoi cioe il gentilhuomo, et il contadino iquali vendono, sono per questo modo arrichiti, li (fo. 164v) altri duoi, Tertia ragione Risponso Obiectione

---

^{a} ai B ^{b} inchiusi B ^{c} claustri B
^{d} guelli B ^{e} acgua B ^{f} delli huomini B
^{g} bronzo B ^{h} per adventura B ^{i} care B
^{j} Word interlined in E ^{k} cio E ^{l} Word lacking in B
^{m} direte B

Lo risponso che compranno sono impoveriti. A tal ragione se[a] risponde per duoi modi. Primo dico che si ha da desiderare[b] che ogni cosa che sia fatta in un'republica fusse p'el utile di tutti generalmente. Ma non potendo, basta che il sia al utile della magiore et principale parte di quella, come si vede qui chiaramente che l'alzamento delle commodità augmentino le richessa[c] delli nobili et contadini, et mostrerò ch'il mercadante et l'artesano non sono per questo modo (fo. 165r) neanche[d] impoveriti. Ma s'ha da considerare che di quatro parte, tre delle comodità del regno sono venduti à i mercadanti forestieri, et va fuora del regno, pero se il marcadante compra caro, egli vende anche caro, senza detrimento di persona alcuna del regno, pero il marcadante quasi sempre

Gli guadagnià, et rara[e] volte perde. Oltra vendeno le mercantie
mercadanti che conducono fuora d'altro paese piu care (fo. 165v) che non
rara[f] volte soleanno, come il vino, tela, ferro, et la seta, talche questi tre sorti
perdono guadagnono, et sono piu ricchi che non erano nel passato.

Obiettione Ma voi direte se[g] i gentilhuomini et i contadini vendono lana, panni, piombo, et le altre commodità piu caro al presente, che non solevano dinanzi; cosi comprano al presente il vino, la seta, tela, et altre cose che li bisognono piu care, che non soleano dinanzi, pero considerando l'uno co'l altro, lor richesse[h] non è augmentata in modo alcuna.[i] (fo. 166r) A questa[j] dico, s'el fusse similitudine ò proportione tra quello che li gentilhuomini et con-

Responso tadini vendino et comprano la ragione sarebbe buona. Ma tra questi, non è proportione alcuna; perche quelli che vendino per mille fiorini, non comprano per dieci, et la causa è che hanno ogni cosa necessario per lor famiglia notriti nelle possessioni proprii,

Gli talche comprano poco. Questo, adunque considerato, se puole
gentil- conchiudere generalmente: (fo. 166v) dove la magiore parte
huomini
comprono delle commodità d'una provincia non escono fuora, ma sono
poco venduto nell'istessa provintia[l] dove nascono, ivi egli è p'el utile
Con- et bene commune di tenere le dette commodità in vili pregio. Ma
chiusion'[k]
generale dove la dette commodità sono la piu parte portate nelle altre regioni, fuora di quel luogo dove i nascono, vi è per il bene commune, che le commodita mantenesserò in grand pregio.

Pero l'alzamento[m] delli commodità in (fo. 167r) Ingliterra ha arrichito tre sorti delli detti huomini, et la[n] quarto vive, cioe

---

[a] si B   [b] de *cancelling* con; de *cancelling two or three letters* B
[c] richezze B   [d] ne anche B   [e] rare B
[f] rare B   [g] e *cancelling* i *in* E   [h] richezza B
[i] alcuno B   [j] questo B   [k] Conclusion B
[l] provincia B   [m] l'azamento E   [n] lo B

l'artesano quantunque non in quella morbidezza che soleanno. Gli altri, che sono piu poveri, iquali per vechiezza, ò per esser cargati con figlioli, non ponno guadagnare il vitto, egli è provisione fatta in ogni parochia per tutto il regno dal publico, et huomini assegnati da ministrarli una volte[a] la settimana d'ogni cosa necessaria, per la tutta. Percio i poveri non vanno circan(fo. 167v)do in Ingliterra, ma l'elemosina li e ministrata à lor casa. Questo[b] opera pia era principiato[c] da Henrico, et confirmato imperpetuo[d] per Edouardo sesto suo figliolo.[21]

Gli poveri non vanno mendicando

Molti se maravaglianno d'onde nasce li grand pretii della lana, panni, et altre commodità del regno considerando che in nessuna età dinanzi era si grand abondantia come gli è al presente. Due sono le cause del alzamento delle commodita. L'una è le strette (fo. 168r)leggi del regno per le quale i subditi tutti, eccetto alcuni gentilhuomini, sono prohibiti di portare veluto ò seta di sorte alcuna ne lor vestimenti se non le cose che nascono dentro il realme. Per questo modo alzano lor proprie commodita, et quelle di altrui si bassano.

Prohibitione de portar' seda

L'altra ragione è l'industria deli mercadanti, i quali non si contentino solamente che li forestieri vengino[e] per tor la comodità (come soleanno), ma egli stessi le trasportino, non solo in (fo. 168v) Fiandra, Germania, Dacia, Francia, Spagna, Portugalia, et Italia, ma in Barbaria, nel levante, et dell'altra parte per lo mare settentrionale fin à Tartaria et Moscovia, dove al presenti l'hanno grand libertà et privilegii cocedutili,[g] per questo[h] honorevole industria infiniti huomini vengon nelle cose marine esperti, il re di buoni navi proveduto, i popoli molto arrichiti, et il regno apresso tutte nationi per famosissimo cognossu(fo. 169r)to. Questo e'l vero vello d'oro,[22] per amore del quale venne portato dentro il realme ogni anno un thesoro inestimabile.

Industria de'[f] marcadanti

Privilegii delli inglesi in Moscovia

Il vello doro

Nella millitia[i] quanto sia la virtu delli inglesi, l'infinite vittorie havuti da li regi di Francia et di Scotia per mare, et per terra fanno chiaro testimonio al mondo senza che io ne parlo di quella.

La militia

Nel principio della guerra, le leggi militari sono publicate, con tal severi(fo. 169v)tà, che colui che giogerà[j] à le carte o dati, che menerà femine nel campo, che sfodrà la spada contra suo compagno, che farà torto ad persona, la quale porterà cosa alcuna

---

[a] volta B   [b] Questa B   [c] principata B
[d] in perpetuo B   [e] venghino B   [f] dei B
[g] concedutili B   [h] questa B   [i] militia B
[j] giogara B

di vendere nel campo, sara condemnato a morte. Usino di portare nella guerra il vallo secondo l'anticha[a] costume romano,

Arme delli inglesi co'l quale sono diffesi, et al presente l'arcabuso, la pica lunga, una
spada pesante et puniale corte, come l'alemani. Ma la gloria dell'
inglesi acquistata con molte vittorie, nacque (fo. 170r) parte delli
archi lungi, li quali tiranno con tanta sforza[b] anzi sendo à cavallo

Archi lungi che gittano facilmente un huomo armato in terra, et penetranno
la sua armatura. I piu destri huomini à cavallo per conto di
ligieri, sono li walli et gli genti che habitanno nelle parti settentrionali appresso la Scotia, iquali portino la lanza firmata à la
coscia et la reggono con tal desterita che non fallino punto di
ferire l'inimico, ò vero il suo cavallo, come gli pare piu advan(fo.
170v)tagio. Giudicanno piu honorevole di morire, che voltare la

Magnanimita schiva ò cedere luogo al nimico per paura, et pero quando danno
segno à la bataglia tutti i nobili dismontano, accioche gli altri
cognoscino ch'el pericolo et la gloria sara eguale à tutti, et che
non rimagne speranza in altra cosa di lor honore et vita che

Obedienti nel campo nella virtu sola. Sono obedientissimi[c] nel campo, a li capi, et
osservino con grand studio l'ordini militari. (fo. 171r) Sono
d'animo invitto, nelli pericoli pronti. Quando sono ala[d] cam-

Invitti d'animo pagna cercano in ogni modo venire ala[e] suffa[f] c'ol nimico, sono
patienti del[g] fame, et massime comportono il freddo.

Il re che circa[h] gloria per via de giustitia[23] non puole publicare

Il parlamento nuove leggi ne rompere le vecchi, fare guerra, conchiudere pace,
commandare tributo ò essattioni del popolo senza con(fo. 171v)
sentimento del commune consiglio detto il parliamento,[i] la[j]
quale consiste in tre gradi d'huomini, cioe nobili,[24] vescovi, et nel
popolo. Li duoi primi sono in ogni parliamento[k] certi. L'altro
incerti, perche li sono cavalieri in ogni parliamento[l] diversi, eletti
per la magiore voce del popolo. In questo parliamento[m] gli e licito

La liberta del popolo per ciascaduno delli detti tre ordini à dire tutto cio che li pare
honore et uti(fo. 172r)le p'el bene publico, et negare tutto quello
che sara contraria senza guardare huomo nel[n] viso.[25] Egli non e
cosa alcuna conchiusa in questo consiglio si le detti tre ordini non
accordono primo di quella, et anche il re per sua absoluta authorità
non le confirma.

---

[a] l'anticho B   [b] forza B
[c] obedientcentissimi *with* cen *cancelled* B   [d] a la B
[e] a la B   [f] zuffa B   [g] della B
[h] cerca B   [i] parlamento B   [j] lo B
[k] parlamento B   [l] parlamento B   [m] parlamento B
[n] nel *cancels* in *in* E; *the sense requires something like* tema di *before* guardare

Nella pace il re non tenne altri soldati che ducenti archieri à cavallo et cento alberdieri à piedi per la guardia di sua persona. L'ordinaria intrada della corona (fo. 172v) d'Ingliterra, la quale venne da li antichi tributi d'alcuni provintie, delle gabelle et custumi[a] che pagino li[b] marcantie che sono trasportate fuora del realme, de la prerogativa che el re ha delle marcantie vendute nelle fere publice, et del patrimonio suo nel quale è il ducato di Lancastria et altre provincie monta al valore di diece milia et trecento libre d'oro di peso. Oltra questa intrada certa, il patrimonio delli pupilli ha augmentato grandemente l'intrada della corona,[26] perche (fo. 173r) i figlioli in Ingliterra non hereditanno innanzi che vegnino[c] à la età di vinti uno, et si per caso il padre morisse dinanzi che i figlioli arrivano à quella eta, rimangino pupilli del re, ilqual[d] gode lor intrade, et fa li ensegnare nelle corte le litere et fatti d'armi. Se le sono femine son chiamate donselle[e] del re, et non ponno maridare senza licentia sua.

Io non parlo delli beni delli monasterii et altri luogi sacri, per esser egli inestimabile, li quali Henrico adgiunse a la (fo. 173v) corona.

Il re ha molte[f] palazzi, nobilissimi et di maravigliosa magnificentia fabricate,[g] tra i quali è Hantona, Nonsuche, Richemonde, Whithaule, Grinwyche, St. Jacomo, Wodstoke, Granta, Wyndsore, Bridwelle,[h] Schourbourne, con molti altri dilettevoli per li siti, et in ogni conte ornati realissimi, nel quale[i] se vede superbi logge, alti torri spatiosi corti, magnifice sale, morbide camere fornite con (fo. 174r) drapi d'oro ricchissimi, ameni giardini pieni d'odoriferi fiori, copiosi di varii frutti, con i barchi spaciosi pieni d'animali salvatigi,[j] et boschi verdigianti copiosi di fagiani, pernici, con i[k] piacevole piscieri,[l] nelle quale se vede ogni sorta di[m] pesci in frotta non senza grand diletto notare. Pero i regi d'Ingliterra si nel grand nomero delli superbi palazzi, come in molte altre cose superanno l'altri principi christiani.

I regi d'Ingliterra si intitolono del (fo. 174v) regno di Francia et le ragione principale son queste:[27] Philippo pulchro re di Francia[28] (il qual regno nel'anno di Christo 1286 hebbe di Joanna suo[n] mogliere tre figlioli maschi: Ludovico detto huttino,[29]

[a] costumi B	[b] paghino le B	[c] venghino B
[d] il qual B	[e] donzelle B	[f] molti B
[g] fabricati B	[h] Briduielle B	
[i] neli quali, *first* i *added later, second* i *cancelling* e B		[j] salvatici B
[k] le B	[l] peschere B	[m] sorte de B
[n] sua B		

Philippo lungo,[30] et Carolo pulchro,[31] et due figlie, l'una morse nella infantia, l'altra chiamata Isabella era maridata ad[a] Edouardo secondo re d'Ingliterra, de la quale Isabella nacque Edouardo tertio che primo si intitoli del regno di Francia. (fo. 175r) Questi tre maschi regnorno, et primo Ludovico huttino, il quale hebbe due mogliere, Margaritta[b] et Clementia. Di Margarita[b] generò una figliola sola, detta Johanna, la quale era maridata al conte de Euburavico, ma ella non hebbe mai figlioli. Di Clementia genero un maschio, il qual morse nell'infantia. Talche morendo Ludovico, non lasso altri figlioli che Joanna, et pero Philippo lungo il secondo fratello succedeva nel regno (fo. 175v) (quantunque de dritto il regno dee venire a Joanna figliola di Ludovico huttino) il qual Philippo dopo cinque anni morse senza figlioli. Finalmente Carolo pulchro regno qual hebbe una figliola sola nomata Biancha,[c] la qual morse insieme c'ol padre Carlo. Donde la stirpe regia di Philippo pulchro mancò in Carlo suo figliolo.

Edouardo tertio vero herede del regno di Francia Siche[d] non rimaneva altro che Edouardo tertio re d'Ingliterra, nato (fo. 176r) d'Isabella figliola di Philippo pulchro et per consequente vero et legitimo herede al regno di Francia. Questo era il principio duna[e] guerra crudelissima, et la lite dura anchora.

La seconda ragione L'altra ragione è questa: Carolo sesto re di Francia,[32] nel'anno 1420,[f] vedendo li guasti delle campagne, i brusamenti de le citta, et l'iminente roina del regno, et havendo forse un secreto rimorse[g] di conscientia nel tenere ingiustamente l'heredità di (fo. 176v) altrui fece pace con Henrico quinto re d'Ingliterra, et lo[h] dette in matrimonio Catarina suo[i] figliola unica, con questi conditione[33] che il detto Henrico sarebbe governatore di Francia mentre che Carolo viveva, et dopo la sua morte iure hereditario possedere il regno di Francia. Et si per caso il detto Henrico morisse dinanzi Carolo, et lassasse figlioli legittimi nati della detta Catharina, che tali figlioli similmente, per quel medemo iure, succedessero nel regno di Francia, et (fo. 177r) disheredito Carolo suo unico figliolo come non legittimo nato, et lo publicò nimico alla patria.

Il tributo che Lodovico divo pago a Henrico tertio Henrico tertio re d'Ingliterra[34] vendeva la Normannia ad Ludovico detto divo, re di Francia, per cento et cinquanta mila scudi, et diece mila ogni anno di tributo. Francesco re di Francia pàgo ad Henrico ottavo cinquanta mila fiorini al anno.

Il tributo che Francesco re pago ad Henrico octavo

[a] al, l *cancelling* d B   [b] Margarita . . . Margaritta B
[c] Bianca B   [d] Si che B   [e] d'una B
[f] *Date underlined in* E   [g] rimorso B   [h] li B
[i] sua B

Tra l'altri singolari doni, che Iddio (fo. 177v) dette al Ingliterra, questo è grandissimo, che in ogni età l'havuta principi ottimi de li[a] quali ne faro mentione d'alcuni nelli guerre piu famosi. Et lassando indrio le cose troppo vecchie commincierò di Adelstano re,[35] il qual ruppe i scotesi,[b] [36] prese Constantino lor re, suggiugò il regno, et fece una monarcha[c] di tutt'l'isola. Per questo i regi di Scotia fin ad nostri giorni soglion dare giuramento a i[e] regi d'Ingliterra. Ma egli osservino la fede tanto quanto li pare utile, et non altramente. (fo. 178r) Sono fedifragi, superbi, dediti a la gola et a l'otio.[f] I regi di Scotia sono stati (per esser dispregiatori delle promesse, et violatori de li[g] giuramenti) maravigliosamente castigati da Dio, come lor istorie chiaramente monstrino, perche di cento et cinquanta regi, che hanno regnati in Scotia in manco di nuove cento anni, cinquanta tre di quelli sono stati amazzati parte nelle guerre civili, et parte nella campagna da l'inglesi. (fo. 178v) Contendino continuamente con li inglesi delli confini, et con tanto odio et contumacia di core, che nulla calamità o adversa fortuna (quantunque piu volte son sforsati dare giuramento e pagare tributo a l'inglesi) li puole vincere, et tenereli in obedientia, perche per ogni minimo[h] occasione che si offri dismentiganno le promesse, la fede, et i giuramenti. Malcolmus re di Scotia[i] [37] primo nego questo giuramento, et per la vilta di Rufo re d'Ingliterra, pensò de haver ricoperato l'antica lor libertà, ma egli insieme (fo. 179r) con suo figliolo Edouardo eran uccise[j] da Roberto conte di Northumbria appresso il castello di Alnevico.

La prima discordia[38] che nacque tra li francesi et inglesi et la causa della prima guerra era tale: nel anno 1118[k] che regno Henrico primo re d'Ingliterra nacque discordia tra Ludovico crasso re di Francia[39] et Theobaldo campano conte di Blesensio, la sorella di cui era mogliere di Henrico d'Ingliterra, per questo affinitado il conte lo trasse facilmente (fo. 179v) in suo aussilio contra Ludovico. Ludovico sdenandosi[l] che il re d'Ingliterra era venuto in aussilio del conte contra di lui, volse tutto lo sdegno non al conte Theobaldo, il qual lo haveva offeso, ma contra Henrico, et si mosse con un essercito grande di tor il ducato di Normannia quale era l'heredita del detto Henrico. Ma egli non solo non diffese il suo, ma ruppe l'essercito di Lodovico[m] apresso la villa di

Margin notes:
Illustri principi
Adelstano
I re di Scotie[d] danno iuremento al re d'Ingliterra
La natura dei scocesi
La vendetta di Dio
Lodio de scocesi
Malcolmo re scotio ucciso
La causa della prima guerra tra Ingliterra et Francia

---

[a] deli B
[b] scocesi B
[c] monarchia B
[d] Scotia B
[e] ai B
[f] al'otio B
[g] deli B
[h] minima B
[i] Scocia B
[j] uccisi B
[k] Date underlined in E
[l] sdegnandosi B
[m] Ludovico B

Nicasiana,[40] uccise Balduino (fo. 180r) conte di Fiandra, ilqual[a]
sequitò le parte francesi, et se impatronisse d'una parte di Francia
per la[c] qual le guerre se continuorno hora con le treughe hora con
pace, ma sempre incerta, fin al tempo di Edouardo tertio, il qual
vendicò il regno di Francia iure materno.

Mentre che Henrico era in Francia, Guilhelmo re di Scotia[41]
dismentigando il suo promesso et fede, assaltò il regno d'Ingliterra, ma suo essercito era tagliato in pezzi et egli menato prigion-
ero a (fo. 180v)Londra.

Da Richiardo primo re[42] (del suo magnanimo detto il core di
lione) i regi d'Ingliterra se intitolono di Hierusalem. Egli con
quaranta mila inglesi ando à la espugnatione della citta santa.
S'impatronisse del regno Cypro iure belli, amazzando un tyranno
che si[d] regnava, et dette il detto regno à Guido portugalese in
cambio di Hierusalem, per la qual ragione i suoi successori davano
il medesimo titolo.

(fo. 181r) Tra gli altri regi Edouardo primo meritava eterna
memoria, che primo ridosse i walli à la obedientia de li inglesi,
pacificò gli tumolti delli guasconi, ruppe l'essercito scocesi,[43]
espugno Edinburge citta regia, prese Gioanne re, il soggiogò tutto
il regno di Scotia, lo[e] dette nuove leggi, et in tutto riformò,
menando Giovanne re à Londra prigioniero, vi lascio inglesi
governatori nel suo nome.

Edouardo tertio monstro primo il (fo. 181v) valore delli inglesi
nel continente,[44] perche nel principio del suo regno rauno un
essercito grandissimo, et per mare et per terra assaltò il regno di
Francia per ricoperare la sua heredità, et hebbe gloriose vittorie,
primo à Sclusa porto di Fiandra (lo quale era preso alhora da gli
francesi) dove sommorse et prese cinquanta navieri francesi. Poi
per terra appicò una bataglia crudele ala villa de Cresiaco con
Philippo re di Francia nella quale (fo. 182r) la magiore parte della
nobilta di Francia cascorno, et Philippo re[45] fugendo se[f] salvo.
Delli uccisi[46] era Giovanne re di Boemia, che era venuto in
aussilio di Philippo, Carolo fratello di Philippo, Rodolpho duca di
Lorena, con trenti mila altri. Costui prese la villa di Cales posta nel
litto oceano, nel continente, et la fece una colonna d'inglesi, prese
Guina, castello fortissimo sei mila da Calez,[g](fo. 182v)nelli paludi
posta. Lui era tal flagello che in nessuno altro tempo accadeva a i

Marginal notes (left column):

Henrico s'impatroni d'e[b] una parte de Francia

Guilhelmo re de Scotia prigioniero

Core di lione

La causa perche i re d'Ingliterra se intitulono di Hierusalem

Li illustri gesti d'Edouardo

Giovanne re prigioniero

Vittoria a Sclusa

Vittoria di Edouardo

Morte Giovanne re di Bohemia

Cales

Guina

---

a il qual *B*   *b* de *B*   *c* *B adds* guerra *before* qual
d li *B*   *e* li *B*   *f* si *B*
g Cales *B*

francesi perche prese non multo poi Giovanne re di Francia[47] con mille et quatro cento delli nobili,[48] et li meno triomphante in Ingliterra.

I scocesi[49] giudicando cosa facile di sogiogare l'Ingliterra, considerando che il re con tutta la forza del regno (come li pareva) era in Francia, assaltorono il realme, brusando (fo. 183r) le ville, ammazando li huomini scorsero fin ad Dorphame,[b] dove Giovanne Copplando li affronto con un essercito (la magiore parte) di pastori et preti, i quali con tanto furore combattorno per la diffensione della patria che misserò i scocesi in fuga et menorno David lor re à Londra prigioniero.[50] Talche Edouardo hebbe fortuna di pochi regi, haveva continuamente a la sua tavola duoi regi prigionieri. (fo. 183v) Costui ordino la somma ordine delli cavallieri in Ingliterra, detto il giartero.

La gloriosa vittoria di Dagincorta (nella quale mancorno quinze mila francesi) ha fatto sempiterno il nome di Henrico quinto, senza l'altri suoi illustri fatti, prese Roana, et tutta la Normandia, occupò la Francia fin ad Orleans, edificò in Roana, in Parise, et lungo la riviera di Segnana molti castelli quali (fo. 184r) seranno memorie imperpetuo della virtu de inglesi, et lascio il regno di Francia al suo figliolo Henrico sesto, il qual era coronato re di Francia nella chiesia[d] di Nostra Donna in Paris, et gli principi giurati al nome suo.

Non faro mentione delli illustri fatti d'Henrico ottavo sempre invito, et arbitro delle pace et guerre ecclesiastici et temporali. Per esser anchora in memoria di tutti, lascierò fin ad (fo. 184v) un altro tempo piu convenevole.

Per i grandi damni che gli inglesi hanno fatti et gloriose vittorie che gli hanno havuti delli scocesi et francesi gli sono invidiati, odiati, et temuti[f] sopra modo da loro. Altri inimici l'Ingliterra non ha, ne la tema potentia alcuna perche i luoghi dove puol arrivare i navi sono fortificati et bene guardati, l'altri sono per natura delli alti rocchi fortissimi. (fo. 185r) Oltra queste ragione el regno e fortissimo per li buoni ordini di quello contra ogni inopinato assalto, perche nelle[g] luoghi piu alti per tutto il regno son posti albori di grand altezza, à la cima delli quali sono barili di pice, et homini per tutte l'esterne parti del regno dal commune pagati di guardarli, et vedendo arrivare à presso il lito alcuno nomero di

Marginalia:

Flagello delli[a] franciosi

Giovanne re di Francia prigioniero

David re di Scocia preso per i pastori et preti

La felicità[c] di Edouardo

Ordine di cavallieri

Preclari gesti

Henrico quinto

Henrico sesto coronato in Francia

Henrico ottavo arbitro delle[e] pace et guerre

La causa della invidia delli francesi et scocesi verso l'inglesi

L'inglese non temono potentia che sia

La fortezza del regno per li buoni ordini di quel

---

[a] deli B
[d] Sic B and E
[g] nelli B
[b] Dorphanne B
[e] della B
[c] felicità B
[f] m cancelling n in E

navi, metteno incontinente fuogo à i detti barili, et similmente
(fo. 185v) fanno gli altri che sono piu dentro il regno, et cosi in
un medesimo tempo tutto il regno (vedendo pericolo) sara su
l'armi. Perche sono obligati quatro dogni parochia vedendo li
detto*a* segni à correre livi*b* con l'arme dove troveranno capitani,
che li conduceranno et monstrerano cio che si ha da fare.

Vescovadi   Sono parochie in Ingliterra cinquanta tre mila.[51] Vescovadi
Contadi   venti duoi. (fo. 186r) Archivescovadi due. Contadi trenta nuove.

L'autorità   L'ufficio del grand cancelliero e d'esser giudice principale sotto
del grand   il re in tutte le cause civile, egli puo*c* gratiare et condemnare
cancelliero   come gli piace, senza consenso del re. Puole conferire i beneficii
tutti (i quali sono sotto la somma di quaranta scudi per anno) à
cui li piace, senza consenso del re. Tiene il grand sigillo del regno
con lo quale le (fo. 186v) littere regale sono sigillate.

Hibernia   Molti sono l'isole soggiete a l'Ingliterra dele quale Hibernia[52]
e*d* principale, et di grandezza quasi d'Ingliterra, ma piena d'aspri
Natura   monti et disutile palude. I popoli sono rossi,*e* incolti, abhoriscono
delli   le delicie humane, come gli vestimenti ricchi, et varii cibi, si con-
hiberni   tentino c'ol latte, formagi, favi et pisci. Tutti portino un sorti*f* di
I vestimenti   vestimenti (fo. 187r) cioe una roba lunga di panno grossissimo
senza manica ò altra fascione solamente ligata con una stringa al
collo. La magior parte non portino calze ne scarpi, ma una
camisia lunga[53] di dodeci brazza di tela lavorato con seta, per
intorno, la quale è fatta giala con safrano non si muta mai fin che
la non sia tutto trita et straciata in pezzi. Stanno la magior parte
nelle tende (fo. 187v) tutto l'anno, i quali sono coverte con li pelli
d'annimali. Non si curino ne del vento ne del sole. Non portino
cosa alcuna à la testa eccetto la*g* salata,*h* i capelli[54] crescono
horridi senza mai pettinare li*i* fin à le spale. Radono la barba
eccetto della labra superiore, la qual stortino per parer' piu
horribile.*j* Tengino*k* poco conto del adulterio o fornicatione.
Abhorriscono l'agricoltura et ogni (fo. 188r) altro fatiga eccetto la
caccia, et la militia, in quella sola è tutta*l* lor piaceri et honore
Il diletto di   posta.*m* Pero gli soldati sono in grand estimatione, et i cavalieri
hiberni   primi, poi i gravi armatura, quali egli chiamano in lor languagio
galloghas. I cavalieri portino la lancia et la briglia nel man
sinestra, fin che ha gittato gli suoi dardi. Gli huomini a piedi

a detti B   *b* ivi B   *c* puoe E
d e *cancelling* i *in* E   *e* rozzi B   *f* una sorte B
g Word interlined in E   *h* Possibly for insalata, *mockingly*
i pettinarli B   *j* horribili B   *k* Tenghino B
l tutti B   *m* posto B

portino li dardi, archi, et la spada greve, la qual d'una banda taglia dell'altra la sega. (fo. 188v) Fuora di*a* lor paese non piglianno mai prigionieri, amazzono tutti. Saltano et corrono velocissimamente. Non usino advocati, perche se la lite non finisse al primo convento, la determinon con l'armi. **Immanitá*b*** **Costume**

L'isola non produce alcuna sorte d'animali velenosi. La produce cavalli dilicatissimi*c* chiamati hobbini. Celebranno le morte[55] di lor amici non con le lacrimi, et pianti, come in altri luoghi, ma con canzoni, et con li arpi. **L'essequie delli hiberni**

(fo. 189r) Dopo Hibernia, l'isola chiamata Vette anticamente, hora l'isola di Wight eccella tutte le altre, et per la grandezza et richezza, et di questa si glorianno sopra tutte l'altre nationi, che vi non e nel'l'isola ne frati, advocati, ne volpi.

---

a *Word interlined in* E
b B *adds and cancels a redundant* Immanita *immediately before* Costume
c delicatissimi B

PORTRAIT OF ENGLAND
COMPOSED BY GEORGE RAINSFORD

Division of England is divided into four principal regions:[1] Northland,
the realm Wales, Cornwall and Kent. These differ in language and customs,
and even in laws, and each of these four contains many districts
and counties.

Northland (fo. 141v) Northland is the largest and extends from the Thames
to the River Tweed (which divides England from Scotland) and
from the North Sea on the east to the town of Hereford located in
the western part of the kingdom.

Most of the principal barons live in this part, and it is all
inhabited: there are no mountains or great forests, but most
Abundance fertile plains, which produce (fo. 142r) wheat, barley, oats,
beans, peas, fruit and vegetables for man and for animals in great
abundance. The people near Scotland are good soldiers, and are
always armed. Their houses are low and small and covered with
straw. They tie their horses to the feet of their beds, and their
lances, which are long, at the head among the covers.

In the inhabited areas, peace between the peoples of Scotland
and England (fo. 142v) is never firm, and truces are always
The enmity uneasy. No friendship or kinship, no pacts or agreements between
between the the rulers can restrain these peoples from continual skirmishes,
English and raids and robberies against one another, as is their practice and
the Scots has been for a long time.

Justice is done among them according to power and not according to reason. They know better than others that the goods of
fortune are variable and uncertain, because if one of them has
forty head of cattle tonight, tomorrow he (fo. 143r) will have
nothing. Their horses are excellent and swift, and they handle
their lances with such dexterity that at a full gallop they can pick
up a musket ball, or a clod of earth of that size, without falling
off. They make cloth in great quantity. For lack of wood, (fo.
143v) they burn a certain hard, black stone mined from the earth,
'Sea-coal' which gives a great deal of heat, and which they call 'sea-coal'.[2]
York The principal city of the region is York, notable for the death
of the Emperor Severus.[3] It came to be called Northland because
it is the windy region, for North in that language is equivalent to
'settentrionale', and land is 'terra'; hence the name means
northern parts.

Wales is to the west, (fo. 144r) and is almost an island, bounded on three sides by the sea, and on the east partly by the River Severn, and on the other side by the city of Hereford. | Wales

The land[4] is fertile towards the south, and produces grain, fruit and vegetables in the lowlands. But towards the east, because most of the region is harsh and mountainous, the people lead a hard life. They eat oat bread, and their only beverage is honey and water, cooked together, like the beverage of the (fo. 144v) Turks. They call it in their tongue metheglyn. They are generally taller than the English. They are fierce in war and hate the quiet life. | Hard life

Formerly they were unwilling subjects of the English and they rebelled many times, but at present they are most obedient. They retain the ancient language of Britain, and, by permission of the king, they keep their own laws. They are exempted from the usual royal exactions, (fo. 145r) and pay instead an annual tribute[5] of 40,000 *scudi*. In war they send 6,000 horsemen, 14,000 foot soldiers and keep as many more ready for what fortune may bring. | British language — Peculiar laws — The tribute of the Welsh

The region produces a gross fabric, which they call frieze, in great abundance. In winter, clothing made from this is worn throughout the kingdom, both by the (fo. 145v) gentlemen and by the lower classes. The region produces goats and cows and good war horses. The region has many castles and fortresses, of which some are well fortified and guarded. Carmarthen is the principal city. | Many castles

Because of the antiquity of the people, because many of them are good soldiers, and because they keep faith with the English, the eldest son of the King of England is called the Prince of Wales, and he lives among them. Not far from (fo. 146r) Carmarthen are the gold mines. | The eldest son of the King is called Prince of Wales

The third region is called Cornwall, because it extends towards Spain in the shape of a horn for ninety miles. The earth is barren, and if anything is produced there, it is because of the great labour and industry of the men, and not because the land is good. From Cornwall come lead, bronze, tin and other metals which are exported all over Europe. Because of the mines, the people live in (fo. 146v) great wealth.[6] The inhabitants are agile and vigorous at running, jumping, kicking and throwing the iron,[7] wrestling, very good at all the other bodily exercises, and yield to the men of no other region. They have their own language, different from the Welsh and likewise from the English.[8] Exeter is | Cornwall — Barren — Abundant in metals — The people vigorous — Exeter their principal city, where they make fabric for stockings finer than (fo. 147r) those made in any other region.

Kent   Kent is the smallest region of the four, but for its size it contains more nobles, more rich people, and more abundance than
Fertility   the others. The air is temperate, the earth is fertile, and produces wheat, fruit, vegetables and every other sort of grain, sheep and other animals in great abundance. The finest and best cloth of the kingdom is made here. Some of the people are lazy, obstinate,
The people   (fo. 147v) and impatient, and do not suffer insults without taking revenge. Canterbury is the principal city, adorned with many beautiful estates, by a great river, deep woods, and pleasant hills on which sweet and various flowers bloom all year, whence comes
A saying of   the saying of foreigners that the earth is good but the people
foreigners   wretched. In every part of the region the air is temperate. The sky is serene in summer, the nights are clear. The days are eighteen (fo. 148r) hours long, but the warmth of the summer, caused by the length of the day, is mitigated by the pleasant winds that blow continually. In winter it often rains, but there are no storms, no hail, and no snow.

England has an abundance[9] of everything needed for human
The bounty   life. It has every kind of animal except the elephant, the camel, the
of [the   mule and the ass. It has no poisonous or dangerous animals,
earth]   except for the (fo. 148v) fox, so that herds of sheep and other animals can be safe without guard every night grazing in the pastures. It has good horses, gentle and mild, most of them cas-
Horses   trated and used for carrying. The best war horses are in the Northland, near Scotland, and in the eastern part of Wales. They have sheep and other beasts in great quantity because one fourth (fo. 149r) of the country is pasture, and feeds these animals as well as deer and rabbits. The English find raising sheep more profitable than tilling the earth. Their beef and their mutton is rich and tastes better than that of other countries. England produces all kinds of birds, both wild and domesticated, hens, capons, geese, ducks, guinea hens, pheasants, partridges, bitterns and other aquatic birds. (fo. 149v) They also have no lack of fish, either salt or freshwater. In the earth they have mines of gold, silver, lead,
Mines   bronze, tin and iron (though little of this last).[10]
The cities   In England there are many great cities, and they are very wealthy, but they are not so beautiful or so magnificently built as in other countries. The reason is that the gentlemen do not like to live in the city, and the merchants, when they have (fo. 150r)

reached a comfortable standard of living, also leave the city and
buy property in the villages where they live happily, having
everything they require both for necessity and for pleasure.

London is the principal city and the capital, adorned with
many beautiful palaces, and with a bridge of marvellous con-
struction, above which are seen beautiful shops full of every kind
of merchandise.[11] London is governed by (fo. 150v) excellent
laws, and is bathed by the Thames, which is in every season and
in every place navigable because of its great depth. Even the
largest ships come safely up the Thames sixty miles to London,
laden with various kinds of merchandise from far-off countries.
The banks of the Thames are everywhere beautified by green
meadows and rich pastures, full of wandering sheep, to the great
delight (fo. 151r) of passing mariners. Other cities are Bristol,
Coventry, Norwich, York, Hull, Chester, Oxford, Exeter,
Southampton, Canterbury, and many others, but these are the
main ones.

London

Bridge on the Thames

There are two famous universities, Oxford and Cambridge,
which have more than forty very large colleges made of native
stone. The colleges enjoy a great income, which they use for the
good of the commonwealth, paying for lecturers, and for an
infinite number of other scholars. Most (fo. 151v) of the endow-
ments were established by kings and bishops, who have the
greatest incomes of all the English, and by other good men whose
purpose has been to maintain letters and learning, without which
every kingdom is ruined.

Universities

The English are tall,[12] well made, and fair complexioned;
by nature full of humanity, modest, kind, especially the gentlemen, who love virtue and cherish virtuous men, invite (fo. 152r)
foreigners to feast at their houses, and receive them with warm
welcome. The plebeians, because they are educated differently,
are of a different sort, as in other countries. Some of them are discourteous, lazy, insolent, impatient of insults, and many of them
hate foreigners. This is because they have never been outside of
their country, and they think that the sun does not shine anywhere
but in England, and that there is no country on earth that can be
(fo. 152v) compared to their own. There is also another reason
why they hate foreigners, and that is because in the past they
have suffered from the cruelty of the Danes, the raids of the
Scots, and the harsh rule of the Normans. Their possessions have
been destroyed, their goods taken, their friends and relations

The stature of the people

Humanity of the gentlemen

Nature of the plebeians

The reason they dislike foreigners

D

killed. These things also happened quite often in the period when the factions ruled: first one side, then the other, called (fo. 153r) foreigners into the country as mercenaries,[13] who indulged in plundering the poor people like thieves rather than serving them as soldiers against the enemy. Although these injuries are past, nevertheless the memory of them remains among the English, and they are unable to forget them. And because they have had no more to do with foreigners than this, they are unable to change their ways, nor to hide their hostility.

The women are generally beautiful, courtly, and not lacking in (fo. 153v) the graces considered appropriate in that country. They are familiar in speech and conversation, and their husbands are

The honesty of the women

not at all suspicious, because they have great trust in the honesty of their women. And the women, likewise, love their husbands and their honesty so much that they never give cause for thinking ill of their behaviour.

The gentlemen live outside the cities

The gentlemen do not live in the cities, but outside where they have houses provided with everything; (fo. 154r) not only those things they need to maintain an honourable estate, but also those things from which any honourable pleasure can arise. They all have private parks, where they keep stags, deer, rabbits and hares for hunting with a great number of dogs of every sort, for

The sports of the gentlemen

deer, hares, and foxes, as well as for bears, bulls and hunting horses, and they delight greatly to see with what fury and hatred these animals, (fo. 154v) which are kept in continual practice, fight with their great mastiffs of marvellous strength. The gentlewomen also ride and go to deer and hare hunts.

The English take no pleasure in rich tapestries, or in garments of velvet or silk, but their pleasure is to have a number of good horses in the stable, to see a hundred or so suits of armour hanging

Magnificence

in the great hall, (fo. 155r) and to have at their service some forty, one hundred, or even two hundred (more or less, depending on their means) brave young men always in their livery, and to have them eat and sleep in their house in addition to the stipend which they give them, which is honourable. They invite one another continually to feast,[14] and it is astonishing how much meat is consumed in a year in one of these houses. All the vessels used at (fo. 155v) the table are made of silver.

They rarely come to court, and they do not seek offices, honours or dignities; except for the younger brothers, who do not inherit land in England. They consider it more precious to have the friendship and hearts of the region in which they live, and to have domestic liberty, than all the honours that the court can give, and in such liberality and magnificence they spend their income. (fo. 156r) Whoever wishes to come will always find an abundance of meat at their tables, and will not need an invitation. To entertain men gladly at their tables is held among them to be the highest humanity. They esteem domestic liberty more than the honours of court

They have laws called 'municipal'. Laws

They do not divide estates and patrimonies among survivors,[15] as is done in Germany and Italy, but only the first-born is the heir. The other brothers must be patient, and attend the kindness of the first-born. (fo. 156v) Therefore all the younger sons become soldiers, or serve at court, so that by those means they may attain a standard of living comparable to that of their elder brothers.

In the judgment of their affairs, both criminal and civil, the English use this procedure:[16] they choose twelve reasonable men from different parishes, but from the same region and county as the accused. These, being well informed of the case on both sides, are sworn by the divine mysteries to judge (fo. 157r) rightly and fairly, without favour or hostility to either side, and they adjourn together to another house, where they are locked in so that no one can leave until they have agreed upon a verdict. This is done so that they cannot be corrupted. And then they appear before the judge, and he asks them if the accused is guilty as charged. And if they find him (fo. 157v) guilty, the judge, speaking for them, condemns him, and pronounces the sentence prescribed by the laws for his crime. Method of settling cases at law

By law, the penalty for theft is death, if the value of the theft is greater than seven pence. The same penalty is set for murder. However, if a man has committed larceny or homicide and (fo. 158r) can read, his life will be pardoned by virtue of that, providing it is his first offence, and that he has not killed a man on the highway, broken into a house, committed sacrilege, or plotted against the royal majesty. Such a man is freed from the royal prison, and is placed in an episcopal one. (Each bishop has his own prison.) And from that, unless his enemies prevent it, he will be freed after a few days in accordance with this law. The accused will be judged anew by twelve scholars called clerks, who, if they do not find (fo. 158v) anyone to accuse him, will free him by the same authority as the other jury had condemned him. But this judgment by scholars is limited to those who are thus handed The penalty for theft Privileges of literacy

Episcopal
prisons

over to the episcopal prisons, and is not for others. And if one who has been freed because of literacy is again apprehended in a similar misdeed, reading will not help him any longer. And so that such men may be (fo. 159r) known, the insides of their hands are branded with an iron in the shape of a letter which indicates whether the crime was theft or homicide.

The
ignominious
punishment
for adultery

Adultery[17] is punished with great severity in England. When they are caught, the man and the woman are both shut in a great cage of wood placed in the middle of the street, out of which, after having chanted *peccavimus* and (fo. 159v) *mea culpa* for three days, they are led, to their present calumny and perpetual shame, and are made to mount a most vile cart (one of those used to carry dung and ordure out of the city) and in that they are led in view of the people, to the extreme sorrow of all their relatives and friends, and then the man is outlawed from the region in which he has in this way triumphed in his chariot, and the woman is forced (being shut within the walls (fo. 160r) where no men come) to live an honest and chaste life. The place in which such women are shut was formerly a Franciscan monastery, in one part of which are 800 orphans and poor children, and in the other part of which are the said women, separated from the consort and company of men. The orphans are taught various trades, and some are taught to read, according to their wit and capacity. The women who don't know any (fo. 160v) praise-worthy trade are also taught to cook, to weave, and to work silk. They are watched over by governing matrons. By this means, shameless women have become the daughters and heirs of the holy fathers, quite apart from the intentions of the founders. So by yielding to straitened circumstances, the women find a dwelling without rent; and also for life, because if no one comes to ask the city for one of them as a wife, or unless someone (fo. 161r) promises a large sum of money, as assurance of their honesty and chastity from that time forward, they will remain there for ever. But since there are few who want them for wives and scarcely any who will allow themselves to get involved and put their feet in a snare for the honesty of those who themselves value it so lightly, the poor women remain imprisoned, making a long expiation for a brief pleasure. And there are there at present a number (fo. 161v) of young, beautiful, and gracious women, adorned with every ladylike quality except chastity. Other crimes are punished as in countries under the civil law.

The English are now richer than they have ever been before. The reason why the English are now richer than ever before In order to show that more clearly, I shall divide the people into four kinds of men. The first consists of the gentlemen, who live on income and holdings; the second, farmers who cultivate the land; (fo. 162r) the third, merchants who engage in trade; and the fourth, artisans who work with their hands. Of these four, the gentlemen and the farmers are the base and foundation of the kingdom, and they maintain its great reputation among nations, both for strength in war, and for the produce of the land. One reason for their wealth is that the income of the monasteries and other holy places, which made up one fourth of the realm, is at present divided: part (fo. 162v) free to nobles, and part sold and rented to merchants and farmers. Thus each of the four classes has succeeded in drawing gain from these properties, which before the time of Henry were so shut within the cloisters that only the king and a few poor people benefited by them, whereas now everyone gains by them, and the crown is much enriched, not without, however, the infamy of the first usurper.

(fo. 163r) Another reason for their wealth is that many most The second spacious places which formerly were marshy or submerged in water, and many other waste places full of deer, rabbits and other useless animals have now, by the industry of the men, been reclaimed[18] and made good for seeding and grazing more useful animals, whence arises a greater supply of grain, a greater number of sheep, and consequently a greater (fo. 163v) quantity of wool and all sorts of foodstuffs.

The commodities of the kingdom are wool, broadcloth, kerseys, Commodities of the realm 'cottons',[19] worsteds, lead and bronze.

The third reason for their wealth is that the said commodities Third reason are more expensive now than they have ever been.[20] If anyone should happen to tell me that it is not in the public interest to have Response high prices for the commodities of a nation, (fo. 164r) I should answer that he would be right if the said commodities were in the hands of a few, but as the greater part by far of the kingdom sell such goods (that is, the nobles and the farmers), it follows that they are enriched, for the wool which formerly sold for one hundred now sells for two hundred. You will say that if these Objection two classes are enriched, the (fo. 164v) other two classes, who buy these things, will be impoverished. I answer in two ways. First, I Response say that it is desirable to do everything in a commonwealth for the good of everyone, and when that is not possible, it is enough if something benefits the majority of the people, as the price increase clearly does, increasing the wealth of the nobles and farmers. And secondly, I shall show that the merchants and artisans are not in any case impoverished (fo. 165r) by this increase. It must be remembered that three fourths of the commodities of the kingdom are sold to foreign merchants, and leave the kingdom. Since the merchant buys dear and also sells dear without detriment to anyone in the kingdom, he almost always gains, and rarely loses. In addition the merchants sell what they bring from other countries dearer (fo. 165v) than they used to—wine, linen, iron and silk, so that three classes gain and are richer than they were in the past.

The merchants rarely lose

Objection But, you will say, if the gentlemen and the farmers sell wool, cloth, lead and other commodities dearer at present than in the past, so they buy at present wine, silk, linen and other things that they need more dearly than before, and therefore their wealth is not at all increased. (fo. 166r) To this I reply that you would be right if there were any proportion or similarity between the things that they buy and the things that they sell; but there is not, because those who sell 1000 florins worth do not buy even ten, and the reason is that they have everything necessary for the nourishment of their own families, and they buy little.

Response

The gentlemen buy little

General conclusion These things therefore being considered, it can be concluded that (fo. 166v) when the greater part of the commodities of a nation do not go out of it, but are sold within it, it is in the common interest for those commodities to be low priced. But when commodities are for the most part exported, it is in the common interest that high prices be maintained.

Therefore, the price increase in commodities in (fo. 167r) England has made three classes rich. The fourth, however, the artisans, do not live in that delicacy to which they were formerly accustomed. For those who are very poor, who, because of age or being burdened with many children, cannot make a living, there is provision made in each parish of the land for them to receive charity at public expense, and men are assigned to distribute necessities to them once a week. And therefore the poor do not (fo. 167v) go begging in England, but alms are given to them in their own houses. This holy work was instituted by Henry, and confirmed in perpetuity by Edward his son.[21]

The poor do not go begging

Many marvel whence arises the great price of wool, cloth and the other commodities of the realm, considering that there is

greater abundance of these things than there has ever been before.
There are two reasons for the price increase. One is the strict (fo.
168r) laws of the kingdom, under which all subjects, excepting
only certain gentlemen, are prohibited from wearing velvet or
silk of any sort in their clothing, and can only wear clothing made
of domestic fabric, whereby they raise the price of their own commodities, and those of others are lowered. Prohibition
on the
wearing of
silk

The other reason is the industry of the merchants, who are not
content to let foreigners come for the commodities, as they used
to, but transport them themselves, not only to (fo. 168v) Flanders,
Germany, Denmark, France, Spain, Portugal and Italy, but
also to Barbary in the Levant, and to places on the North Sea up
to Tartary and Moscow, where at present they enjoy great freedom, and where privileges have been granted them. By this
honourable industry of the English, large numbers of men become
competent sailors, the king is provided with good ships, the
people are much enriched, and the kingdom has become most
famous among all nations. (fo. 169r) This is the true golden
fleece,[22] and love of it brings an inestimable treasure into the
kingdom every year. Industry
of the
merchants Privileges
of the
English at
Moscow The golden
fleece

The strength of England's armies is attested to by the innumer-
able victories they have gained over the kings of France and
Scotland, by sea and by land. The world knows this well and I
do not have to speak of it. The military

At the start of a war, martial laws of great (fo. 169v) severity
are proclaimed, prohibiting playing at cards and dice, bringing
women into camp, attacking a comrade, and stealing from anyone carrying goods to sell in the camp. These offences are
punished with death. In war they practise entrenchment in the
Roman fashion, which defends them well. At present they use
the arquebus, the pike, the heavy sword, and the short dagger,
like the Germans. But the glory of the English, (fo. 170r) acquired
in many victories, has been due in part to the longbow, which
they draw with great force, so that when mounted they can
fell an armed man and penetrate his armour. The most skilful
horsemen, because of their light weight, are the Welsh and the
people who live in the North near Scotland, who carry a pike
strapped to their thigh, which they manage so well that they
never fail to wound their enemies, and even their enemies'
horses, if that seems (fo. 170v) advantageous. They consider it
more honourable to die than to run from an enemy or to yield Arms of the
English Longbows Magnanimity

ground to him out of fear, and therefore, when the sign of battle is given, all the nobles dismount, so that the others will know that danger and glory alike will be shared by all, and that no hope of honour or of life remains in anything except valour. The English

Obedient in camp are most obedient to the officers in battle, and they observe military regulations with great diligence. (fo. 171r) They are of unconquerable spirit and ready for danger. When on campaign

Unconquered in spirit they seek every opportunity to bring the enemy to fight. They endure hunger and cold very well.

The king who seeks glory justly[23] in England cannot promulgate new laws, nor can he break old laws, make war, conclude a peace, or command tribute or exaction from the people without

The parliament the (fo. 171v) consent of the common council called parliament, which comprises three classes of men—the nobles,[24] the bishops, and the commons. The first two are the same in each parliament. The third part varies, for different knights are elected to each parliament by the majority voice of the people. In parliament,

The liberty of the people each member of the three orders is permitted to say anything which seems to him honourable and in the common (fo. 172r) interest, and to deny those things which seem contrary to the common interest, without fear of any man.[25] Nothing can be concluded by this assembly unless the three classses agree upon it, and unless the king also confirms it by his absolute authority.

The personal guard of the king In peace, the king has no soldiers except for 200 archers on horseback and 100 halberdiers on foot for his personal guard.

Ordinary income of the kingdom The ordinary income of the Crown (fo. 172v) of England, which comes from ancient tributes exacted from certain regions, from the salt tax, from duty paid on exported goods, from the royal prerogative on goods sold at public fairs, and from the patrimony of the duchy of Lancaster and other regions, is 10,300 pounds of gold in weight. Beyond this fixed income, the income

Income from wardships from wardships has greatly increased the income of the crown.[26] Children (fo. 173r) in England cannot inherit before they reach twenty-one, and if a father should die before the children arrive at that age, they become wards of the king, who enjoys their income, and has them taught letters and deeds of arms at court. If they are women, they are called damsels of the king, and they cannot marry without his permission.

I will not mention the goods of the monasteries and other holy places which Henry added to the crown income. They are inestimable.

(fo. 173v) The king has many most noble palaces of great magnificence, among which are Hampton, Nonsuch, Richmond, Whitehall, Greenwich, St. James, Woodstock, Grafton, Windsor, Bridewell, Sherborne, and many others, delightful in location, and furnished most royally in every county, in which may be seen superb loggias, high towers, spacious courts, magnificent salons and luxurious chambers furnished with (fo. 174r) rich hangings of gold, pleasant gardens full of fragrant flowers and various fruits, large parks full of wild animals, verdant woods full of pheasants, partridges and pleasant fishponds in which are shoals of every sort of fish, delightful to behold. Thus the kings of England, in their great number of superb palaces as in many other things, surpass the other princes of Christendom. *Royal palaces*

The kings of England claim the title of the (fo. 174v) kingdom of France, and the principal reasons are these:[27] Philip the Fair, king of France,[28] who ruled in the year 1286, had by his wife Joan three sons: Louis called the Simple,[29] Philip the Tall,[30] and Charles the Fair,[31] as well as two daughters, one of whom died in infancy, and the other of whom, named Isabelle, married Edward II of England, by whom she bore Edward III, who first held title to the kingdom of France. (fo. 175r) The three sons of Philip ruled in turn. First Louis the Simple, who had two wives, Margaret and Clementia. By Margaret he had only a daughter, named Joan, who was married to the count of Evreux, by whom she had no children. To Clementia was born a male child, who died in infancy. So that when Louis died, he left only Joan; Philip the Tall, the second brother, then succeeded to the crown (fo. 175v) which by right should have passed to Joan, daughter of Louis. Philip died after five years, childless. Finally, Charles the Fair reigned. He had only one daughter, named Blanche, who died when he died. Thus the royal line of Philip the Fair failed in his son Charles so that there remained only Edward III of England, son of (fo. 176r) Isabelle, daughter of Philip the Fair, and consequently he inherited the true title to the kingdom of France. This was the beginning of a cruel war, and the struggle has lasted until this day. *The claim of the English to the crown of France* *Edward III true heir to France*

Another reason for England's title to France is that in 1420 Charles VI of France,[32] seeing that the countryside was being ravaged, the towns burned, and the kingdom on the point of ruin, and having perhaps a secret remorse of conscience because he unjustly held the inheritance of (fo. 176v) another, made peace *The second reason* with Henry V of England and gave him Catherine his only daughter in marriage, on the understanding[33] that Henry would be governor of France while Charles lived, and that after his death, he would rule the country in hereditary possession. And if Henry should die before Charles, leaving legitimate children by Catherine, such children by the same agreement would succeed to the throne of France; and the king (fo. 177r) disinherited his only son, Charles, as illegitimate and proclaimed him enemy of his country.

The tribute St Louis paid to Henry III

Henry III of England[34] sold Normandy to St. Louis, king of France, for 150,000 *scudi* and 10,000 per year in tribute. Francis I paid Henry VIII 50,000 florins per year.

The tribute King Francis paid to Henry VIII

Among the singular gifts which God (fo. 177v) gave England, this is the greatest, they have had excellent princes. Leaving to one side deeds of too great antiquity, I shall begin with King Athelstan,[35] who beat the Scots,[36] took Constantine their king, subjected their country, and made one monarchy of the entire island. Because of this, the kings of Scotland must swear loyalty to the kings of England to the present day. But they make of this faith what suits them, and no more. (fo. 178r) They are breakers of faith, proud, given to gluttony and laziness. Because of their scorning of promises and violations of agreements, the kings of Scotland have been marvellously punished by God. Their history shows this clearly, for in less than 900 years, 53 of the 150 kings who have reigned in Scotland have been killed, some in civil wars and some in campaigns against the English. (fo. 178v) They fight with the English continuously at the border, and with such hatred and contumacy that no calamity or misfortune can conquer them and keep them in obedience, no matter how many times they are forced to give pledges and pay tribute to the English. On any slight occasion that offers itself, they forget their promises, their pledges and their faith. Malcolm of Scotland[37] was the first to deny loyalty to England, and, because of the baseness of King Rufus, thought to have recovered Scotland's former liberty. But he, together (fo. 179r) with his son Edward, was killed by Robert, earl of Northumberland, near the castle of Alnwick.

Famous princes

Athelstan

The kings of Scots swear loyalty to the king of England

The nature of the Scots

God's vengeance

Hatred of the Scots

Malcolm King of Scots killed

The cause of the first war between England & France

The first discord[38] which arose between the French and the English and the cause of the first war was this: in 1118, when Henry I was king, there arose a dispute between Louis the Fat of France[39] and Thibault of Champagne, count of Blois, whose sister was the wife of Henry, by which relationship the count drew him easily (fo. 179v) to his aid against Louis. Louis, feeling himself dishonoured because the king of England was helping the count against him turned all his anger not upon Count Thibault, who had offended him, but against Henry, and came with a great army to take the duchy of Normandy, which was the inheritance of Henry. Henry not only defended his own, but destroyed Louis' army near the town of Noyon.[40] He killed Baldwin, (fo. 180r) count of Flanders, who took the French side, and he took possession of a part of France. From which time the wars continued, sometimes with truces, sometimes with peace, but always uncertain, until the time of Edward III who avenged himself upon France to which he held title through his mother. *Henry took possession of part of France*

While Henry I was in France, William of Scotland,[41] betraying his promise and faith, attacked England, but his army was cut to pieces, and he was led prisoner to (fo. 180v) London. *William King of Scotland prisoner*

From Richard I,[42] for his courage called Lion Heart, the kings of England have held title to Jerusalem. He went to conquer the city with 40,000 Englishmen. He had become the ruler of Cyprus by rule of war, having killed a tyrant who ruled there, and he exchanged Cyprus for Jerusalem with Guy of Portugal, by which the kings of England have held title to Jerusalem ever since. *The Lion Heart* *Why the kings of England hold title to Jerusalem*

(fo.181r) Among the other kings, Edward I merited eternal memory, who first reduced the Welsh to obedience to the English, quieted the revolts of the Gascons, broke the Scottish army,[43] conquered Edinburgh, took King John of Scotland, subjected his whole kingdom, proclaimed new laws and reformed all things there, and then led John to London prisoner, leaving Englishmen there to rule in his name. *The illustrious deeds of Edward* *King John a prisoner*

Edward III first showed the (fo. 181v) strength of England on the continent,[44] for at the beginning of his reign he assembled a great army and attacked France both by sea and by land to recover his inheritance. He had glorious victories, the first of which was at Sluys, the port of Flanders, then held by the French, where he captured or sank fifty French ships. Then by land he found occasion for a cruel battle at Crécy with Philip of France,[45] in which (fo. 182r) the greater part of the French nobles fell, and from which Philip had to flee to safety. Among the slain[46] were King John of Bohemia, who had come to aid Philip; Charles, brother of Philip; Rudolf, duke of Lorraine, and 30,000 others. Edward took the town of Calais on the coast, and made it an *Victory at Sluys* *Victory of Edward* *Death of King John of Bohemia* *Calais*

English colony; he also took Guînes, a fortified castle six miles from Calais (fo. 182v) on the marshes. Edward was the greatest scourge the French had ever had, for soon afterwards he took prisoner King John of France[47] and 1400 nobles[48] and led them in triumph into England.

The Scots[49] thought it would be easy to conquer England since the king and the whole strength of the kingdom was in France. They attacked, burned (fo. 183r) the towns and killed the men. They got as far as Durham, where John Coupland confronted them with an army composed for the most part of shepherds and priests, who fought with such fury for the defence of their country that they put the Scots to flight, and led David their king prisoner to London.[50] Thus Edward had the fortune of few kings, and always had two captive kings to dinner. (fo. 183v) He founded the highest order of knights in the land, the order of the Garter.

The glorious victory of Agincourt, in which 15,000 French were killed, and which made eternal the name of Henry V, was only one of his illustrious deeds. He took Rouen and all of Normandy, occupied France up to Orléans, built many castles as perpetual memorials of the strength of the English in Rouen, on the Seine, and in Paris, (fo. 184r) and he left the kingdom to his son Henry VI, who was crowned king of France in Notre Dame of Paris, and the princes swore loyalty to him.

I shall not mention the glorious deeds of Henry VIII, ever unconquered, arbiter of peace and war, both temporal and ecclesiastical, because they are still in the memory of all, and I leave them until (fo. 184v) another, more suitable time.

Because of the great deeds the English have done, and the great victories they have won over the Scots and the French, they are envied, hated and feared by them beyond measure. They have no other enemies, and they fear no foreign power, because the places where ships can land are well fortified and guarded, and those that are not guarded are protected by high and strong cliffs. (fo. 185r) In addition, the kingdom is strong because of the provisions it makes against unexpected attacks. In high places all around the kingdom are placed masts of great height, at the top of which are barrels of pitch, and men in every outlying part of the country are paid by the public to keep watch, and when they see any ships near the shore they set the barrels of pitch on fire, and this is (fo. 185v) a signal to others further inland to do the same, and so in time of danger the whole country can quickly take up arms. Four men from every parish are obliged, when they see such signs, to take up arms and to run to where they will find captains to tell them what is to be done.

There are 53,000 parishes in England,[51] twenty-two bishoprics, (fo. 186r) two archbishoprics, and thirty-nine counties. **Bishoprics Counties**

The office of lord chancellor is to be principal judge under the king in all civil cases. He can free and condemn as he thinks right without consent of the king, and he has in his gift all benefices under 40 *scudi* per year, which he gives to whomever it pleases him without the consent of the king. He holds the Great Seal, with which (fo. 186v) royal letters are sealed. **The authority of the lord chancellor**

Many islands are subject to England, of which the largest is Ireland,[52] and it is almost the size of England, but full of harsh mountains and useless swamps. The people are tough and uncultivated. They hate human delights like fine clothing and various diet. They are content with milk, cheese, peas and fish. They all wear one sort of clothing, (fo. 187r) which is a long robe of very rough cloth without sleeves or other additions, bound with a string at the neck. Most of them do not wear shoes or stockings, but a long tunic[53] of twelve layers of cloth, worked with silk on the outside and coloured yellow with saffron, which they never change unless it is tattered and torn into shreds. Most of them live in tents (fo. 187v) all year, which are covered with animal skins. They take no notice of the wind or the sun, and wear nothing on their heads except for the foliage of their hair,[54] which grows uncombed down to their shoulders. They shave their beards, except for their moustaches which they twist to seem the more horrid. **Ireland Character of the Irish Their clothing**

They take little notice of adultery and fornication. They abhor agriculture and all (fo. 188r) other work except for hunting and fighting, which are their only pleasures and honours. Therefore their soldiers are held in great estimation, and most of all their horsemen, who wear a heavy armour which they call 'galloghas'. The horsemen carry both their lances and their reins in their left hand, so that they can throw darts with the other. The foot soldiers also carry darts, bows, and a heavy sword with one straight and one serrated edge. (fo. 188v) Outside their country they take no prisoners, but kill everyone. They run and jump very quickly. They do not have lawyers, because if a dispute is not settled at the first meeting, they determine it with arms. **The pleasures of the Irish Cruelty Customs**

The island does not produce any kind of poisonous animal. It produces most delightful horses called 'hobbins'.

Irish funerals   They commemorate the deaths[55] of their friends without the tears and complaints that are usual in other places, but with singing and harp playing.

(fo. 189r) After Ireland, there is the island that was formerly called Vette, and is now called the Isle of Wight. It excels the others except Ireland in size and in riches, and they glory in this above all other nations, that on their island there are no monks, no lawyers, and no wolves.

NOTES

1. Cf. Polydore Vergil, *Anglica Historia* (ed. Basel, 1534): 'Britannia . . . dividitur in partes quatuor: quarum unam incolunt Angli, aliam Scoti, tertiam Vualli, quartam Cornubienses. Hi omnes vel lingua vel moribus . . . inter se differunt' (p. 3). Rainsford's 'England' includes Wales and Cornwall, but not Scotland. Thus to retain the quadripartite division of his literary model, he divides what Polydore called England into Kent and the curious 'Northland'.
2. Polydore has 'cum rarae hic sylvae, ignem faciunt ex lapide nigro, quem ex terra effodiunt' (*Angl. Hist.*, p. 7). But his subjects are the inhabitants of the southern part of Scotland, not the northern part of England. Other details in this description of 'gli popoli verso la Scotia', such as the straw-covered houses and the bringing of animals indoors (fo. 142r), seem to have been borrowed from Polydore's description of Scotland proper.
3. Lucius Septimius Severus died in 211.
4. Cf.

   > Regio agrum habet magna ex parte sterilem, ac minus fructuosum, propterea quod cultione caret: unde fit, ut agrestes vitam duriter degant, qui panem avenaceum edunt, atque lac aquae admistum serumque bibunt. (*Angl. Hist.*, p. 8)

5. Wales paid no tribute in the sixteenth century.
6. Polydore does not mention bronze as a commodity of Cornwall, but is otherwise the source of this passage:

   > Terra admodum sterilis, fructum magis ex cultorum industria, quam ex sua bonitate, praebet: sed fert ubertim plumbum nigrum et album, hoc est stannum, in quo effodiendo maxime consistit vita incolarum. (*Angl. Hist.*, p. 9)

   Polydore also mentions that Cornwall is ninety miles from Spain, and that it is shaped like a horn.
7. I know of no game in which anything made of iron is thrown or cast using the feet. Scribal error may be responsible for this odd phrase.
8. Rainford has either misunderstood a passage in his source, or else disagrees with it: 'Lingua autem ipsa longe alia est ab Anglica, cum Vuallica vero nonnihil affinitatis habet' (*Angl. Hist.*, p. 9).
9. Cf.

   > Abundat Anglia omni pecudum genere, praeter asinos, mulos, camelos, et elephantos: at nullum gignit venenosum animal aut rapax, praeter vulpem, et olim lupos . . . quare vagum pecus, et nullo fere custode, innocuum est: videre enim licet armenta boum et equorum ac ovium greges interdiu noctuque passim errare . . . Id circo equis testiculi amputantur, ut cantherii facti sub dio, maiori compendio pascantur. (*Angl. Hist.*, p. 13)

10. Cf.

    > Fert item aurum, argentum, plumbum album, id est stannum, plumbum nigrum, cuprum. Nascitur etiam in maritimis regionibus ferrum, sed eius exigua est copia. (*Angl. Hist.*, p. 14)

11. Cf. Polydore's description of London Bridge (*Angl. Hist.*, p. 4).
12. This is clearly taken from *Angl. Hist.*, p. 14:

    > Sunt Angli procera statura, venusta et candida facie . . . suapte natura ad omne humanitatis officium propensi, et cum primis nobilitas, vel erga alienos, sed plebs praesertim urbica non item.

Rainsford expands considerably Polydore's poor opinion of the English lower classes: but while he amplifies abuse, he also makes something of an apology for them, pointing to the fact that they are not unlike plebeians in other lands, and excusing their hatred of foreigners by reference to their insularity and the effect upon them of a long history of foreign invasion and oppression by mercenaries.

13. Rainsford's argument at this point reflects several of Gardiner's principal themes: the factions of the nobility as the cause of popular misbehaviour, and the ill-effects of mercenaries.

14. Cf.

Amicos domum suam invitant, hospitioque benigne et in prandiis ac coenis hilare, nitide, lepide, atque ampliter accipiunt: idque officium humanitatem vocant. (*Hist. Angl.*, p. 14)

But Polydore was far from sharing Rainsford's positive attitude towards this custom: he continued 'etsi, ut Tacitus ait, pars est servitutis non modica, alieno tantum cum taedio, indulgere palato'.

15. This passage is taken from Machiavelli's *Ritratti delle cose della Francia* (ed. Giunta (1532), p. 59), quoted in the introduction above, p. 57. Since the anonymous *Ritratti del regno de Inghilterra* (ed. and trans. C. V. Malfatti in *Two Italian Accounts of Tudor England* (Barcelona, 1953) (see above, pp. 57–8)) may have been used by Rainsford for the passage immediately following this, and since that work, too, discusses primogeniture, it is worth citing here:

I Feudi non si dividono tra gli heredi, ma il primogenito heredita ogni cosa; et così si fa anchora nel resto della robba che non è feudo, et gli altri fratelli si vanno a guadagnare il vivere con servir altri alla costuma di Francia non punto aiutati dal primo fartello [sic], et di qui nasce che gli huomini che crescono in alcun merito, la maggior parte sono secondi fratelli facendoli la necessità industriosi et astringendoli la necessità alla virtù. (p. 96)

16. Cf. *Ritratti del Regno de Inghilterra*, p. 94:

Nei Giuditii criminali hanno per costume in quel Regno di far elettione di 12 huomini di molti che eleggono, i quali sono poi quelli che giudicano secondo la lor conscienza qual si voglia persona che sia chiamata in giuditio, con tutto che non habbino lettere nè sorte di esperientia; questi ascoltato tutto quello che sarà opposto all' accusato, et similmente le difese sue, sono commandati a dir il lor parere, li quali sono chiusi tutti in una camera et non l'aprono prima che si siano accordati tutti insieme o di assolvere o di condannare l'accusato ... nel qual tempo mentre che stanno così serrati non gli danno mai da mangiare acciochè astretti dalla fame venghino presto alla conclusione.

The parallels seem insufficient to claim this as Rainsford's source.

17. Public penance for adultery was common (see T. P. Oakley, *English Penitential Discipline* (New York, 1923), p. 46). The *Ritratti del Regno de Inghilterra* (pp. 97–8) sheds light on the particular form of it which Rainsford describes:

Gli huomini che trovano con alcuna donna li mettono prigioni in una publica fatta a quest'effetto et per la maggior parte nelle piazze nelle quale sono veduti da tutta la Terra, et in quel luogo lo fanno stare un giorno intero, et talhor due et tre secondo il delitto commesso, cioè che sia stato con maritata, con vedova o con donzella. Et questo costume era in uso al tempo del Re Edoardo, perchè conforme alla nova sua religione intendevano che ognuno si havesse a maritare.

But the custom was short-lived, and, according to this author, 'con la mutatione del governo si è anchora mutata questa legge, essendo venute di Spagna molte cortiggiane, le quali si comportano senza sorte alcuna d'ingiuria'. The issue of prostitution may thus have been a live one in 1556, and Rainsford's stress on severity here, coming as it does in a treatise addressed to Philip, may be a kind of protest against Spanish influence in this matter.

18. Land-reclamation was not, in fact, extensive until the Stuart period. (See P. Ramsey, *Tudor Economic Problems* (London, 1965), p. 23.)

19. Not cottons in the modern sense, but rather woollen cloths like frieze.

20. For a discussion of Rainsford's economic theory, see above, pp. 64–8.

21. By 27 Henry VIII, cap. 27, and 5 and 6 Edward VI, cap. 2.

22. Cf.

> Hoc vellus vere aureum est, in quo potissimum insulanorum divitiae consistunt: nam magna auri atque argenti copia a negociatoribus eiusmodi in primis coemendae mercis gratia, in insulam quotannis undique apportatur, ibique perpetuo manet, quia alio terrarum referri omnibus lege vetitum est: unde fit, ut opes maiores nusquam gentium sint. (*Angl. Hist.*, p. 13)

23. Here Rainsford is influenced in his phrasing ('Il re che circa gloria per via de giustitia' is typically Machiavellian in its diction and in its telling specificity— there are kings who seek glory by non-constitutional means as well) by Machiavelli, and also undoubtedly by Gardiner's way of using Machiavelli, a way in which constitutionalism and classification of princes according to how they chose to rule was characteristic.

24. Note that Gardiner's regular term was *baroni*, barons, a term falling into disuse in the mid-sixteenth century. Rainsford's *nobili*, nobles, was the more up-to-date locution. Ramsey (*Tudor Economic Problems*, p. 122) conjectures that the shift in terminology was caused by the fact that the barons had declined in governmental and military importance, and the older term carried connotations of their former function. Compare Rainsford's discussion of 'gentlemen' and 'nobles' and the role they played in society with Gardiner's somewhat anachronistic account (fo. 118 seq.) beginning 'i baroni in Ingliterra et Francia participanno del stato co'l re, et i hanno privilegii et authorità grandissima co'l popolo'. Gardiner stressed their military importance, for example, and this was certainly on the wane.

25. This was the freedom to speak freely in opposition to government bills, first requested by Thomas More in 1523. (See J. E. Neale, *Elizabeth I and her Parliaments, 1559–1581* (London, 1953), pp. 17–19.)

26. The institution of Wardship, a very profitable one indeed for the Crown, is fully discussed in J. Hurstfield, *The Queen's Wards* (London, 1958).

27. Cf.

> Philippus Pulcher rex Franciae, tris ex Ioanna uxore creavit filios, Ludovicum Hutinum, Philippum Longum, et Carolum Pulchrum: filias vero duas, unam quam infantem mors rapuit, et alteram Isabellam nomine, quae nupsit Edoardo secundo regi Angliae, ex qua natus est Edoardus tertius, de quo nunc sermo est. Illi tres filii deinceps regnarunt. Successit Philippo pater Ludovicus maximus natu filius, is ex Margarita priore uxore, filia Roberti ducis Burgundiae Ioannam filiam suscepit, quae mox data fuit in matrimonium Ludovico Eburovicomiti, sed nullis ex se genitis liberis, haud diu superstes fuit. Alteram uxorem Clementiam nomine, filiam Martelli, qui pater fuit Roberti Siciliae regis, moriens gravidam reliquit, quae puerum peperit, cui nomen Ioannes est impositum, qui pauculos dies vixit. Post hunc Ioannem regnat Philippus Longus, quamvis nonnullis inclamantibus regnum Ioannae Hutini filiae deberi, id quod Odo Burgundiae dux avunculus puellae cum primis faciebat, plus tamen vis potuit, quamque ius. Philippus deinde post annum quintum, quam regnum occuparat, sine liberis moritur. Postremo Carolus Pulcher regnum obtinuit, is septimo post anno mortem obivit, relicta Ioanna uxore gravida, quae paucis post diebus

filiam nomine Blancham enixa est, quae statim patris fatum secuta est. Per hunc igitur modum, regia virilis stirps Philippi Pulchri in Carolo filio defecit, ex quo de regno inter Francum et Anglum contentio orta est, quae, ut ante diximus, etiam nunc sub iudice restat. (*Angl. Hist.*, pp. 355–6)

28. Philip IV 'the Fair' (1285–1314).
29. Louis X 'le Hutin' (1314–1316).
30. Philip V 'the Tall' (1316–1322).
31. Charles IV 'the Fair' (1322–1328).
32. Charles VI (1380–1422).
33. Cf.

Forma foederis eiusmodi fuit, ut Henricus usque eo dum viveret Carolus, regnum Franciae gubernaret, administraret, regeret, idque post Caroli mortem, eodem obtineret iure, quam qui optimo: et si contingeret, ut Henricus prior moreretur, eius filio magno natu ex Catherina genito regni haereditas veniret, ac principes Franci conceptis verbis, ipsi Henrico iusiurandum darent, atque Carolus Delphinus omni deiectus honore quem gerebat, hostis patriae perpetuo haberetur. (*Angl. Hist.*, p. 449)

Machiavelli also gives an account of this treaty in the *Ritratti delle cose della Francia* (ed. Giunta (1532), pp. 65–6).

34. Henry III (1216–1272).
35. Athelstan (925–939).
36. At the battle of Brunanburh in 937.
37. Malcolm III (1057–1093).
38. This passage is based loosely upon *Angl. Hist.*, pp. 185–7.
39. Louis VI 'the Fat' (1108–1137).
40. Henry I defeated the French at Brémule, near Noyon, in 1119.
41. William 'the Lion' (1165–1214) succeeded Malcolm IV (1153–1165). He was captured in 1174, taken to Normandy, and set free in return for his homage to Henry II of England: Rainsford here confuses Henry I and Henry II. (Cf. *Angl. Hist.*, p. 226)
42. For the passage on Richard I, cf. *Angl. Hist.*, p. 246.
43. Edward I acted as arbiter between contenders for the crown of Scotland in 1292. He decided in favour of John de Balliol (1292–1296), but when Balliol asserted his independence in 1295 by making peace with France, then at war with England, Edward invaded Scotland and took him prisoner. He surrendered his crown in 1296, and was held in England until 1299.
44. English forces were victorious at Sluys in 1340, at Crécy in 1346, and at Poitiers in 1356.
45. Philip VI (1328–1350).
46. Cf.

Ceciderunt in ea pugna triginta circiter Francorum millia, in quibus fuere viri principes Ioannes Boëmus rex, Carolus Alenconii comes, Philippi frater, item duo Ludovici, dux Lotaringus, et Flandriae comes, compluresque alii. (*Angl. Hist.*, p. 371)

47. At Poitiers in 1356, where Edward, the Black Prince, captured John II, king of France 1350–1364.
48. Polydore's figure is 1070 (*Angl. Hist.*, p. 376).
49. Much of this paragraph is based upon *Angl. Hist.*, pp. 371–2.
50. David II (1329–71) was captured at Neville's Cross, near Durham, in 1346, and was imprisoned for eleven years.
51. For some reason, Machiavelli's description of France includes this information, somewhat out of context, concerning England: 'Li arcivescovadi d'Inghilterra sono duoi. Vescovadi XXII. Parrochie LII mila.' These are the closing words of the treatise (ed. Giunta (1532), p. 66). The information was very common-

place, but Rainsford's eye may have been on his Machiavelli text, for he goes on to borrow Machiavelli's description of the office of Chancellor:

> L'uffitio del gran Cancelliere è; merum imperium et puo gratiarum et condemnare suo libito, etiam in capitalibus sine consensu Regis: Puo rimettere i litiganti contumaci nel buon di; puo conferire i benefitii cum consensu Regis tantum: perche le gratie si fanno per lettere Regali sigillati col gran sigillo Reale: però lui tiene il gran sigillo (ed. Giunta (1532), p. 63).

52. The account of Ireland is based largely on *Angl. Hist.*, pp. 217–19.
53. 'Tunicam ex panno lineo confectam induunt, et eam non mutant, donec contrita sit.' (*Angl. Hist.*, p. 218)
54. Cf.

> Capillum parum supra aures circuncidunt: aliqui tamen more vetusto, capillo usque ad occipitium reciso, in parte capitis anteriore longos gerunt crines. Barbam frequenter radunt, labio duntaxat superiore ad terrorem, ut credere par est, intonso. (*Angl. Hist.*, p. 219)

55. Polydore describes Irish mourning in *Angl. Hist.*, p. 219.

III

THE LETTER-BOOK OF THOMAS BENTHAM, BISHOP OF COVENTRY AND LICHFIELD

edited by

ROSEMARY O'DAY, B.A., Ph.D., F.R.Hist.S.

and

JOEL BERLATSKY, B.A., Ph.D.

The letter-book of Thomas Bentham, Bishop of Coventry and Lich-field (1560–79), is to be found in National Library of Wales MS. 4919D. The volume was purchased in May 1923, being one of some 500 volumes sold by Captain Ivor McClure on his removal from London to Malvern. Mr (later Sir) John Ballinger travelled up to London to examine the library on behalf of the National Library of Wales. Personal letters between the Librarian, Mr Ballinger, and Captain McClure survive for this period but provide no clue as to the origins of the library in general or of this volume in particular. The correspondence, moreover, does not indicate how the sale was made. The National Library of Wales Librarian's Report to the half yearly meeting of the court of Governors, held on 30 October 1923, makes no mention whatsoever of this purchase. It is known that at least three other rare books were bought from the same collection—a seventeenth-century Ethiopic psalter; the *Divinae Institutiones* of Lactantius (Latin, fifteenth century); and *Roman Inscribed and Sculptured Stones* (nineteenth century).

The letter-book is contained in a folio volume of eighteenth-century full calf tan binding. This is scratched and has no armorial bearings. The document was beautifully repaired after purchase in 1923 and this has obliterated any sewing marks which may have been present. There is no record of the state of the document before this repair was performed. The volume as it now stands consists of some 36 paper folios, numbered from 29 to 100. In addition there are two end pieces at both the beginning and the end of the volume. The dorse of the first endpaper at the front of the volume contains pencilled notes in a modern hand under the heading 'some names

mentioned in these letters'. The numbering of the folios suggests
that the letter-book as it now exists was originally a continuation of
another book but the document contains no indication of the nature
of this original manuscript. The average folio measures 8½ by 12
inches and there are about 45 lines to the average page. The dorse
of fo. 76 is blank.

For the most part the book is written in a very legible hand. The
script is basically secretary hand with some characteristics of human-
istic script. It is possible, if unlikely, that more than one person was
involved in drawing up the book; for example, the script on fo. 34r
appears to differ markedly from that on fo. 35r. It is more probable
that the work was undertaken by the bishop's personal secretary
who scrupulously *copied* the script of the few letters received which
were to find a place in the book and also the bishop's own signature.
Parts of the document have been badly damaged by damp: this is
especially true of some of the final folios. In other cases damp has
caused the ink to blotch badly and to render the letters almost illegible. Folios 47 to 57 and 65 to 74 are badly affected in this respect.

The contents of the letter-book consist almost entirely of copies of
letters sent, or paraphrases of the contents of such letters issued, by
the bishop from Eccleshall, his Staffordshire residence. A few items
represent letters or documents received by the bishop. There are a
few copies of letters sent from the Staffordshire rectory of Hanbury
and from an unspecified residence in London. The letters span the
period 20 June 1560 to 30 May 1561. Some of the entries are now in
an out-of-date order: folios 29 to 43 cover the months June to November 1560; folio 45 doubles back to May 1560 and this sequence
is continued. There are 254 items contained in the document.

Thomas Bentham

Thomas Bentham was born in Sherburn, Yorkshire, in 1513. In
November 1546 he was admitted a perpetual fellow of Magdalen
College, Oxford, where he proceeded M.A. in 1547. He became
known as a theologian and as one learned in Latin, Hebrew and
Greek. In 1553 he was one of six fellows of the college removed at
Gardiner's visitation. In 1554 he appeared at Zürich, remaining
there from April to October. Shortly afterwards he travelled to
Basel and registered as a student there for the year 1555–6. He be-
came preacher to the exiles in Basel but in 1557 moved on to Frank-
furt, where he acted as arbiter in the quarrel between Horne and
Asheley. During that year he received an invitation from Geneva to

co-operate on the Genevan Bible and in November he answered the call. At some time between November and January he married Maud Fawcon of Hadleigh, Suffolk. Shortly thereafter he returned to England to minister to the Protestant congregation in Marian London.

In 1559 he was appointed one of Elizabeth's visitors in the Royal Commission to Lichfield, Oxford, Lincoln and Peterborough. Elizabeth chose him as her bishop of Coventry and Lichfield and he was consecrated by Matthew Parker in March 1560. He was then 46 years of age. It seems probable that he did not enter the diocese until late May or June 1560. The contents of the letter-book seem to indicate that he set up his official residence at Eccleshall, using the parsonage of Hanbury as a summer residence once he gained control of it. Much of February and March 1561 was spent in London, seeing to financial and legal business. Henry Machyn tells us that Bentham preached at court in the spring of the following year, 1562. In 1568 he translated the books of Daniel and Ezekiel for the Bishops' Bible. Bentham died a decade later, in February 1579, leaving a wife and four children.

The Diocese

The diocese of Coventry and Lichfield contained four archdeaconries: Coventry, Derby, Salop and Stafford. There were over 500 congregations, between 388 and 420 of these being parishes properly under the jurisdiction of the bishop, the remainder consisting of donatives, peculiar jurisdictions and churches of uncertain status. According to the household census of 1563 the population of the diocese numbered approximately 125,144, which was distributed most unevenly through the area. The archdeaconry of Coventry contained the largest urban centres of the diocese (Coventry (*c.* 2,200), Birmingham, Solihull, Sutton Coldfield, Aston, Nuneaton and Hampton) although it was not the most populous archdeaconry. Technically the archdeaconries of Derby and Stafford were more populous but they covered much wider areas and population was, therefore, not so dense as in the smaller Coventry archdeaconry, there being few sizeable towns. Perhaps most significant was the fact that the diocese contained many areas of peculiar jurisdiction, outside the bishop's control. This was particularly problematical as many of the reasonably large urban agglomerations were thus made exempt from the bishop's jurisdiction. These included Lichfield (400 households); Wolverhampton (323); and the parish of Bakewell with seven chapelries, representing an enclave of population within Derbyshire equivalent in size to that of Coventry. Other peculiar jurisdictions were Bridgnorth, Shrewsbury and Prees in Shropshire and a multitude of parishes controlled by the dean and chapter of Lichfield. Both administrative and pastoral problems were posed by this situation, as the contents of the letter-book amply illustrate.

By 1560 the number of possible episcopal residences available to a bishop of Coventry and Lichfield had been reduced to three— Eccleshall castle, Hanbury parsonage house and Coventry palace. Of these, Coventry palace had been leased out for 99 years by bishop Sampson in Henry VIII's reign and the bishop had to defeat the claims of several persons in courts of law before he was able to take full possession of Hanbury. The bishop had no place of residence in the Derby or Salop archdeaconries. Episcopal revenue was drawn from ten manors; nine appropriate rectories; one prebendal church (Gnosall); certain meadowland tenths, synodals, and pensions. Additional to an anticipated revenue of £796 or thereabouts, there were the profits of office, including the profits of seal for institutions and orders, and the proceeds of woodsales, manorial courts, episcopal fairs and so forth. By Bentham's time very little of the episcopal demesne was held in hand. Hanbury was repossessed by the bishop in 1560/1 but was leased out again in December 1566, leaving the bishop only the home farm of Eccleshall, and stretches of park and woodland which were not leased out.

The value of the Letter-Book

To anyone attempting to construct a picture of Thomas Bentham's episcopate or of the diocese of Coventry and Lichfield at the start of Elizabeth's reign, the value of the letter-book here edited is self-evident, for apart from it there is little or no archival material upon which to draw. The episcopal register (L.J.R.O. B/A/1/15) contains some folios of institutions for the period 1560–84, but the information is incomplete for three of the archdeaconries concerned, listing Salop institutions only up to 1563, Derby to 1578 and Coventry to 1582. To some extent this material can be supplemented from the bishops' certificates in the P.R.O. and from B/A/2ii/1 at Lichfield. There is little visitation material for the episcopate, which lasted 18 years—six books containing *comperta* and two being *libri cleri*. There are instance court books for the period but no extant office court books until 1582/3: it is just such books as these which would yield information about the response to the Reformation and to the Elizabethan settlement within the diocese. Chapter Act Book IV gives some valuable material about episcopal leasing, mainly by Bentham's predecessors, and about the appointment of officials. There are extant one set of visitation articles and injunctions, a letter to the Privy Council, and several returns of recusants. Clergy subscriptions in 1559, records of the royal visitation, wills of clergy and of a few officials, and some central court records yield supplementary information. It is the letter-book, however, which enables the historian to assess the position in this diocese at the beginning of Elizabeth's reign on the basis of a solid corpus of material.

The historian must also view the letter-book in the context of other extant source material for the early Elizabethan church and, more particularly, the episcopate. The Correspondence of bishop Parkhurst of Norwich, recently edited by Dr Ralph Houlbrooke, is the only surviving Elizabethan episcopal letter-book of comparable quality.[1] This, however, covers a later period when the initial shock of the exiles' return to reality had passed. It is only in Bentham's letters that the bishop's fumbling attempts to deal with the problems of an impecunious and large diocese immediately after the Marian Reaction can be studied in detail. The letters were written before the newly-returned exiles had finally resigned themselves to the fact that Elizabeth had no wish to see a 'further reformation' of the church and had little intention of alleviating the financial position of her chosen bishops. They were written at a time when the returned exiles were being favoured at court—many became bishops, deans and archdeacons, and many more were accorded indirect patronage.

The letters also afford considerable insight into the diocesan administration of the period. The bishop's dependence upon his chancellor and his registrar are well demonstrated. Here, as nowhere else in the Lichfield archives, the relationship between the bishop and his archdeacons and chief clergy are sketched in. The pre-eminence of Lever as archdeacon of Coventry is made very clear: that this was partly due to the fact that Coventry was traditionally *archidiaconus major* is true, but Thomas Lever's personal status among the exiles probably contributed much to his position in the diocesan administration. Bentham's delicate relations with the dean and chapter and, specifically, with the dean and chapter peculiars are highlighted. Exclusive jurisdictions such as these, without the full co-operation of the official, made it extraordinarily difficult for the bishop to

---

[1] *The Letter-Book of John Parkhurst*, ed. R. A. Houlbrooke, Norfolk Rec. Soc., vol. xliii (1974–5).

stamp out popery or nonconformist practices or, indeed, to ensure that any episcopal policy was fully enforced. The letters also provide much interesting information regarding Bentham's attempts to make his presence felt in the administration. This may be seen in his realization that the diocesan registrar had been given too much freedom in the past. Effectively, he had controlled recruitment of the clergy, being permitted to approve and authorize the institution of examinees without consulting either bishop or chancellor. In at least one instance the registrar had abused his charge by authorizing the institution of a simoniacal vicar. As a result Bentham ruled that in future the registrar was to act in concert with either the bishop or the dean, and not alone. Bentham also inaugurated a pastoral ministry. He sought to influence the appointment of clergy. The letters show that he preached in various churches in Staffordshire and Shropshire. He also intervened in disciplinary jurisdiction in a manner unparalleled before or after in the records of the diocese in the sixteenth and early seventeenth centuries. Whether Bentham held a formal court of audience or not is a moot point, although from external evidence it appears that he did so. He certainly called before him on several occasions persons presented for offences in visitation in order to act as arbiter and judge. In matters concerning divorce and probate, however, he appears to have felt himself incompetent and to have bowed to the technical expertise of his chancellor and registrar.

As has been shown elsewhere, the letters are most valuable in underlining Bentham's financial predicament during 1560/1 and in demonstrating his attitude to the problem and his attempted remedies.[2] To some extent the letters provide information regarding the new Protestant bishop's relations with the surrounding landowners. The need for money, either in the form of loans or the repayment of debts, placed him in an ambivalent position. He wished to treat the local notables as equals, yet there was a note of subservience in his letters which was not solely the result of existing conventions but which was partly dictated by his financial predicament, and by his very real need for support among the, to him unknown, gentry of the diocese. His position was probably made even more delicate by the uncertain response of the local notables to the Elizabethan settlement. Bentham's relations with officials whom he inherited from the last administration are less ambiguous. Some,

[2] R. O'Day, 'Thomas Bentham: a case study in the problems of the early Elizabethan episcopate', *Journal of Ecclesiastical History* (xxiii, 1972), 135–59.

like Richard Walker, archdeacon of Stafford and Derby, appear to have been approved but carefully controlled. Bentham assumed that Lever would pursue a Protestant line in visitation (indeed he had to be told not to be too radical) but Bentham felt that he had to watch Walker to ensure that he toed the line. Others, most especially Thomas Bolt, collector, and Thomas Chedulton, official of Stafford, were suspect from the start and soon fell foul of the new bishop. As has been shown, Bentham was eager to fill vacant positions with his own men—this policy extended to parochial benefices as well as to ecclesiastical and manorial offices. To a limited extent he drew his own officials from prominent local families as a palliative to the gentry.

The letters also contribute to our knowledge of religious feeling in the diocese at this time. As there is little visitation material for the first years of the episcopate, this is very welcome. The archdeaconry of Stafford was already reputed to contain numerous Roman Catholics ready to cause trouble at any time, and from the letter-book it appears that these pockets of resistance had found a haven in the many peculiar jurisdictions scattered throughout the county. The one which forced itself upon Bentham's attention was situated in the episcopal manor of Eccleshall. The historian may find it noteworthy that it was the part of local women in this popular resistance to Protestantism which Bentham found significant. It is likely that Bentham's role in the 1559 Royal Visitation of the diocese had given him a valuable insight into the probable trouble spots of the area. He certainly seems to have watched closely the clergy deprived under Mary for marriage who had been re-instituted at Elizabeth's accession. Thus we find Bentham rebuking Henry Techoo, vicar of Montford in Shropshire, for his behaviour in marrying and yet worshipping images. Bentham believed, probably with some justice, that the Catholics within the diocese were retaining their altars and images in the hope that the new regime would soon be overturned and the old religion restored—history, after all, seemed to suggest that such a possibility was not unlikely.

The historian of the Elizabethan settlement will find particularly interesting the light which the letters throw upon relations between the returned exiles. Bentham felt himself to be still intimately connected with the group of Marian exiles, especially with those who had been at Magdalen College with him or with whom he had had close links in Zürich, Basel and Geneva, and with the members of the Protestant congregation in London who had been with him in

1558 and 1559. He knew that the returned exiles were in favour with Cecil and Bacon at court, and he tried to take advantage of this fact by appealing directly to these men and by lobbying them through exiles such as Nowell and Mistress Asheley. On another level he tried to procure preferment for Cuthbert Hughes, a fellow exile; and he used his influence with Haddon to obtain favours for friends. The gradually emerging split between those exiles who had been offered and had accepted bishoprics, and those who had not, is evident. Bentham's relations with Thomas Lever were even this early in his episcopate strained on occasion. Lever thought that Bentham was spending too much time away from his pastoral charge and that he was not doing enough to discipline the recalcitrant. Relations with Thomas Sampson were even worse.

Of course, the letter-book does not provide the historian with all the facts necessary for an account of Bentham's administration at Lichfield. It covers less than two years of his eighteen-year episcopate. Moreover, the letters sent out present us with an accurate picture of the image of himself and his situation which Bentham wished to project to his readers rather than with an exact reflection of the state of affairs in this midland diocese. The reader must therefore approach the letters critically and with caution. Yet the value of the book is unchallengeable—Bentham's own appreciation of the various problems facing him in administering the see at such a critical juncture in the English Reformation makes this a unique piece of documentation; through the book's pages the historian can also trace the delicate relationships maintained by this Protestant bishop with local gentry, with the surviving officials of the Marian see, with his clergy, with the companions of his exile, and with the government.

The editors wish to thank the National Library of Wales for permission to publish this document and for assistance accorded during its preparation. They also wish to express their gratitude to Ann Rycraft, who generously transcribed items 191 and 193, and to Jane Isaac, of the Lichfield Joint Record Office. Keith Thomas gave much valuable advice in the initial stages of preparation of the typescript.

ABBREVIATIONS USED IN THE NOTES

Bateson, *Original Letters*	*A Collection of Original Letters from the Bishops to the Privy Council*, ed. M. Bateson, *Camden Miscellany IX* (1895)
B.L.	British Library
C.P.R.	*Calendar of Patent Rolls*
D.N.B.	*Dictionary of National Biography*
Foster, *Alumni Oxonienses*	J. Foster, *Alumni Oxonienses . . . 1500–1714* (8 vols, Oxford, 1891)
Garrett, *Marian Exiles*	C. H. Garrett, *The Marian Exiles* (Cambridge, 1938; reprinted 1966)
Gee, *Elizabethan Clergy*	H. Gee, *The Elizabethan Clergy and the Settlement of Religion, 1558–64* (Oxford, 1898)
Landor, *Staffordshire Incumbents*	W. N. Landor, *Staffordshire Incumbents and Parochial Records (1530–1680)*, Collection for a History of Staffordshire, William Salt Archaeological Society, 1915
L.C.L.	Lichfield Cathedral Library
Letters & Papers . . . Henry VIII	*Letters and Papers, Foreign and Domestic, of the Reign of Henry VIII*
L.J.R.O.	Lichfield Joint Record Office
P.C.C.	Prerogative Court of Canterbury
P.R.O.	Public Record Office
Valor Ecclesiasticus	*Valor Ecclesiasticus temp. Hen. VIII*, ed. J. Caley and J. Hunter (6 vols, 1810–34)
V.C.H. Staffs	*Victoria County History, Staffordshire*
Venn, *Alumni Cantabrigienses*	J. Venn, *Alumni Cantabrigienses* (pt 1, 4 vols, Cambridge, 1922–7)

1. [*To Edmund Grindal, Bishop of London,*[1] *20 June 1560*]

(fo. 29) For as moche as three poore men beyng Spanyods and fley-nge theyr ther countree for religions sake have requested me to speake to your good Lordshippe in theyr behalffe. These ar to signi-fye that they were commended unto me by the letters of ii godly and lerned men that is of one Mr Spenser,[2] and of one Mr Cole.[3] And since theyr comyng hither, they have godly and diligentlye applied theym selfes to labor and studye, so farr as I know or can understand. Whiche thyng I thought good to signifye unto your good Lordship to thend that in case they shall desyre your helpe herafter for theyr better savetye, your Lordshipe may understand how they cam in to Inglande, and withe what commendation, and so helpe to ease theyr troble, yf the case so requyre. Thus desyreng yor good Lordshipes helpe unto theym when nede shalbe, I sett theyr names under here folowying. Wryten this 20. of June 1560.

                    Your good Lordshipes to commaunde,
Cyprianus Valera,[4] studiosus Cantabrigiae.

Franciscus Cortes   ⎫
              ⎬ degentes Londini.[5]
Ferdinandus de Leon ⎭

2. [*To Sir Francis Knollys,*[6] *Vicechamberlain to the Queen, 1 July 1560, from London*]

(fo. 30) In most consyderate wyse my dewtye remembred to your ho-nor these may be [to] desyre the same, so favorablye to accept this berer Mr Reniger[7] as to helpe to preferr his suete unto the Quene,

[1] Edmund Grindal, bishop of London 1559–70.

[2] Possibly John Spenser, M.A., archdeacon of Chichester 1560–71.

[3] Either Thomas Cole, archdeacon of Essex 1559–71, or Robert Cole, clerk, rector of St Mary-le-Bow, London, 1559–76. If the latter, see item 154. Both were exiles.

[4] Cyprianus Valera. Born in Seville *c.* 1532; he was renowned for scholarship, and translated the Bible into Spanish. See Venn, *Alumni Cantabrigienses*.

[5] Unidentified.

[6] Francis Knollys, 1514–96. An exile in both Frankfurt and Strasbourg, he is said to have been a member of Magdalen College, Oxford; he was appointed to the Privy Council in December 1558 and became vicechamberlain of the royal household. See *D.N.B.*

[7] Michael Reniger, 1530–1609. Born in Hampshire, he was a student at Cambridge, then demy and fellow of Magdalen College, Oxford; he vacated his fellowship before 29 July 1553, and went into exile at Strasbourg (1554), and Zürich (1554; 1556); he was appointed chaplain to the Queen, 1561. See Garrett, *Marian Exiles.*

for the assignment of his byll. The matter beynge ordinarye, ys easye
to be preferred by any that have occasion; the man hym selfe ys
suche one as ys worthye in my symple iudgement to have not onely
that lyvyng but allso a greater, his learnyng ys knowen to be good
and grownded in Laten and greike, besyde his diligent studye in the
Hebrewe, which I know once to be greate. Wherefore so moche as
your honor shall further his cause, so moche I beleve you shall helpe
Christs churche with a worthye minister. He was at Zuriche, when
I and others were there also: for which cause I thynk hym mete to
be preferre. And yet cheyfly I wryte this moche because that I do
knowe his learnyng and lyvying to deserve good preferrment. Yf I
had any suche benefyt in my hand presently I wold thynk yt well
bestowed upon suche an one. This most earnestlye desyryng your
honors furtherance in this case, I commytt you to the goodness of
God almyghtye. Wryten at my poore lodgyng in London this fyrst
of July, 1560.

> your good honors to command

3. [*To Lawrence Nowell,*[8] *Dean of Lichfield, and the Chapter, 11 July
1560, from London*]

(fo. 30) Whithe my hartye commendations to your worships, thes ar
to signifye unto the same, that receavynge letters frome my Lord
Tresorrer[9] for the collection of the subsidyes[10] whiche ar to be payd
within my diocese I went unto hym and pleaded partlye upon ignor-
ance of the case partlye upon other good reasons as semed unto me.
Notwhithestandynge he wylled me to use diligence in that behalfe
and earnestly to call upon you for the collection of the same. Wherefore thes ar to move and requyre you to helpe the furtherance of that
collection whithe sped, so as your diligence may deserve thankes. And
what I can do I wyll do at my comyng downe which I purpose God
wyllyng to hasten nowe: In the meane tyme commytynge you to God

[8] Lawrence Nowell: brother of Alexander Nowell, dean of St Paul's; he had a
long-standing connection with the diocese of Coventry and Lichfield; deprived of
his benefice, *c.* 1553, for failure to take priest's orders within twelve months of
institution, he went into exile in Germany; he was made dean of Lichfield in
March 1560; he may also have held the archdeaconry of Derby 1558–77; but see
items 23 and 199. See also *Calendar of State Papers, Domestic, 1547–1580*, p. 393, and
Venn, *Alumni Cantabrigienses.*
[9] William Paulet, first Marquis of Winchester, ?1485–1572. He was Treasurer to
Queen Mary, an appointment confirmed by Elizabeth; he voted against changes
in church services but was essentially a trimmer, and on good terms with Cecil.
[10] See item 9.

and me to your godlye prayers. Wryten this xi^th of July 1560 at my poore lodgyng in London.

your freynd most assuredlye

4. [*To Sir Nicholas Bacon,*[11] *Lord Keeper of the Great Seal,* (?) *July 1560*]

(fo. 31) In most humble wyse compleyninge sheweth unto your good Lordshippe your dayly orator Thomas by the permission of God bysshoppe of Coventry & Lichfield. That where as one Raufe[12] late bysshoppe there was amongest other landes, tenamentes and herediitaments lawfullye seised in his demesne as of fee, as in the right of his saide bysshopricke, of and in the castell Lordshippe and manor of Eccleshall[13] with thappurtenances in the countye of Stafford and of and in all and singuler messuages, lands, tenaments & hereditaments, profytts, commodytes and emoluments to the same belongynge or apperteanynge. And so beyng thereoff seased, about one yere now last past, was accordynge to the lawe (in that case provyded) deprived and deposed from the said bysshopricke. Sithens whiche deprivation your said orator (the sea of the said bysshoprike beyng voyde) was named, elected and chosen by the deane and chapiter of the cathedrall churche of Lichfeild aforesaid to the said bysshoprick and after consecrated, invested and instituted in due forme and order of the lawe in and to the same,[14] by force whereof your said orator was and is also seased of and in the said castell lordshippe and maner and other the praemisses with thappurtenance accordyngly. So yt is yf yt may please your good Lordshippe that one Humfrey Swynerton Esquyer,[15] together with one Sir George Blount knyght,[16] by color and pretence of a certane and surmised and feaned lease thereof made unto one Francyes Evered[17] by the reverend father in God Richard

[11] Nicholas Bacon, 1509–79. He was created Lord Keeper of the Great Seal on 22 Dec. 1558. See *D.N.B.*
[12] Ralph Baynes, bishop of Coventry and Lichfield; nominated 25 Oct. 1554; consecrated 18 Nov. 1554; deprived 26 June 1559; died Nov. 1559.
[13] Eccleshall, Staffs. *Valor Ecclesiasticus* gives castle and manor of Eccleshall as being worth £86 7s. 1¼d.
[14] Nominated 27 Dec. 1559; consecrated 24 Mar. 1560.
[15] Humphrey Swinnerton. A general pardon cites him as late of Swynnerton, Staffs, alias of Hilton, Staffs (*C.P.R., 1558–1560*, p. 163). Will proved in P.C.C., 1562.
[16] George Blount. A general pardon cites him as late of Kinlet, Shropshire, alias late of Knightley, Staffs (*C.P.R., 1558–1560*, p. 235). Will proved in P.C.C., 1581.
[17] Francis Evered. L.C.L., Dean & Chapter Act Book IV, fo. 154v: confirmation of Francis Everard as bailiff of the manor of Eccleshall, Feb. 1549; fo. 156r:

E

Samson,[18] sometyme bysshopp there, do pretend a feyned title in and to the premisses,[19] whereas in very dede the said Francys dyd after apon a certane composition made betwene hym and the said Raufe, late bysshop of the same bysshoprick, surrender the said lease in to his handes as your said orator by dyverse good and sub-stantiall wytnesses is able to prove. And for as moche as the said surmysed title can not be other wyse disproved then by the examin-ation of certane old and aunciant persons abydynge as well within the City of London and whithin the said county of Stafford as els where who ar very aged, impotent and unable to travell without daunger of theyr lyves, and so in continuance of tyme throughe ob-livion and forgetfullnes thereof your said orator and his successors might be dishereted and defeted of theyr right title and interest in and to the premisses. May it therefore please your good Lordshippe the premisses considered to graunt forth the Quens majesties most honorable wryte of commission to be directed to certane worshipfull & discrete persons by your good Lordshippe to be named and apoynted, authorizing theym thereby to call before theym and to examyne suche of the said ancyant persons as best can and wyll testifye the truethe in this matter. And the said examination so herd and taken at a certane day to certyfy in wrytyng in to this honorable court there to remayne of recorde *In perpetuam rei memoriam* to thin-tent (fo. 32) that the right, title, and interest of your said orator and his successors in the premisses may the better be hereafter preserved, defended and kept frome all suche persons as pretend any feyned and untrue title to the same. And your said orator shall dayly pray to god for the preservation of your good Lordshipp in honor longe to contynue.

5. [*Interrogatories, (?) July 1560*]

(fo. 32) Interrogatories to be ministered on the part and behalfe of the reverend father in God Thomas bysshoppe off Coventree and Lichfeld.

    1.   Item wether this deponent do knowe the castell lordshippe & manor of Eccleshall in the countye of Stafford.

---

confirmation of a lease to Francis Everard, gent., of the manor of Eccleshall for 99 years at an annual rent of £44, 15 Mar. 1550.
   [18] Richard Sampson, bishop of Coventry and Lichfield 1543–54; he died 25 Sept. 1554.
   [19] A bill confirming grants and leases made by bishops deprived was read on 11, 18 and 21 of Feb. 1559 (*Journals of the House of Commons*, i, *1547–1628*, p. 54).

2. Item wether this deponent do knowe of any lease made to one Francys Evered of the said castell lordship and manor, by the reverend father in God Richard Sampson sumtyme bysshopp of the said bysshoprike of Coventry & Lichfeld.

3. Item wethere this deponent do knowe wether the said Frauncys Evered did after upon a composition betwene hym and one Rauffe late bysshoppe of the said bysshoprick surrender the said leas in to his handes or not and upon what conditions and to what uses etc.

4. Item howe longe yt is sithen the said Evered decessed and whethere he made a wyll and, yf he did, then who where his executors.

5. Item wether any writyngs or muniments or other esspecialtyes concernyng the said demyse, surrender or composition ever cam to the handes of the said executors sithens the death of the said Evered and yf they dyd where and in whose custody they nowe be.

6. Item wethere this deponent have any knowledge where any maner of evidences, court rolles or other muniments concernynge aswell the said manor of Eccleshall whithe thapportenances as any other lands, tenamentes and hereditaments apperteynyng to the said bysshoppricke byne become and in whose custodye they be.

6. (fo. 33) *Certane remembrances concernynge Eccleshall.*

1. First the saide manor or castell of Eccleshall whithe the whole lordshippe was lett in a large and ample maner to one Francys Evered by Bysshoppe Sampson.

2. Item the same lease was redemed by Bysshoppe Bayne, who paiyd yerely for the redemption thereof xxiiij[li] or there about to the saide Francys & his wyfe, and to the longer surviver of theym.

3. Item covenaunts towchynge the payment of the saide some of xxiiij[li] was confirmed by the dean and chapiter of Lichfield under theyr seall.

4. Item the saide Francys Evered was bound to deliver in to the bysshops handes all and all maner of wrytynges concernynge the same lease.

5. Further, one Mr Clerke dyd surrender or deliver up all the said wrytynge whithe the lease in to Bysshopp Bayns hands.

6.   Last of all the said bysshope haithe made a conveans of the saide
     lease unto one Humfrey Swynerton Esquyer.

7. (fo. 33) *For Hanbery*[20]

1.   The personage of Hanberye beynge forthe also at that tyme
     under the yerelye valour was likewyse redemed by the late
     bysshoppe.[21]
2.   Item there ys yerely payd for the redemption thereof to one Mr
     Pope[22] x[li]
3.   Item the said parsonage ys nowe lett forthe agayne under the
     yerely valor of yt and so the bysshopricke burdened whith that
     x[li] more than yt was before.
4.   Last of all the said lease or indenture is not confirmed by the
     deane and chapiter[23] as in lawe yt owght to be.[24]

8. [*To William Paulet, Lord Treasurer of England, 9 Sept. 1560*]

(fo. 34) My dewtye remembred unto your good honor, may it please
the same to understand that at my comynge in to this countree I
convented first of all the deane & chapter of Lichefeild concernynge
the collection & paymentt of the subsydyes,[25] wherefore at that
tyme I receaved your honors letters. And I have apoynted the accostomed collector; and processe is directed forthe accordynge to lawe

   [20] Hanbury, Staffs. The advowson belonged to the lordship of Tutbury until the
reign of Edward VI, when the rectory was appropriated to the bishops of Coventry
and Lichfield; *Valor Ecclesiasticus* gives vicarage worth £43 15s. 2d; tenth,
£4 7s. 5d; vicarage with annexed chapel of ease at Marchington, Tamworth
deanery, in 1563.
   [21] Baynes.
   [22] L.C.L., Dean & Chapter Act Book IV, fo. 155v: confirmation of the lease by
bishop Sampson of the farm of Hanbury rectory to William Pope, gent., for 60
years, on 30 July 1549.
   [23] There is no confirmation of the lease of Hanbury to Baynes and Grene in the
above act book, although fo. 164v gives confirmation of the grant of office of
custodian and bailiff of Hanbury by Ralph Baynes to Christopher Grene for life
at 40s. p.a. (10 Feb. 1559).
   [24] L.J.R.O., CC. 124100 *Temporalia Episcopalis*, p. 13, states 'No concurrent
lease is good without the confirmation of the deane and chapter And unles it
comence in ye habendum from the making thereof.
Item leases made before 1⁰ Elizabeth confirmed by deane & chapter were good:
not so by president & chapter.'
   [25] See items 3 and 9.

for the same, so that suche sped as may be is used therein; And promyse ys made unto me of the collector to gather it up in hast.[26] For
my part I have neither bene forgettfull nor negligent in this behalfe,
wherefore I desyre your honor so to thynk of me and I wyll call upon
theym daylye for yt so that this your honors letter which I receaved
the vii[th] day of this moneth of Septembre shall with all possible sped
be accomplished. Further concernyng my owne matters, I most
hartely desyre your good honors furtheraunce: for as yet I have not
receaved my mony of Mr Harecourt[27] which I shold by your lordships letters receave. The cause ys partly that we do not agre upon
the same some, which your honor dyd drawe forth unto me, because
he saith nowe that he haithe not receaved so moche as he dyd wryte
of then but I am able to prove that he haithe receaved xxiij[li] more
sence that tyme. An other cause is that he haithe bene at great charges in kepynge the castell of Eccleshall the vacation tyme; wherein
I most earnestly desire your honors favor that mr Harecourt may be
recompensed at the Quens hand for so long tyme as he kept yt in
her maiestyes name[28] and to my power I wyll be ready to gratify
or satisfy hym for my tyme. Beyng thus ordered, I was never brought
to suche necessitye and rebuke therewhith in disapoyntynge my
creditors. I thought your order wold have served me but I fynd yt
not so and so I knowe not what way to turne me neither can I
receave money to pay my detts nor to kepe my howse, nor yet to pay
the Quene. Wherein I beseche your honor beare whithe me yf I kepe
not my day. Thus desyring your honors favor & furtherance I beseche God to blesse you & yors with healthfull & quyett lyfe to his
pleasure. Wryten this ix[th] of Septembre at my castell of Eccleshall
1560.

your good honors to comaund

26 Thomas Bolt. Subscribed in 1559 (Lambeth Palace Library, C.M.XIII/58);
a pluralist rector in the diocese since 1549; he died in 1579. See Foster, *Alumni
Oxonienses*.

27 Simon Harcourt, of Ranton and Ellenhall, Staffs, armiger. Glover (*Visitation
of Staffs, 1583*) gives 'of Stanton Harchourt, Oxon.'; a relative, Sir John Harcourt,
had been sheriff of Stafford and chief steward of Ranton priory; on 12 Dec. 1559
Simon Harcourt was granted for life the office of receiver-general of the revenue
of lands in Staffs, Hereford and the city of Hereford, late in the survey of the Court
of Augmentations and now in that of the Exchequer, as from Easter 1559, at an
annuity of £20, plus 20s. portage, on every £100 paid into the Exchequer (*C.P.R.
1558–1560*, p. 250); he acted as sequestrator of revenues of the episcopal castle and
manor of Eccleshall during the vacancy of the see; see items 20, 42, 68. See also
item 87. Bentham named him before the Privy Council as an adversary of religion
in 1564. He was noted as one of a 'knot hurtfull to Justice & great Mainteineres'
among J.P.s in Staffs (Bateson, *Original Letters*, p. 42).

28 As receiver-general.

9. [*To Mr Bolt,*[29] *at Lichfield, 9 Sept. 1560*]

(fo. 34) After my harty commendations etc. Thes ar to signify unto you that I have receaved my Lord Treasurers letters nowe agayne for the subsidies dew anno iiij[to] & v[to] Phillipi et Mariae.[30] Wherein I pray you use boyth diligence & expedition for the quene haithe nede of her moneys as my Lord wrytethe.[31] Thus trustyng to your faithefull diligence and lyke expedition, I byd you most hart-elye fayre well frome my castell of Eccleshall this ix[th] of Septembre 1560.[32]

yor freynd to commaund

10. [*Letter to an unknown correspondent, 9 Sept. 1560*]

(fo. 35) Right honorable and my very good Lord my humble comen-dacons considered, this is to desier your Lordship to geve me leave to make you privye in what state I found the howses that were assigned to my bisshoppricke by the quenes majesty for me to lye att within my dioces: first, Eccleshalle Castle, all the stuff, implements and standerds of howshold, as well in the kitchine as in the barnehouse, not only taken away but also the commodityes, as the cornes and the fisshe, in a manner spoyled so that the state of the howse joyned with my poore hability I know not howe I may conveniently ly ther yett, and nevertheles ame borne in hand by such as ar of worshippe here and hability in the countrey not longe to enioye itt, but by colore of a lease shalbe pluckte out of it; and my rents due to me recepted by others before my coming I can not gett them. So that I ensure you my Lord yf I had knowen as much afore as by proufe now to my great disscomfort, I would have ben leyd in priesone befor I would have taken so weighty and chargable an office in hand with so much unquietnes as I am like to sustaine if your good Lord-ship be not my pattrone in my iust causes which ar so full of trouble and combraunc lefte unto me by my predicessors that if it be not by

[29] Thomas Bolt.

[30] *Journals of the House of Commons,* i, *1547–1628*: 22 and 24 Feb. 1558, readings of bill for clerical subsidy; the subsidy was one of 8s. in the pound, payable over 4 years at a rate of 2s. in the pound p.a. on 9/10ths of incomes (*Statutes of the Realm,* iv, 332–5).

[31] Under the terms of the act the bishops, and their delegates as collectors of the subsidy, were empowered to enforce payment by sequestration, censure etc.

[32] According to the terms of the act, the subsidy for 1560 should have been paid to the collector by 25 Mar. 1560, and have been paid into the Exchequer by 10 June 1560 at the latest.

your comfortable assistaunce I will yet be willing with the Quens majestys favor to yeld it upe ageine. Thother howse assigned to me by her Majesty is the parsonage of Hanbury in the county of Stafford which was taken by my predicessor Bisshopp Sampsone as parcell of some recompenc for such lands he departed with;[33] which parsonag hous and tiths was not only in the manuell occupacon of the said bisshop during his life but also in the late Bisshop Banes handes untill he perceived that God would once agein restor his gosspell here in England to the overthrow of papistrye, in which time, though he had ben both vehement in times past to persecut and very earnest to recon ageine the stat of his sey spoyled yet he then seing thaltracon of the world contrary to his corrupt fantacy could be content to shew his good will to leave his successors never howse to lye in as it appeireth by a lease made to twoo of his servaunts[34] a litle afore his deprivacon, which I ame (fo. 36) enformed by my learned counsell for certain causes here under written is void and that I may mak my entry there which I have done without any damage or trouble, praying your Lordship to stand my good Lord so far as the equitye of my cause will bear and that I may not be dissposessed agein therof untill my title be heard affor your Lordship yf that we doo not quietly end the case before by freynds:[35] whiche as I most desyre, so I trust it wyll come to passe. And so desyrynge your good Lordship to iudge the best therein and to help when nede shall requyre, I commytt the same to almyghtye God. Wryten this ix[th] of Septembre 1560 at my poore castell of Eccleshall.

Your good honors at
commaundement.

11. (fo. 36) *Causes whye the lease ys not good.*

1. First and principally because it wanteth the confirmacon of the deine and chapiter.[36]

---

[33] In fact it was Bishop Lee who thus received Hanbury (*Letters & Papers . . . Henry VIII*, XII(I), pp. 357, 363, 439, 526; XII(2), p. 346; XIII (I), p. 63; XIV(I), pp. 403, 404).

[34] P.R.O., C/3/13/63: Christopher Baynes declared that Bishop Baynes was his 'naturall uncle'. L.C.L., Dean & Chapter Act Book IV, fo. 164r: Baynes was constable of Eccleshall castle as from 7 Jan. 1559; fo. 164v: Christopher Grene was bailiff of Hanbury.

[35] P.R.O., C/3/13/63: Case in Chancery against Christopher Baynes. 2 folios, being a letter from Bishop Bentham to Nicholas Bacon, signed by R. Forsett, and Christopher Baynes' answer to the charges made in the presence of R. Rede.

[36] See item 7.

2. secondarylye[a] because it hath not byne[b] usually sett and lett at any time befor.

3. Thyrdly because thold rent is not reserved.
   [c]is lett forth in fraudenc as most planelye doethe appere.

4. Fourtly becaus that it is iudged of the most part to be antedated.

5. Lastly onely to defraud the successor at this tyme, as is most constantely affyrmed.

12. [*Covenants between Bishop Bentham and Christopher Baynes and Christopher Grene, Sept. 1560*]

(fo. 37) Certaine covenants and agrements made and subscribed unto by the reverend father in God, Thomas bysshoppe of Coventry & Lichfeild on the one partye: And Christofer Grene & Christofer Bayne gent on the other partye: concernyng the parsonage of Hanberye in the countye of Stafforde, the sevent day of August in the second year of the reagne of our soverayne ladye Elizabethe by the grace of God Quene of Inglande Fraunce and Ireland defender of the faythe etc.

First that where as the aforesaid Christofer Grene, and Christofer Bayne, do pretend a title and interest in the said parsonage of Hanbery by vertue of a lease (as they say) yt is nowe covenanted and agreed betwene the above named persons, that the same title, right and interest shall from henceforthe cease and be of none effect untyll further and better tryall of the validity thereof whithe common consent may be hadd.

Item that whereas the above named Thomas by the permission off God etc. haithe as in his right mad an entre in to the said parsonage, he lykewyse shall forbeare to take or gather any part or percell of the fruytes and commodytyes of the said parsonage untyll the right, tytle and interest be further tryed and better knowen: but as shall folowe.

Item that in the meane tyme for the better preservation of tythe haye and corne and suche other fruytes and commodytyes: the gatherynge in, kepynge and bestowynge of the same shalbe at the apoynetment of boyth partyes indifferently by common consent.

[a] *Word interlined.*
[b] *Word interlined.*
[c] *Word preceded by* 4 because that yt, *struck out.*

Item for the better quietnes and ease of all partyes, as well the mansion howse of the parsonage as the pastures and meadows shalbe by vertue of thes covenants and common consent indifferently used.

Last of all, that the right, title and interest of the saide lease be examined and tryed either by indifferent persons to boyth partyes or els by suche lerned counsell as either of the partyes shall name and chuse for the hearynge and determination of the same whithe in three or foure monthes (at the furdest) after the date hereoff.

Item for the performance of thes covenants either party shalbe bounde to the other in an obligation of CC^{li} and interchangeablye to thes covenants sette theyr handes and seales.

13. (fo. 38) Anno 1560 *The copy of requests*

This byll made the seventhe day of August in the second yere of the reagne of our soverayne ladye Elizabethe by the grace of God Quene of Englande, Fraunce and Ireland, defender of the faythe etc. wyttnesseth that we Christofer Grene and Christofer Bayne gent ioyntly and either of us severally do owe unto the right reverend father in God Thomas by the permission of God bysshopp of Coventree and Lichefeild two hondrethe pounds of good and lawfull money of Ingland, to be payd to the said reverend father, his heires, executors, assignes or administrators at the feast of the natyvity of our Lord next after the date hereoff. In whitnes whereof, we bynd us and either of us, owre heires, executors, assignes, and administrators by thes presents dated the day and yere above wrytten and signed whithe our handes and seales.

> The condition of this obligation is suche that yf the above bounden Christofer Grene and Christofer Bayne and every of theym do well and fathefully kepe and observe all suche covenantes and agrements as ar made and enterchangeably subscribed whithe the handes of boyth partyes above named in one draught of covenantes made concernynge the parsonage of Hanberye, that then this obligation to be voyde and of none effect or els to stande in his full streinghte.

14. [*To the Queen, 9 Sept. 1560*]

(fo. 39) In most humble & obedient wyse suethe unto your highnes
your poore & dayly orator Thomas, by the permission of God and
your graces collation bysshoppe of Coventry & Lichfield, That where
as your graces highnes haith bestowed upon your said suppliant the
afore named bysshopprike and he at the takynge upon hym the said
offyce of ministerye, beynge a man of poore aestate & callynge, and
sence that tyme put to suche greate charges as well^a extraordinary
as ordinarye whiche^b then he is not able to susteane & beare, and
last of all nowe fyndyng his bysshopprick in that case & stayte that
the greatest part thereof is so intangled with divers leases and so incombred with suetts & trobles of lawe that hitherto neither he
haythe ne can receave the greatest part of his rents either to discharge his deatts which be greater then the hole rents unpayd wyll
discharge or to kepe house & famylie mete for his callyng & expectation of the contrey, or els to answere your highnes accordyng to
the lawe for first fruytes.[37] In consideration whereof may it please
your majesties highnes so mercyfully to tender your poore suppliant
state as to releve & comforthe the same whithe release of some part
of his first fruytes and especially of the first payment nowe at michaelmas or els he shall be able, neither to pay any part of his detts,
whiche to him is great greyfe, neither to make necessarye provision
for house kepyng, nor to kepe any howse at all, whiche he iudgethe
wyll redowne moche to the slaunder of the gospell, whereby he
shalbe unable either to serve God or your highnes as his dewtye &
wyll is. Wherefore as he most earnestlye desyrethe God to move yor
graces heart herein, so moche humbly and lowly he besechethe your
highnes to pardon his rude boldnes, whereunto by extreme necessitye he is dryven presentlye And he shall not cease to praye to the
mercy seate of almightye God for the longe, peacefull & healthfull
preservation of your maiestyes reagne. Frome my poore & colde
castell of Eccleshall this 9 of Septembre 1560.

youre majesties humble orator

---

^{a} *Followed by* ordina, *struck out.*
^{b} *Word struck out and then inserted again above the line.*

---

[37] The income from temporalities, pensions and appropriated churches was
£795 17s. 6¾d (*Valor Ecclesiasticus*).

15. [*To Sir William Cecil, Principal Secretary to the Queen, 9 Sept. 1560*]

(fo. 39) With most faithfull remembrance of my dewtye unto your good honor, may it please same to stande my freyn so moche that I may be bold to desyre your favor & furtherance in my poore suet unto the Quens highnes. So yt is, right honorable, that*a* by extreme necessitye I am dryven to desyre the Quens maiesties highnes for some release of my first fruitts. The causes be thes: My greate charges at my longe*b* beyng at London; my smale recepts of rents; and the greate trobles and incombrancyes wherewhithe I am wrapped & intangled in the most part of lordshippes & benefyces belongyng to my bysshoppricke. Wherein yf I shall not have better & stronger helpe then my selfe I shalbe thrust to the walls.*c* Wherefore as yor honor haithe bene my syngulare and onely freynd heretofore, so I beseche you nowe lett me have your good word & furtherance to the Quens highnes. Yf I were not so farr indetted by borowyng of moneye at London to pay ordinarye fees and other charges I wold in no case attempte so boldlye to request her highnes and yf (fo. 40) your honor had bene at London at my departure I shold have desyred your helpe and counsell then. Thus trustyng to your good honors helpe at my nede, I desyre God to blesse and preserve you in healthe and quietnes to his pleasure and your comforthe. Writen this at my poore castell of Eccleshall this 9 of Septembre 1560.

> Your good honors at commandement,

16. [*To Dr Haddon,*[38] *Master of Requests, 9 Sept. 1560*]

(fo. 40) My harty commendations remembred unto your good worshipe, Thes may be to desyre you most hartelye to be so freyndlye unto me as to helpe the furtherance of a rude supplication whiche by necessitye I am compelled to send and offer unto her highnes, wherein as I do symplye and planelye declare my poore state nedye of present helpe so I beseche your worshippe yf the same shall come to your handes to speake of and commend the same as charytye shall move you. I can requyre nothing of desert yet for that smale tyme

---

a right honorable, that *interlined.*   *b* *Word interlined.*
c thrust to the walls *written in the margin in pencil in a modern hand.*

---

[38] A Master of the Requests and Master of the Prerogative Court of Canterbury.

your worshippe was in Magdalene colledge,[39] I trust you wyll remembre my poore estate. Wherein what pleasure so ever you shall shewe me I shall not onelye presentlye most thankfullye acknowledge the same: but readye at all tymes either to recompence or deserv yf it shall lye in my poore power, as knowethe the Lorde, to whose good gyd[yng] I commyt your worshippe. Wryten this ix[th] of Septembre at my poore castell of Eccleshall 1560.

Your good worshipps to command

17. [*To Mrs Asheley*,[40] *10 Sept. 1560*]

(fo. 40) As I have bene alwayes bolde with you present right worshippfull Maistres Asheley, so I have great ned of your helpe beyng absent. It is so that necessitye haithe compelled me to wryte unto the Quens highnes a rud supplication whiche I bes
che you helpe to deliver yf nede shall requyre or els when it is delivered to speak a good word to prosper yt for surelye yf I had knowen this moche beyng at London I shold hardleye have come in to this contrey, but nowe, seyng I am in the brears, I must get forthe when I may and as I may. In the mean tyme havynge nede of all good mens helpe, I pray you speake for me when you see best occasion and most apt tyme. And althoughe I be not able to deserve yt, yet I wyll hartely pray God to recompence yt, to whose blessed protection I commytt yor worshipe. Writen this x[th] of Septembre 1560 at my poore castell of Eccleshall.

your good worshippes to command

18. [*To Alexander Nowell*,[41] *Dean of St. Paul's, 10 Sept. 1560*]

(fo. 40) After my most harty commendations unto you gentill Mr Nowell, beynge glad to heare of your healthe & preferment, I meane your mariage, whereatt I hartelye reioyce, knowynge the godlines of your wyfe,[42] to whome I praye you have me commended. Thes ar

---

[39] From Sept. 1552–Aug. 1553 (resigned). Haddon had been President of Magdalen College, Oxford. He was a prominent reformer.

[40] Katherine Asheley was Woman of the Bed-Chamber to the Queen; she was wife of the exile John Asheley gent., of Norfolk, Elizabeth's Master of the Jewel House. See John Asheley in Garrett, *Marian Exiles*.

[41] Brother of Lawrence Nowell, dean of Lichfield, he was a prominent exile who became dean of St Paul's in 1560.

[42] He had married a widow named Blount.

at this tyme most earnestlye to desyre but suche helpe as you con-venientlye may shew me; that is in helpynge that a poore supplica-tion may be delivered unto the Quene for surely yf her majestie do not helpe me I shall not onelye be almost clerelye undone but also so defaced and discoraged in this contrey that I shall never be able to do any good. I have (fo. 41) writen letters up to suche as I trust most unto, desyryng theyr furtherance & helpe. God sped yt as it shall please his goodnes to exercyse me. In the meane tyme I have moche a doo not onely whithe myne adversaryes but in that I can not gett in my rents dew at our lady day past. What incombrancys there be a man wolde hardly beleve for either I must receave as every man haithe corrupt his lease or els nothyng at all. Thes I wryt for no other cause surelye but onely to crave your helpe in this my nede for I doubt not but a fewe wordes of you shall do as moche good. And so I commyt you to the goodnes of almightye God and me to your good prayers. Writen this xth of Septembre 1560 at my poore castell of Eccleshall.

your freynd to commaunde

19. [*To Mr Godfrey*,[43] *17 Sept. 1560*]

(fo. 41) After my harty commendations unto you gentill Mr. God-frey, Thes may be to desyre your lawfull favor nowe at my neces-sitye towching the first payment of my fruyts whiche by order of compowndynge must be before michaellmasse. And for as moche as I can not gett in my rents before the day apoynted, I pray you suffer me a litell after the day, and whithe all spede I wyll make yt readye, Yf I can not gett a warrant frome the Quens majesty for the same. And verelye what favor you shall shewe me herein, yt shall not be forgotten when so ever I shalbe able with any lyke pleasure to gratifye you, as knowethe God, to whose kepynge I commytt you. Writen this 17 of Septembre 1560 at my castell of Eccleshall.

Yor freynd most assuredlye etc.

[43] Thomas Godfrey was Remembrancer of First Fruits. The procedure was that the Remembrancer consulted the *Valor*, and in event of failure of payment issued a warrant to the sheriff of the appropriate county to extract the debt by any means, including arrest and/or process against the underwriters of the incumbent's composition with the Office.

20. [*To William Paulet, Lord Treasurer, 18 Sept. 1560*]

(fo. 41) Right honorable & my verye good Lord, my dewty rightlye considered thes may be to desyre your good honor to be so favorable & freyndlye unto me as at my extreme necessitye to helpe me with my moneye, whiche either is payd in to thexcheker or els remanethe in Mr Harcourts handes. I have asked yt planelye inoughe but as yet I have not receaved yt, wherefore I beseche your good honor to stand my freynd so moche as to move hym earnestlye to pay me that whiche he confessed before by his letters that he had payd in to thexcheker. And where as your honor well, I trust, remembrethe thexchange of the manors of Ichyngton and Tachebrook for the whiche in recompence I shold have my tenthes and one smale parsonage of xii^li valewe whithe the tenthes of the prebend of Alderwas, I beseche your honor that I may have your warrant to receave nowe at michaelmas boythe the rent of the parsonage & also the tenthes of the prebend from michaelmas last seiyng that the Quene haithe the hole rent of Ichyngton, for yf the same shalbe payd in to the Exchecker then shall I have as moche ado to receave yt agayne as I have about the rest alreadye payd in. Wherefore I pray your good honor to let me have your warrante to receave in tyme the same rents & yor good honor shall bynd me to acknowledg the same most thankfully as knowethe almightye God, who preserve your honor in health to his pleasure. This 18 September 1560 at my poore castell of Eccleshall.

yor honors at commandment

21. [*To the Officers of the Exchequer, 2 Oct. 1560*]

(fo. 42) After my most humble commendations to your good honors, may it please the same to understand that as I have receaved a letter of *sub pena* to appere before your good Lordshippes and the rest of the Quenes officers of the exchequer in the octaves of St Michaell,[44] so my state is suche present and the tyme so short that yf I shold personallye apere yt shold be to my utter undoyng. Whitche thynge as I trust is not the meanyng of the lawe so I beleve certanlye standythe not with the pleasures of your good honors. Wherefore I am the

---

[44] Within the week following the feast of Michaelmas (29 Sept.).

bolder to desyre your favors. And so moche the rather I beseche you to shewe me your lawfull favors for that (I protest before god and all the world) I never knewe nor herd of the matter before that I was served with the wryte: which yf I had the case shold not have come to this passe for I receave not one farthynge gayns by it. Not whith standyng yf it be annexed to my bisshoppricke by order of lawe I wold gladlye use the same, onely for correction of synne which in that chappell haithe bene moche unpunyshed as I am informed. Howbeyt nowe beyng absent I wyll not pleade but, submyttyng me to your charitable orderynge and moche humblye besechinge you lett myne attorney answere in my cause, I desyre your honors to thynke neither contempte nor disobedience*a* in mye absence, even so desyr-inge allmightye God to blesse you all and kepe you in his feare. Writen this second day of october at my poore castell of Eccleshall.

your good honors at commaundement

22. (fo. 42)   28 Octobris 1560

Moved aswell by the knowledge and intelligence that we have as also by the honest testimonye that Maistres Marye Hayles and Mrs Lucye[45] haithe geven of one Elizabeth Thickyns, whithe whome she haithe bene conversant a many of yeres; beyng allso requested to geve our iudgement of the said Elizabethe, do judge of here that she ys an honest and sobre woman and suche a one that for her con-ditions is worthye to be cowpled with some honest and discrete mate. In whitnes whereoff we the bysshoppe and justices of peace have sett our hands to this byll.[46]

per me

a Followed by my, *struck out.*

---

[45] Possibly Mrs Lucy of Charlecote, Warwickshire.
[46] The twenty-ninth Royal Injunction of 1559 recognized clerical marriage, but the consent of the diocesan and two J.P.s, as well as the goodwill of the woman's parents, kin, or master, was required.

23. [*An acquitance to Richard Walker for the sinages*[47] *of Derby and Stafford, 16 Oct. 1560*]

(fo. 42) Receaved this xvi[th] of October 1560 at the hands of ⎫
Mr Richerd Walker for the sinages of tharchedeaconrye of ⎪ xiij[li].
Darbye and of Stafforde xiij[li] xiijs xd dew for this yere.[48] ⎬ xiijs.
In wytnes whereoff I have to this acquitaunce sette my hand ⎪ xd.
the day & yere above wryten ⎭

By me

24. [*An indenture concerning Hanbury, 27 Nov. 1560*]

(fo. 43)   The copy of an indentre
This indenture made the xxvij day of November in the yere of the
reagne of our soveraygne ladye Elizabethe by the grace of God of
England Fraunce and Ireland Quene, defendor of the faythe etc.,
the thyrd, betwyxte the right honorable and reverend father in God
Thomas of Coventree & Lichefeild bysshopp on the one partye and
Christofer Grene & Christofer Bayne gent on the other partye.
Wytnessethe that where certane articles were concluded and agreed
upon betwyxe the said partyes to thes indentures as well for the concernynge the gatherynge in, kepynge and bestowynge of the tythe
hay, corne, other fruytes and commodyties belongynge to the rectory
or parsonage of Hanberye as allso the mansion howse of the said
rectorye or personage, pastures and medowes shold be indifferentlye
used by common consent durynge three or fowre monthes,[49] lyke as
by the said articles made betwyxe the said partyes to thes indentures
bearyng date the vij[th] day of August in the second yere of the reagne
of our said soverayne ladye the Quenes majestie that nowe ys[a] at
large more planelye[b] may appere. Neverthelesse that for as moche
there haith and doethe some ambiguityes, questions and doubt
rysen and growen upon this word or terme, monthes, for how longe,
or tyll what day yt ought to endure. Knowe ye nowe that for a playne
diffynition and explanation thereof, yt is fully concluded, condis-
cended and agreed betwyxe the sayd partyes to thes indentres that

[a] *Followed by* more.   [b] *Followed by* doth appere.

---

[47] Probably what are commonly known as synodals—dues of approximately 2s.
p.a. paid by each parish priest to his bishop as a token of homage and fealty, which
were customarily paid on attendance at the diocesan synod. According to L.J.R.O.,
CC. 124100, the total of diocesan synodals in 1623 was estimated at £18 13s. 4d.
[48] See item 3.   [49] See items 5 and 6.

the said tyme and terme monthes ys and shalbe expounded to contynue and endure frome the day of the date of the aforesaid first
articles untyll the seventhe day of December next, any question,
ambiguitie, doubt or other thyngs that shall or may thereupon ryse
or growe to the contrarye in any wuse not whithe standynge. In
whitnes whereoff the partyes above said to thes present indentures
interchaungeablye have sette theyre hands and seales the daye and
yere first above wryten.

by me Christofer Grene

25. (fo. 44) *A breache of covenants by Christofer Grene & Bayne etc.*

1. First beynge demaunded and required to lett the barne dore
   of Marchyngton[50] be locked with ii lockes or els to have ii keys
   for one locke indifferently for boeth partyes wyllfullye the
   refused so to do and so kept one key continually to theym
   selfes etc.
2. Item they beyng requyred to lett my servants have the use of
   the chambers indifferently for theyr ease refused to do the
   same.
3. Item they kept the keys of all the doores to theym selfes and
   wold not suffer my men to have any but kept theym in the
   parsonage lyke prisoners.
4. Item the xxvi[ti] of November I required to have the chambers
   accordyng to the covenants and promise but I cold not so have
   theym.
5. Item the same day and before Christofer Grene and Bayne
   had both men and women hired to kepe owt my servants by
   force of armes.
6. Item the 27 of November when yt was agreed that for the use
   of the mansion house and chambers Mr Vernam, Mr Adder-
   laye,[51] Mr Aston[52] of Mugleston and Mr Banister shold vewe
   and allott to either party chambers metelye and convenientlye
   they wold not open some of the chambers because that theyr
   hired men were locked in theym.
7. Item Cristofer Grene openlye said they contynued there by
   vertue of theyr lease, whytche wordes ar a playne breache of
   the fyrst covenant and therefore I wylled all men present to

---

[50] Chapel of ease of Hanbury.
[51] See item 178.   [52] Robert Aston, rector of Mucklestone; see item 180.

beare wytnes thereof as Mr Vernam, Mr Adderlay, Mr Aston, Mr Banister, Mr Chetewood, Mr Shefford etc.

8. Item where as an agrement of a certan dowbt by common consent was made and boethe partyes shold seale and subscribe the same: Christofer Grene & Bayne requyred that no advantage myght be taken at theyr wordes and then they wold subscribe the same agrement, whitche requeste was denied because they were so uncertane and inconstant in all theyr doynges.

9. Item Christofer Bayne refused to gyve my servants the key of that chamber where they lay sayng yf they wold he wold lend theym yt because the house was theyrs.

10. Item Christofer Bayne said that he wold rather make his bedd in the hall then my servants shold have any interest to come in or to go forthe, which in the ende he dyd.

11. Item when Christofer Grene was blamed for withholdyng the keys he sayd yt was but for one day to wytche yt was answered that yt was inoughe to breake the covenants and so to forgett hys obligation etc.

26. [*To Alban Langdale,*[53] *D.D., 2 May 1560, from Edmund Grindal at London*]

(fo. 45) We wyll and requyre you in the Quenes maiesties name all excuses and delayes sett apart that you make your parsonall apparance before us her highnes commyssioners or other owr colleags in the longe chappell whithin the cathedrall churche of Saint Pawle in London[54] the eight day next after the receipt hereof, yf it shall be then court daye, or els the next court day then immediatelye folowyng, Then and there further to do and receave as shall apperteane. And so fare you well frome London this second of May 1560.

> yor lovyng freynds
> Edm. London
> Willm Mey
> Thomas Huyck

[53] Alban Langdale. Appointed prebendary of Lichfield in 1559; he was chancellor of Lichfield Cathedral in 1559–60; he was never, as Landor (*Staffordshire Incumbents*, p. 367) implies, chancellor of the diocese; see also P.R.O., S.P. Dom. Eliz. Add. xi, no. 45 (according to Gee, *Elizabethan Clergy*, the report of the Commissioners of recusants, dated August 1562) for description of his obdurate recusancy.   [54] The consistory place.

27. [*To the Queen, (?) May 1560*]

(fo. 45) In most humble, obedient and dewtifull wyse suethe unto your maiesties highnes your poore orator and obedient chaplayne Thomas Coventry & Lichfield: That where as your graces highnes haithe bestowed upon the said suppliant your bysshoprick of Coventry & Lichfield which beyng moche in decay, partlye by former echange of landes, by old and large leases demysed forthe of the same, partlye by incombrances made and left by my predecessor the late bysshopp thereof with suche arrerages as at this present ar very burdenous to beare, so that your said suppliant & chaplayne ys not able either to repayre to his mansion house or to make suffi-cient provision for his house kepynge withowt your graces especiall helpe and liberalitye therein, Susteanynge at this present suche greate charges, partlye by ordinary fees alreadye payd and here-after to be payd at the restitution of his temporalties, partlye by the goyng forthe of the bysshoprike by paten, partlye by tenthes, first fruytes and other exten[   ] alleved owt of the same. In consider-ation whereof may yt please yor graces highnes so to tender your humble suppliant and poore orators case that for his better helpe and necessarye furniture for howse he may receave suche profyts as have fallen and risen in and upon the sade bysshoprike sence the deprivation of the last incombent thereof or els one moytye of Michaelmass rent past, whiche graunt your saide suppliant shall acknowledge as a most free and liberall benefyte to make hym the more able to provyd furniture of howsehold and to go toward the better & the rather to serve God & yor highnes in his dioceses, which he moche desyreth, yf yt may please your graces highnes to assigne his restitution to that end for the whiche onelye he haithe tarryed here sence Aester, as knowethe the Lorde God, who kepe and blesse your highnes in all your graces most godly affares.

28. [*To Dr Weston, Chancellor, 3 Aug. 1560*]

(fo. 46)   At Eccshall 1560 Augusti.
A letter wryten to Dr Weston[55] to take up the matter betwene Mr
Myddelmore of Brymmyngham[56] & Mr Short of London.

29. [*To Mr Lever, Archdeacon of Coventry, 4 Aug. 1560*]

(fo. 46)[a]A letter wrytten to Mr Levir[57] towchyng 3 causes; the fyrst
for borowynge of xl[li] of Mr Dudley of Coventrey[58] with an obligation for the receapte thereoff;

30. [*To Mr Lever, 4 Aug. 1560*]

(fo. 46) Item to convent the parson or curate of Solyhull[59] for dis-
order about the communion; last to ryd to Salop to preache yf he
can.

31. [*To Mr Dudley at Coventry, 5 Aug. 1560*]

(fo. 46) [b]a lettere also to Mr Dudley for the borowynge of the said
money.[60]

32. [*To the Summoner of Shrewsbury, 5 Aug. 1560*]

(fo. 46) a lettere to the somner of Shrewsbury to call before me one
David ap Edwarde and Margaret Wendlock upon Fryday beyng the
9 day of this month.

    a *Word preceded by figure 4, probably signifying the date.*
    b *Word preceded by a figure 5, probably signifying the date.*

55 Robert Weston. Born in Weeford, Staffs; he was the brother of the diocesan
registrar, James Weston. He was chancellor of the diocese between 1560 and 1567,
and in 1564 Bentham recommended him as a J.P. (Bateson, *Original Letters*, p. 47).
He was to be Lord Chancellor of Ireland from 1567 to 1573. Will proved in
P.C.C., 18 July 1573. See Foster, *Alumni Oxonienses.*
    56 Birmingham. These two men are unidentified.
    57 Thomas Lever, 1521–77, was archdeacon of Coventry from 1560 until death;
he does not appear to have held another benefice in Coventry, but was preacher
there before appointment as archdeacon, perhaps as minister of St John's, Bablake.
    58 See item 31.
    59 John Bavand, rector of Solihull, was deprived 1570.   60 See item 29.

33. [*To Ralph Egerton at London, 5 Aug. 1560*]

(fo. 46) a letter wryten to my brother Raphe Egerton[61] to London for the forbearynge of his money whiche I do owe hym.

34. [*To James Weston, Registrar, 5 Aug. 1560*]

(fo. 46) Item a lettere wryten to James Weston[62] to make letters dimisorye[63] for one Thomas Trubshawe to take orders where he wold etc.

35. [*An agreement between Christopher Baynes, Christopher Grene and Bishop Bentham, 7 Aug. 1560*]

(fo. 46) An agreyment betwene Christofer Grene & Bayne with me for a tyme.[64]

36. [*To Lawrence Nowell, 8 Aug. 1560*]

(fo. 46) [a]A lettere to Mr Deane of Lichefeild[65] to go & preache at Segyngton[66] & heare the parson Sir William Heys[67] confesse his faultts.

[a] *Word preceded by figure 8, probably signifying the date.*

---

[61] The exact relationship to Bentham is uncertain; perhaps he was Sir Ralph Egerton of Wrinehill, Betley, Staffs (d. 1596), whom Bentham recommended as J.P. in 1564; he was a J.P. in 1577; appointed commissioner-general of the diocese, 18 April 1561 (L.C.L., Dean & Chapter Act Book IV, fo. 28r).

[62] James Weston, died 1589; son of John Weston of Lichfield and brother of Robert Weston (see item 28) and Katherine, who married into the Dyott family, he was diocesan registrar to death; will proved in P.C.C., 2 May 1589.

[63] Non-graduates had to possess letters dimissory from their own diocesan if they wished to be ordained outside their native diocese or place of long dwelling (Royal Injunctions, 1559).

[64] Concerning Hanbury.

[65] Lawrence Nowell.

[66] Seckington, Warwickshire.

[67] Instituted to Seckington 5 Aug. 1560, on the death of the previous incumbent; he was presented by Thomas Burdett, armiger.

37. [*To Thomas Ryley, Coventry, 12 Aug. 1560*]

(fo. 46) A lettere wryten to Mr Thomas Riley of Coventrey and an obligation for the borowyng of xl[li].[68] A letter to the churche-wardens of Upton under Hamon.

38. [*To Henry Cumberford, 12 Aug. 1560*]

(fo. 46)   To Mr Comberford.[69]

After my harty commendations unto you Mr Comberford thes ar to signifye unto you that although I have great occasion to make my complaynt for divers iniuryes done unto me, as well in my evidences as other thyngs which of right I owght to have: yet my meanynge is quietly to request myne owne befor I complayne of any man. And therefore, understandynge that you have moche of my evidences and other thynges also, thes ar to wyll you send theym unto me with all convenient spede that I may knowe my right. And though per-adventure I do not charge you particularely with this thyng or that yet I trust that your conscience is suche a regester that you knowe all thyngs what of right you owght to deliver unto me and therefore wyll so doo mostwyllyngely. My hope is that equity of yor conscience is suche that respectynge the iustyde & iudgement of God that you wyll deteane nothynge but that whereof you purpose to make an accompt before god who seythe and knoweth all thyngs. Besydes my evidences, counterfayns of leases, with suche implements of howse as I presently do requyre, I must nedes put you agayn (fo. 47) in remembraunce of the greater seall, which was used in the office of the chancelorshipp at Lichefeild Which divers persons do affirme unto me that you have. I doubt not but some of my freynds will put you in remembrance of those thyngs which I must nedes have. And so trustynge to your equitye in all the said matters I commytt you to God. Wryten the xii[th] of August at my castell of Eccleshall.

                                        yor freynd to command

[68] Thomas Riley, alderman of Coventry. See item 232.
[69] Henry Comberford or Cumberford; lately precentor of Lichfield Cathedral and rector of Norbury, Derbs.; articles were brought against him by Lichfield bailiffs for 'lewde preaching and misdemeanour' in Feb. 1559 (*Acts of the Privy Council, 1558–70*, p. 64); he was deprived.

39. [*To John Cocke, Aug. 1560*]

(fo. 47) A letter of an attorneye for John Cock[70] concernyng the sellyng of certane tenths in Hadleigh in Suff.[71]

40. [*To William Cruche, Aug. 1560*]

(fo. 47) A letter of an attorney for William Cruche to gather &
receave my rents.

41. [*To Mr Basforthe of Fenny Bentley, Aug. 1560*]

(fo. 47) Item a letter wryten to Mr Basforthe of the paryshe of
Bentleye[72] for whitholdynge the parsons dewtye,[73] movynge hym
for his worshippes sake & for the church sake which ys to moche
iniured by suche detention in many places to paye the parson his
dewtyes & complayne orderlye of his faultes & they shalbe corrected
etc.

42. [*To Clement Throckmorton, Aug. 1560*]

(fo. 47) Item a letter wryten to Mr Clement Throckmorton[74] to
signifye howe that I have receaved no money of Mr Harcourt;[75]
what he demaundethe of me; what Mr Blount[76] meanethe to do at
London; & of the agreyment betwyxt me & the fermers of Hanbery
parsonage.[77]

43. [*To Ralph Egerton, London, Aug. 1560*]

(fo. 47) Item a letter to my brother Raphe Egerton to forbeare his
money unto I can receave my rents.

[70] Later described as Bentham's brother-in-law (Item 81).
[71] Bentham's wife, Maud Fawcon, came from Hadleigh, Suffolk.
[72] Fenny Bentley, Derbyshire.   [73] Tithes.
[74] Clement Throckmorton of Haseley, Warwickshire; M.P. on several occasions,
including for Warwick in 1562 and 1572. Fox (*Acts and Monuments*, vii, 18)
describes his acceptance of Protestantism; he died in 1572.
[75] Simon Harcourt.   [76] George Blount.   [77] See item 35.

44. [*To Richard Chambers,*[78] *Aug. 1560*]

(fo. 47) Item a letter to Mr Richard Chamber to knowe in what case my bookes be with Mr Osborne & to admonishe hym of my sutes to be.

45. [*To Thomas Wayre, Aug. 1560*]

(fo. 47) Item a letter to Mr Thomas Wayre for lx els of canvayes for shets, some of xiid the ell[79] & some of viijd or there abowts.

46. [*To Ambrose Cave, 20 Aug. 1560*]

(fo. 47) Item a letter wryten to Sir Ambrose Cave[80] concernyng the vicaredge of Workesworth[81] for Sir Richard Stonynought that the title beyng tryed I wyll do what I can to his preferment.[82] In the meane tyme to iudg the best of the fact.

---

[78] There is a strong possibility that this was the man who acted as treasurer to the exiles; in view of the fact that Bentham was in Frankfurt at the same time as Chambers in 1557, and therefore had personal acquaintance with him, and that Chambers is known to have been active early in Elizabeth's reign, the identification is probably correct; he died in 1566. See *The Zürich Letters*, ed. and trans. H. Robinson (Parker Soc., L–LI, Cambridge, 1842–5), I, p. 148.

[79] Ell = a cloth measure of $1\frac{1}{4}$ yards.

[80] In 1560 Cave was both Chancellor of the Duchy of Lancaster and Joint Lieutenant of Warwickshire; in 1559 he was appointed Commissioner to visit the dioceses of Oxford, Lincoln, Lichfield and Peterborough with Bentham; he served as M.P. for Warwickshire in the parliaments of 1558, 1559 and 1562; he married a Warwickshire woman, Margaret Holte, and died in 1568. See *D.N.B.*

[81] Wirksworth, Derbyshire. *Valor Ecclesiasticus* valued it at £58 10s. 8d; it had 470 households in 1563 and was one of the largest agglomerations of population in the archdeaconry; patron, dean of Lincoln; no external documentation of this case—record of caveats begins just too late, October 1560 (L.J.R.O., B/V/1/13).

[82] Cave's suit was unsuccessful. The dean of Lincoln assigned the right of presentation to a relative, Richard Tayler of Lincoln, who presented John Hyron, 24 April 1560 (L.J.R.O., B/A/1/15). Richard Stonynought or Stannynawght had been presented to the small living of Croxall, Derbyshire, before 1559 and here remained until his death in 1586. His patron was the Earl of Huntingdon; will proved, L.J.R.O., 14 May 1586. Evidence of Cave's patronage can be found in B.L., Lansdowne MS. 443, and in L.J.R.O., B/A/1/15: 30 May 1561.

47. [*To Mr Adderlay at Hanbury, c. 20 Aug. 1560*]⁸³

(fo. 47) Item a letter writen to Mr Adderlay at Hanbury that as at the reqest of Sir Raphe Bagnold, Sir Raphe Egerton and Mr Harcort with others that he shold gather his tithe corne so that it shold [   ] my title, now my counsellor thinks any covenant mad betwene Grene and me. For as I was ready to grant, so I trust that my good wyll & mea[   ] shall nether tend to prejudice my rights nor hurt my cause and so I [   ] to shewe pleasure. So that in the meane tyme the corne I [have] in the barne [   ] for [   ] Whereas he shalbe no further from [
          ] the saide [tythe.]

48. [*To Dr Weston, Chancellor, 25 Aug. 1560*]

(fo. 48) Item a letter wryten to Doctor Weston my chancelor in the behalfe of Sir Raphe Bagnold⁸⁴ to have a citation *quorum nomina*⁸⁵ for certane men of Stooke which deteane theyr tythes. Yf the case be plane and the tyeths accustomed to be payde or yf any controversye be in that behalffe that the lawe may try yt. Also to wyll hym come over to me whithe Mr Fletewoode⁸⁶ yff he come by Lichefeild by cause I wold use boyth theyr counsells in certane matters of myne.

49. [*To Thomas Lever, at Coventry, 26 Aug. 1560*]

(fo. 48) Item a letter wryten to Mr Levir to Coventry concernyng his visitation which I wold have had deferred one weyke longer by reason of harvest. As towchynge the iniunctions,⁸⁷ I lyke theym well, save the first & ii of the last to be more mete for Coventrey & suche

---

⁸³ This letter is badly damaged. The foot of the page is torn and the ink from the reverse side serves to obliterate much of the remaining text.

⁸⁴ Sir Ralph Bagnold, M.P., son of John Bagnold of Newcastle-under-Lyme, Staffs, had his estate at Barlaston, Staffs; he married Elizabeth Whitgreave; a former exile, he was named by Bentham in 1564 as a favourer of religion and fit to continue as a J.P. (Bateson, *Original Letters*, p. 42). See L.J.R.O., B/C/5 (office case v. Henry Trickett 1598/9) for Bagnold's activities in the 1570s.

⁸⁵ A form of citation was issued to the apparitor by the registrar: the apparitor was left to fill in the names of those to be cited. This method was open to abuse for the apparitor received fees for each citation. Canon CXX of 1604 rendered them illegal and required the registrar to enter all names on a citation before its delivery.

⁸⁶ Probably John Fleetwood, esquire, of Colwich, Staffs.

⁸⁷ Injunctions drawn up by Lever for his archidiaconal visitation.

towns then the villages farr distant in the contrey. Movyng hym to add lykewyse interrogatoryes accordynglye as the archdeacon of London[88] haithe done. But concernyng his settyng theym forthe in the name of tharchedeacon of Coventreye havyng not yet his mandate and, indeed, I doubt wether it wylbe preiudyce. Last of all I am aboute my chappell whithe slowe work men but I wyll mayke that haist that I can.

50. [To Mr Lord of Leicester, 26 Aug. 1560]

(fo. 48) Item a letter to Mr Lord of Leicesstre[89] thankyng hym for his gentill letter, promisyng to wryte to the deane[90] & chapiter of Peterboroughe for the staying of processe at Bugbey[91] although they have not deserved that gentilnes.

51. [To Thomas Chedulton,[92] at Stafford, 27 Aug. 1560]

(fo. 48) Item a letter to Mr Chedulton of Stafforde in the behalffe of one Richerd Whittell,[93] clerke of Ladye Churche in Stafforth to pay hym his dewtyes witholden etc.

52. [To Dr Weston, Chancellor, 27 Aug. 1560]

(fo. 48) Item a letter to Dr Weston in the behalfe of William Mansfeild[94] for the parsonage of Boylstone[95] voyde by lapse.

[88] John Mullins.   [89] Unidentified, but see item 73.
[90] William Latymer. [91] Long Buckby, Northants.
[92] Chedulton was official of the archdeaconry of Stafford in June 1558 (L.J.R.O., B/V/1/2, fo. 2); he was prebendary of Denstone in the Collegiate Church of St Mary, Stafford, c. 1548; vicar of Worfield, 1545–62, when he was deprived; in Mary's reign, while acting as canon of Lichfield and Commissary, he was responsible for the deprivation of nine Derbyshire clergy for marriage (J. Strype, Ecclesiastical Memorials, iii, pt 1 (Oxford, 1822), pp. 168–9); he was made vicar of St Mary's, Stafford, in 1548. See Landor, Staffordshire Incumbents, pp. 237, 240–1, 243, 375.
[93] Richard Whittell was noted as receiving a pension of 20s. as vicar-choral there in 1548 (Landor, Staffordshire Incumbents, p. 242).
[94] Mansfeild was instituted to Boyleston on 28 Aug. 1560 on the death of the previous incumbent; he was presented by the bishop (L.J.R.O., B/A/1/15, fo. 31r).
[95] Boyleston, Castellary deanery, Derby archdeaconry; a church with no chapels of ease and 31 households in 1563.

53. [*To the Dean*[96] *and Chapter of Peterborough, 28 Aug. 1560*]

(fo. 48) After my harty commendations to your good worshipps, thes may be to desyre the same stande so freyndlye unto certane fermers of myne, that where as you have directed forthe your ordinarye processe of sequestration[97] for arrerrages of the parsonage of Bugbye[98] & others as I heare say as to stay the same processe or els revoke your sequestration and God wyllyng I shall sue forthe a discharge therefore this next terms. I have not as yett my wrytinges whiche shold discharge yt in my handes but agaynst that tyme I wyll provyd theym. So that as I trust you shall take no harme in so doynge and bynd me to do you the lyke pleasure yf it shall lye in my poore power, as knowethe the Lorde to whose good kepyng I commytt yor worshipes. Wryten this 28 of August at my castell of Eccleshall 1560.

yors to command

54. [*To Thomas Bolt, 4 Sept. 1560*]

(fo. 49) Item a letter wryten to Mr Bolt in the behalfe of my Lord Stafford[99] for a feather bed yf he can deliver yt.

55. [*To Dr Weston, Chancellor, Sept. 1560*]

(fo. 49) Item a letter to my chancelor in the behalf of one Thomas Procter of Draycott als H[aigh] for his counsell in that the said Thomas carried part of his tythe to his owne barne.

56. [*To James Weston, Registrar, Sept. 1560*]

(fo. 49) Item a letter to James Weston to publishe thadministration of orders which shalbe ministred upon sanct Mathewes day viz. 21 Septembris.[100]

[96] William Latymer.
[97] The ordinary would appoint one or more sequestrators to seize the profits (tithes etc.) of the parish.
[98] Long Buckby, Northants.
[99] Sir Thomas Fitzherbert of Norbury, Lord Stafford, died in the Tower of London in 1591.
[100] Apparently Bentham's first ordination. For an example of such a letter, see Guildhall, London, MS. 9535/1 (1550).

57. [*To Humfrey More,*[101] *of Uttoxeter, Sept. 1560*]

(fo. 49) Item a letter to Sir Hymfrey More curat of Uttoxater[102] to come over to me[103] with the churchwardens of the same upon Fryday next which shalbe the xiii[th] day of this present monethe etc.

57a. [*To Lord Stafford, Sept. 1560*]

(fo. 49) Item a letter in the behalf of John Bedulphe[104] of Eccleshall to my Lord of Stafford to release hym & either at other tymes or at other places to let hym fele the weight of his fault nowe to spare hym at my request & I am lothe to medle in matters whereof I have no skyll.

58. [*To Thomas Lever, at Coventry, 9 Sept. 1560*]

(fo. 49) After my harty commendations in the Lord unto you & yours etc. Thes ar to signifye unto you that I have apoynted the xxi[ti] day of this monethe to geve orders upon at Eccleshall, at what tyme I wold have you repayre thither with suche as you knowe mete to enter in to the ministery.[105] Yf you cold come ii dayes before I wold be gladd and then lett Pember[ton] cause the vicare of Coleshill to come also,[106] who as I heare shewethe moche stoburnes, Wherefore I purpose to talke with hym. I intend the same xxi[ti] day to ryd at after noone toward Shrewesberye and therefore I purpose to dispatche betyme. Yf you can well & convenientlye ryd with me, I wold have yor companye. Thus leavyng other thyngs to yor comyng, I commytt you to God & me to your prayers this ix[th] off Septembre at Eccleshall 1560.

yor freynd to command

[101] Resigned 1561/2 (L.J.R.O., B/A/1/15).

[102] Uttoxeter vicarage, Leek deanery, archdeaconry of Stafford; with no chapel and 240 households in 1563.

[103] This is possibly a reference to Bentham's court of audience. See the entry for 30 Sept. 1561 for the only known formal mention of the audience court in surviving Lichfield records (L.J.R.O., B/C/2/5).

[104] See item 78.

[105] It was the archdeacon's duty to examine candidates before ordination. See M. R. O'Day: 'Clerical Patronage and Recruitment in Elizabethan and Early Stuart England' (unpublished Univ. of London Ph.D. thesis, 1972), pp. 24–6 & *passim.*

[106] 1561/2: John Fenton, vicar of Coleshill: died 1566 (L.J.R.O., B/V/1/5).

59. [*To Lord Paget,*[107] *9 Sept. 1560*]

(fo. 49) Right honorable & mye verye good Lord with remembraunce of my de[wty] thes may be to signifye unto your good honor that I wold have bene gla[dd] to have wayted thereupon yf I had knowen of your short departynge. Notwithstandynge, for lacke of convenient tyme, I must desyre your honor to stay my good lord & freynd in those thyngs which ar my right, which your honor knowethe better then I. And I trust that I shalbe as readye at al tymes to do my dewty agayne as to aske anye thynge at your handes. In (fo. 50) [cer]tifying your honor concernyng thes thyngs wherein my chapleyn Mr Walker[108] haithe conferred I wylbe gladd so farr as by common order taken I may. Yt is signifyed unto me that I shold receave yerelye of your honor to the full recompence of thexchange for[a] I am sorye that I cold not come to conferre with you.[109] Thus desyringe your honor to have me excused and also in remembraunce in this behalfe, I commytt you to God. Writen this ix[ti] of Septembre at my poore castell of Eccleshall.

> your good honors to command, etc.

60. [*To Clement Throckmorton, Sept. 1560*]

(fo. 50) Item a letter to Mr Throckmorton to signifye my state; and when I purpose to kepe court; & that I have not yet receaved my money of Mr Harcourt; of Sir George Blounts[110] processe; and of Hanberye etc.

61. [*To Simon Harcourt, Sept. 1560*]

(fo. 50) Item a letter to Mr Harcourt to aske his counsell what is to be done in that processe agaynst my tennants & others wether they

---

[a] *Followed by* the.

---

[107] William Paget.   [108] Richard Walker.

[109] Presumably concerning the grant made to Paget, as one of Henry VIII's secretaries of State, in 1546 of Beaudesert & Haywood and various Staffordshire manors in exchange for several appropriations. See *V.C.H. Staffs*, iii, p. 52, n. 76.

[110] Sir George Blount, of Knightley, 'accounted of good men adversaries to religion & no favoureres thereof, nether in died nor woorde' (Bateson, *Original Letters*, p. 42).

maye be stayed or the persons warned to take hede, because that I am unskylfull in suche matters etc.

62. [*To Dr Weston, Chancellor, 11 Sept. 1560*]

(fo. 50) Item a letter writen to Dr Weston in the behalfe of John Holbage & Margerye Smythe in the countye of Warwicke to mary withowt askynge the baynes, to do what the lawe wyll.

63. [*To Thomas Blount, Sept. 1560*]

(fo. 50) Item a letter to Mr Thomas Blount for the appeerence of William Critche & others. That I wold have bene glad to have talked with the plaintif before or after yf I had any convenient place; in the meane season I dare put my selfe to answere for theyr appearence yf they be within my libertyes. This certifye Sir George Blount, beyng her destitute of counsell & comforthe I can se no more but desyre God to make us all of one mynd and send us that agrement that may ioyne us in God etc.

64. [*To Humphrey Wells,*[111] *Sheriff of Stafford, 14 Sept. 1560*]

(fo. 50) After my most hartye commendations unto your good worshipe, as unacquaynted with the same thes may be to desyre so moche freyndshippe at your worshipes handes that where as certane processe is directed unto you at the suett of Sir George Blount and Mr Swynerton as I am informed, whiche processe beyng served of some of my tennants and of some of my servants, I desyre yor good worshippe so to favor my request as to lett me have a copye of the originall of your wryt; the end thereof is to come to some communication and brynge suche unitye and quyett as shall lye in me. And thus your good worshippe shall bynde me to acknowledge this your pleasurynge and gratifye yt with lyke yf at anye tyme yt shall lye in my poore powre, as knowethe the lord God, to whose good

111 Although noted as an adversary of religion, Bentham regarded him as one of the Staffordshire J.P.s who were 'no favoureres of Religion but better learned than the rest' (Bateson, *Original Letters*, pp. 42–3).

protection I commytt yor worshipp this present xiiiith of September
at my poore castell of Eccleshall.

> yor freynd to commannd,

65. [*To George Bromley,*[112] *Attorney-General of the Duchy of Lancaster, at
Mr Egerton's house at Bridge End, 15 Sept. 1560*]

(fo. 51) After my most hartye commendations to your good worshippe, Thes may be to desyre the same of suche freyndshippe &
helpe as to be with me in ii or iii dayes at michaelmasse at my castell
of Eccleshall, Aboute what tyme as your worshippe did signifye unto
me that you might be best spared frome other your necessarye busynes and at most libertye: so I have apoyncted my great court at
Eccleshall[113] upon Monday after Michaelmas day which court day
shalbe the last day of this moneth of Septembre, wherefore as I shall
at that tyme have the greatest nede of your helpe, so I pray you
most hartelye that I may trust to the same. And yf it shall please
you to bringe your good brother with you for your ease and com-
panyes sake yt shall be to my great comforthe and presently I wyll
be ready to gratifye boythe your paynes as I am able and hereafter
deserve or recompence whith what pleasure I can. In the meane
tyme I beseche you most hartely that I may boldlye trust to this
your helpe, Whereof yf you can signifye unto me but one word you
shall pleasure me greatlye, as knowethe the Lord, to whose good &
mercyfull protection I commytt your worshipe this 15 of Septembre,
1560 at my poore castell of Eccleshall.

> your freynd most assuredly to
> commaund at all tymes,

66. [*To Sir Henry Sidney, Lord President of the Council of the Marches,
(between 15 and 19 Sept. 1560)*]

(fo. 51) Althoughe myne acquayntance be so smale with your good
honor and my deservyng lesse then that upon either of theym I shold

---

[112] 'Georg Bramley of Worfeild, esquier' is noted as 'miet to continew in office',
and Bentham reports 'I know the learning of none much reported, but of Justice
Corbet, and George Bramley' as Shropshire J.P.s (See Bateson, *Original Letters*,
p. 44).
[113] Presumably the great court of the episcopal manor of Eccleshall.

be thus bolde to troble your honorable affayr[es], yett in consider-ynge your naturall clemencye towardes all poor sueters, I trust that my boldnes shalbe taken no other wyse then I meane. As to medle in any case or cause wherein I have no interest I am verye lothe: so to deny my freynd any request wherein I myght pleasure hym, withowt hurt of others, I cold not charitablye doo. Wherefore I am presentlye so bold with your honor to desyre the same be so favorable and freyndlye to the bringer hereof, Richerd Brasey of Buckley in Cheshire,[114] a verye freynd of myne for whome notwhith-standynge I wryt no other then the truethe of his cause wyll beare. That were as the said Richerd Brasey[a]

67. [*Paraphrase of letter to Margaret Einsworth of Uttoxeter, Sept. 1560*]

(fo. 52) Item a letter writen to Margarett Einsworth of Uttoxater to conform her selfe to lyve with her lawfull husband or els to come and shewe some lawfull & good reason why she shold not do etc.

68. [*To Clement Throckmorton, 19 Sept. 1560*]

(fo. 52) After my most hartye commendations to your good woor-shippe, thes may be to thanke you for your gentill wrytinge unto me at this present, signifynge there whithe that I have talked once with Mr Bromeley[115] who haithe promised to helpe me with his counsell. And therefore, as I have apoynted my court the last day of this monethe to be kept, which ys the Monday folowyng michaelmasse day immediatlye, so I have wryten unto hym to come unto me at that tyme and I trust he wyll do so. In the meane tyme I wyll suche counsell as I can gett. I thoughte that Mr Fleetwood wold have come unto me or by me, for so he dyd wryte after your beyng at Hanberye, And yet he is not come neyther can I tell wether he be returned up to London agayne or not. Yf the tyme of the yere whithe weyther and waye were suche that you might well travell and other of your busynes for the Quene well dispatched, I shold thynke my selfe most happye to have you present at my court. As

---

[a] Text incomplete.

[114] Probably a relative of the recipient of item 85.   See also item 116.
[115] See item 65.

yett Mr Harecourt and I are not thorowe but stand as at your beyng whithe me. Whereof I am sorye not so moche for the lacke of my money, whereof I have great nede, but that the worshippfull of the countrey do understand the same and halfe brought in beleve that the fault shold be me, So that I must nedes beare this as a part of my crosse. Thus leavyng other thinges to an other tyme I commytt your woorshippe to the goodness of God be wryten this xix^th of Septembre at my poore castell of Eccleshall 1560.

your most lovyng freynd to commaunde,

69. [*To Richard Chambers, London, 20 Sept. 1560*]^116

(fo. 52) Item a letter to Mr Richerd Chambers of London to helpe to call for an answere at Mr Doctor Haddon concernyng a supplication which I have sent to the Queen's maiestye; And also to desyre Mr Stapleton to helpe me with his counsell in the lawe & to declare unto hym the case & state of Hanberye & other thyngs.

70. [*To James Weston, Registrar, 21 Sept. 1560*]

(fo. 52) Item a letter wryten to James Weston for those whiche I had ordened in to the orders of deacons and for an institution to one of theym.^117

71. [*To Dr Weston, Chancellor, 22 Sept. 1560*]

(fo. 52) Item to Doctor Weston in the behalfe of Margaret Wendlocke to be holpen agaynst her husband who is a^a perverse man.^118

72. [*To Mr Fisher,*^119 *24 Sept. 1560*]

(fo. 52) After my harty commendations to your worshippe &c. Thes may be to signifye unto the same that, receavyng this letter inclosed

---

^a *Followed by* perfect, *struck out.*

^116 See item 44.
^117 Probably Ralph Lompe, instituted at Bradley rectory, 31 Oct. 1560, on the presentation of the dean of Lincoln.   ^118 See item 32.
^119 Thomas Fisher, previously agent to the Duke of Somerset, or his son, Edward Fisher.

F

21 Septembris in other letters sent unto me from London but not understandynge the meanynge thereof other wyse then onely by coniecture, I shall desyre you make answere to the same as may satisfye my Lord Treasorers request and also bryng me to some quiet end and peaceable possession of my right for where as I shold (fo. 53) have receaved the rent of Ichyngton yf there had no exchaunge bene [made] nowe am I inforced to tarrye for the same, wherefore I pray your worshippe consyder that yf I nether can receave that nor yet recompence therefore I shall not be able to contynue here in my bysshoprike any tyme.[120] Thus trustynge to your spedye answere to your letter, I bydd you most hartely fare well. Wryten this 24 of Septembre at my poor castell of Eccleshall.

Your lovyng freynd,

73. [To John Lord at Leicester,[121] 25 Sept. 1560]

(fo. 53) Item a letter to Mr John Lord to Leicestre in the behalfe of the fermer of Blegrave for the subsydies which the next terme God wyllynge I wyll discharg yf my patens wyll serve.[122]

74. [To Dr Weston, Chancellor, 25 Sept. 1560]

(fo. 53) Item a letter to Doctor Westone to make processe for one John Marchald of London who haithe gotten Maud Ashelake with chyld & is rune away because he wyll not gett god fathers to christen yt.

---

[120] Bishop Sampson had surrendered Itchington, Warwickshire, with other land in fee farm to Thomas Fisher in 1546; a nominal rent charge of £50 was soon quashed. Bishop Baynes succeeded in negotiating an £82 10s. p.a. rent charge; Bentham's struggle to collect the same is an intermediate stage in the process which ended when Bishop Overton succeeded in obtaining parliamentary sanction for a rental of £83 p.a. from Edward Fisher. It appears, however, that the Queen exchanged two of the manors, Tachbrook and Itchington, with the bishop, proffering in return appropriate rectories. See F. M. Heal, 'The Bishops and the Act of Exchange of 1559', Historical Journal (xvii, 1974), 240. The exchange is referred to specifically in item 20 of this letter-book.

[121] Chancellor or official of the archdeaconry of Leicester. See item 50.

[122] Belgrave rectory, Leicestershire. The rectory had been leased for 30 years on 20 Nov. 1558 (L.J.R.O., CC. 124100, fo. 8r).

75. [*To George Bromley, at Brian Fowler's house,*[123] *26 Sept. 1560*]

(fo. 53) Commendynge me most hartelye to your worshippe, thes ar to thanke you for your gentill and lovyng letter. And althoughe your worshippe can not be with me by reason of your more weighty and apoynted busynes: yet if it shall please you to call at my house in your returne you shall doo me greate pleasure, that I may have your counsell in one or ii poynts. And so if it may please you to take so moche paynes as to take a pere of saltfysh with me tomorowe at dynner, or els when you shall come this way, I shall thynke my selfe greatelye pleasured therein and glad of your most gentill company as knowethe God, to whose prosperous tuition I commytt your worshippe. Writen this xxvith of Septembre at my poore castell of Eccleshall.

your freynd to commaund.

76. [*To Lord Stafford, 30 Sept. 1560*]

(fo. 53) After my hartye & humble commendations to your good honor, may it please the same to understande that accordynge to your Lordship's request I have sent my servant Mr Audley[124] to be at your Lordship's commaundement, neverthelesse most hartelye desyryng and whysshinge that yf it be for any poynt of his evell demeanour he may fullye answere and satisfy the same: but not knowynge the case, I commytt the whole to your good honors prudencye and judgement, requestynge for my owne part most earnestlye that yf your good Lordship do heare any thyng by me worthye suche correction, I may understand the same*a* by suche most lovynge and honorable letters. Wherein as your lordshipe shall do most honorablye and charitablye, so I shall take the same most lovyngly and thankfullye, as knowethe allmightye God, to whose

---

a Followed by most lovyngly and thankfully, *struck out.*

---

[123] Brian Fowler of Sowe, esquire, one of the 'no favoureres of Religion but better learned than the rest' (Bateson, *Original Letters*, pp. 42–3). His house was at Pendeford.

[124] Bentham's steward at Hanbury.

good protection I commytt your honor this last of Septembre 1560 at my poore castell of Eccleshall.

> your good Lordships at
> commaundement,

77. [*To the bailiffs of Lichfield, 30 Sept. 1560*]

(fo. 54) Item a letter to the baylyfes of Lichefeild to prepare my rent for Michaelmas with spede,[125] because that I have nede thereof, which yf they consider, I wyll recompence you with the like.

78. [*To Ralph Egerton, London, 2 Oct. 1560*]

(fo. 54) After my harty commendations unto you gentill and lovyng brother Raphe Egerton thes ar to geve you thankes for your most lovynge letter therewith to singyfye unto[a] you that nowe, so shortlye as I can gather up any[b] of my rents, I wyll sende you some money, by the grace of God. In the meane tyme, I pray you put none of the bibles nor psalme bookes awaye for I wold have theym all, and rather moo then fewer, and I wold have theym bound as hansomly as may in paist, whithe some golden letters. Further I thank you for payinge of Philipp Nicols for my horses[c] grasse, which you shall have agayne with thanks. At the talk of money I have not above v^li in my house, and that is not nowe increased. I heare say that I am moche slaundered of negligence, coldnes and weaknes, whithe maneye other grevous faults, whereunto I say nothynge, but wyshe theym that slaunder me yf they wold do more and better in my place. What they be I knowe not but I beleve they never felt suche a burden as I am compelled to beare dayly. Beynge so many wayes vexed as I am and havyng so litell helpe & comforthe as I fynd, no marvayle yf I satisfy not all mens expectation, for indede I do not content myselffe. Howe be yt as you have knowen me somethynge exercised and tryed in tymes past, so I trust you wyll answere for

---

a Word repeated.   *b Followed by* money, *struck out.*
c Followed by meats, *struck out.*

---

[125] Rental for this property in the 1580s amounted to £57 3s. 1d (L.J.R.O., CC. 124100, fo. 5r).

me in that behalfe. In no case can I medle where I have no jurisdiction, for at this present I stand in hassard to forfeite to the quene a thousand marks for medlynge in an exempt place, which yet was not done by me, but by some of my offycers: and yet that place was by act of parlament,[126] in Quene Marys dayes, annexed to my bysshoprike. And yf extremitye of lawe be used agaynst me I lose yt every pennye. Howe nedefull then is it for me to go no further then my comyssion wyll serve. This is part of my crosse, whiche I pray God that I may patientlye beare. I dyd wryte but one letter to my Lord Stafford for Mr Bedull[127] and he sent me word agayne that at my request he shold be delivered on Tuesday folowyng, which was not so for I thynk that he spedd nothyng better therefore. And for my part, the wryting of that letter haythe boyth bene cast in my tethe here and allso wryten of from London, that I shold love my enemys better then my freynd. And thus farethe the world, so that no man can lyve well at ease but to passe over this whithe quietnes, I pray you have me most hartelye commended to my sister Anne your wyffe and to Mr Brasey and his wyfe, to my contreeman and all my good freyndes.[128] Wryten this seconde of October at my poore and cold castell of Eccleshall.

your freynd most assuredly to commaund,

79. [*To Simon Harcourt, J.P., at Stafford, Oct. 1560*]

(fo. 54) Item a letter to Mr Simon Harcourt to the Sessions to desyre hym to speke in the behalfe of the poore, that corne and victuals may be brought to the marketts. This I wold wryt to the rest of the commyssioners yf I had lyke acquayntance with theym etc.

---

[126] Possibly the collegiate church of St Mary, Stafford, which was originally a royal peculiar. In 1550 the assets of this deanery passed to Henry, Lord Stafford, who passed them on to a London merchant. The jurisdiction lapsed to the bishop and was safeguarded in 1614 in the Borough Charter but, even at this late date, there were suggested attempts to revive the exempt jurisdiction (*V.C.H. Staffs*, viii, p. 308).

[127] Bedulfe. See item 57a.

[128] Anne Egerton was possibly the sister of Bentham's own wife, Maud or Matilda Fawcon of Hadleigh, Suffolk (C. Martin, *Les Protestants anglais réfugiés à Genève au temps de Calvin, 1555–60* (Geneva, 1915), p. 337).

80. [*To Dr Weston, Chancellor, 10 Oct. 1560*]

(fo. 55) Item a letter to Doctor Weston for Sir Richerd Fox[129] to be presented to the vicarige of Curdworthe[130] & to declare unto hym of the *subsyd pena* wherewithe I was served at Shrewsberye.

81. [*To Richard Chambers, London, 2 Oct. 1560*]

(fo. 55) After my harty commendations unto you gentill Mr Chambers, thes are to thank you most hartelye for your payns takyng in my cause, and therewhithe to signifye unto you that I have receaved your lovynge letter and wold be very glad to folowe your counsell yf I knewe which waye so to doo, but beyng thus far absent it wilbe very herd to do any thynge that may ease me of so many trobles as I am incombred whithe. Yet if I knewe that my comyng up to London might either release me of my greves or discharge me of my office, I wold most wyllingly and most gladlye come: but I am nowe so farr behynd that I wott not well which way to turne me. In the meane tyme good Mr Chambers, the more you do for me there the more diligent wyll I be here. Inded, if I had either suche helpe or comforthe as I wold have, I shold not moche passe upon theyr stomblyng blockes. And yet you shall perceave that I have some busynes for doyng of nothynge for, beiyng at Shrewsbery to preache, and havyng Mr Lever whithe me the 22 of Septembre,[131] to welcome me thyther I was served whithe a *sub pena*. Wherein I must desyre your helpe or els they say it wyll cost me the pryce of yt. Well thes thyngs shold never troble me yf I might quietlye enioye myne owne. Wherefore I pray you lett me have your good helpe and lovyng furtheraunce as I have allwayes had and I wyll the more quietlye lett thes stormes passe. I have sent for some of my busynes suche instructions as I am able by my brother in lawe John Cocke,[132] the brynger hereoff, whome I have sent up cheyfflye for myne answer in the Exchequer and allso for divers other matters. Thus commyttynge you to God and me to your godly

---

[129] This met with no success; Fox had to wait for preferment until 1564 when he was instituted to Baxterley rectory, Warwickshire, on presentation by a relative of the deceased incumbent (L.J.R.O., B/A/1/15).
[130] Curdworth (*Valor Ecclesiasticus*, £5) had 56 households in 1563.
[131] Fifteenth Sunday after Trinity.
[132] Unidentified; see items 39, 111 and 119.

prayers, I pray you to commend me to my good Lord of London[133] and to Maistres Warcoppe[134] with all my good freynds with you. Wryten this second day of October, at my castell of Eccleshall.

your lovyng freynd to his poore powre,

82. [*To Clement Throckmorton, 2 Oct. 1560*]

(fo. 55) Commendyng me most hartelye to your good worshipp, thes may be to signifye unto the same that I wold gladlye have my case of Hanberye well betten forthe before that yt be determined. I beleave that this one poynt wylbe able to defeate yt for that the old rent is not reserved unto the Lord: howe beyt, they say that they pay more, yet not unto me. I have differred my court because that I cold not have Mr Bromley present with me at yt. Notwhithstandynge, he wyll helpe me in my matters at London as he haithe promised me and I have many brablyng matters to be dispatched. But cheifflye I pray you helpe me to an attorney in the Exchequer for I shall have moche ado there daylye. I wold therefore have one of the godliest to be myne attorney. Thus desyringe your accostomed favor to the furtherance of my matters, I commend you to God. Wryten this second day of October at my poore castell of Eccleshall.

Yor freynde most assuredlye,

83. [*To Mr Marrow, 2 Oct. 1560*]

(fo. 56) After my most harty commendations to your good worshippe, with lyke thanks for your singulare affection towards me and presentlye for that yt pleased you to se my poore house, Thes may be to signifye unto you that my trobles do but now begynne: and therefore do I neither knowe howe nor when to end theym. I have alreadye wryten a supplication to the Quens maiestye in one part: howe yt doethe or shall sped I knowe not as yett and therefore my other great and weightye suetts I dare not attempts, except my

---

[133] Edmund Grindal.
[134] Anne Warcup befriended John Jewel, in flight from Oxford, in 1554 (J. Strype, *Ecclesiastical Memorials*, iii, pt 1 (Oxford, 1822), p. 227) and Lawrence Humphrey when he was sequestered for nonconformity in 1565 (J. Strype, *The Life and Acts of Matthew Parker*, I (1711), p. 368); her son, Cuthbert, was a strong supporter of Richard Chambers in Frankfurt (Garrett, *Marian Exiles*, p. 321); will proved, under Cuthbert Warcuppe, in P.C.C., 1559, 44 Chayney.

counsell thynk yt so mete. I dyd wryte to Mr Secretary in that case, which was to obteane a release of the first payment of my first fruyts, because all my lyvyngs ar so intangled that I can receave smale rents as yett, wherefore I lyve very poorely in the meane tyme, beynge so moche in dett as I am. This I signifye unto your worshippe that as you shall have occasion to talk with any of my freynds you may understande my state before. Thus wysshinge your worshippe most comfortable healthe, I commytt the same to allmightye God to blesse and preserve you to his good wyll and pleasure. Wryten this second of October at my poore castell of Eccleshall.

> yor lovyng & poore freynd at commaundment,

84. [To Mr Goodrich,¹³⁵ 2 Oct. 1560]

(fo. 56) After my hartye commendations to your good worshippe, thes may be to desyre the same to stande my good freynde yf any of my matters shall come before you or els yf any of myne shall come and ask your counsell in any matters. I am very sore trobled with manye matters and have nede of many freyndes and moche helpe, whiche causeth me to desyre thus moche at your worships handes. And though I be not able to deserve yt yet I wyll not forgett you in my most hartye prayers unto allmightye God, whome I beseche to blesse and preserve you in healthe, with my good ladye your bedfellowe, to whome I pray you have me most hartelye commended. Frome my poore castell of Eccleshall this second of October 1560.

> your poore freynd to commaund,

85. [To Thomas Brasey, 2 Oct. 1560]

(fo. 56) Item a letter wryten to Mr Thomas Brasey thankyng hym for his letter and wyllyng hym to be bold, because that what so ever comethe frome the heart is full of eloquence. And as towchyng Mr Bedell, I wryte for hym but wether that dyd hym good or not I can not tell and also to wyll hym not to thynk long for his money;

¹³⁵ Very probably Richard Goodrich who died in 1562; he was apparently in the Lord Keeper's household and a near relative of the late bishop of Ely (*Diary of Henry Machyn*, ed. G. J. Nichols (Camden Soc., 1848), pp. 283, 390; B.L., Lansdowne MS. 443, fo. 92r).

favor is suche here that yt may be bought with an egg & lost with the shell. If I had bene in*a* his case I shold have tasted the same sauce etc.

86. [*To the bailiffs of Lichfield, 3 Oct. 1560*]

(fo. 56) Item a letter to the baylifes of Lichefeild for michaelmas rent whereoff I stand nede styll—to deliver x^{li} to John Cock & to send the rest etc.

87. [*To Alexander Nowell, 3 Oct. 1560*]

(fo. 56) Item a letter to Mr Alexander Nowell to speak unto his brother, the Attorney of the Wards,[136] to be a meane to Mr Treasorer for the election of the sheriffe of this shire either Sir Thomas Gresley[137] or Mr Simon Harcourte.

88. [*To Mr Lee, (?) Shrewsbury, 4 Oct. 1560*]

(fo. 56) Item a letter wryten to Mr Lee to bye me ii or iii peces of Irysh rugg to make blankets or bed coveryngs off this wynter for my servants and I wyll content hym or the bringer therefore with thanks.

89. [*To Henry Techoo, vicar of Montford, Shropshire, 4 Oct. 1560*]

(fo. 57) Item a letter to Sir Henry Techoo vicare of Manford[138] to come and answere whye he servethe not his cure as he ought to do and whye he hayth hyd iiii of theyr images with theyr cases or tabernacles which I have charged hym to brynge with hym to be some part of his satisfaction.

a Word interlined.

---

[136] Robert Nowell.
[137] Sir Thomas Gresley of Castle Gresley, Colton and Drakelowe, Derbyshire.
[138] Techoo had been deprived, for marrying, under Mary (B.L., Harl. MS. 421, fo. 59r): he was apparently reinstated at Elizabeth's accession. See also items 101 and 102.

90. [*To Thomas Griffith of West Felton, Shropshire, 4 Oct. 1560*]

(fo. 57) Item a letter to Thomas Griffeth of West Felton to suffer William Kynaston quietlye to occupye and kepe his place or forme in the churche or els to come and shewe reason whye he shold not so doo etc.

91. [*To Roger Sprisco, 4 Oct. 1560*]

(fo. 57) Item a letter to Roger Spristoo to geve place unto Thorperlaye & his wyffe in theyr stale or place in the churche or els he to repayre unto me to shewe some lawfull cause whye Thorperlaye shold not have his place there as he haythe allwayes bene accostomed to have etc.[139]

92. [*To the Chancellor of Lichfield, 7 Oct. 1560*]

(fo. 57) Item a letter to my chancelor for expedition in a case betwene one Thomas Hanley & William Yonge.

93. [*To William Sale,[140] 8 Oct. 1560*]

(fo. 57) Item a letter to Mr Sale for William Kynaston agaynst Thomas Griffith for his forme.

94. [*To John Gifford, 8 Oct. 1560*]

(fo. 57) Item a letter to Mr John Gefforth in the behalfe of my tennaunts of Coldmese.

[139] 9 Dec. 1561: George Torperley against Roger and Anna Sprisco for his church pew (L.J.R.O., B/C/2/5).
[140] He appears as surrogate and commissary of the court in a metropolitical visitation, 1560 (L.J.R.O., B/V/1/4); for his career summary, see Foster, *Alumni Oxonienses* and P.R.O., S.P. Dom. Eliz. xxxvi, 41 & 42.

95. [*To James Weston, Registrar, 8 Oct. 1560*]

(fo. 57) Item a letter to James Weston to mak an institution for Sir John Lawrenson to the*ᵃ* parsonag of Swerkeston.[141]

96. [*To Thomas Yeaton or Eaton, vicar of Wellington, Shropshire, 10 Oct. 1560*]

(fo. 57) Item a letter to vicare Eaton of Wellington to make inquisition for one Ales Johnson of Eamestre, who haith slaundred Bromhalls wyffe & is a slaunderous whoman, to punishe her severely yf the case be so tried owt.

97. [*To James Weston, Registrar, 11 Oct. 1560*]

(fo. 57) Item a letter to James Weston to bestowe the parsonage of Northwinkfield[142] upon one John Cook[143] yf the same be in lapse and in my gyfft.[144]

98. [*To Richard Walker, Archdeacon of Stafford,[145] 11 Oct. 1560*]

(fo. 57) Item a letter to Mr Walker of Lichefeild to come and common with me this next weike, partlye in common matters, partlye in myne owne matters.

ᵃ Followed by vicarag, *struck out.*

---

[141] Swarkestone rectory, Derbyshire.

[142] North Wingfield, Derbyshire. The patron was Mr Langford (L.J.R.O., B/V/1/2). It had 68 households in 1563.

[143] Unidentified except as incumbent of North Wingfield, which he seems to have vacated in 1564/5 for Longford (P.R.O., E.331 C. & L. (2) 4).

[144] Livings left vacant for six months were said to be in lapse, the right of the presentation *pro hac vice* passing to the diocesan, unless it were a crown living.

[145] Born in Lichfield *c.* 1501, he was archdeacon of Stafford 1547–67; will proved in P.C.C., 11 Nov. 1567. See items 3 and 23, and Venn, *Alumni Cantabrigienses.*

99. [*To Nicholas Bullingham, Bishop of Lincoln, 11 Oct. 1560*]

(fo. 57) Item a letter to my Lord of Lincoln[146] partlye to thanke hym for his lovyng counsell at all tymes whishing that for his paynes takyng he susteane no losse which as yt wyll be a burden to hym so yt wylbe a greyfe to his freynds, gevyng hym thanks allso for his favor towards one Cuthbert Hugonius who was with me in Oxforth xx[ti] yers agoo, and also in Germanye.[147]

100. [*To Cuthbert Hughes, 11 Oct. 1560*]

(fo. 57) Item a letter to Cuthbert Hugonius to signify that I am gladd of his state and that I have writen a letter to thank my Lord of Lincolne for his gentilnes towards hym and that I wyll be glad to have hym in remembrance hereafter as occasion shall serve.

101. [*To George Torperley, Shropshire, 12 Oct. 1560*]

(fo. 58) For as moche as I do planly understand by experience of my selfe in many places made that the most part of churches within this part of my diocese haithe not onely yet theyr altars standyng but also theyr images reserved and conveyd awaye contrarye to the Quens maiesties iniunctions,[148] hopying and lookyng for a newe day as may be thereby coniectured. Whiche thynge owght neither to enter in to any true Christiane or faythefull subiects hart. Thes ar to wyll you take suche paynes as to goo, together with my somner, to those churches whiche be neighe unto you and call for theyr images and suche bookes as the Quenes iniunctions doethe apoynt. And in case any man shall either conteniously troble you or wyllfullye resyst you in this doyng, take his name that he may be presented unto me with convenient spede and I shall take order therein. Thus trustyng to your faythf[u]ll quyett and sober doyngs, I commytt you to God. Wryten at my castell of Eccleshall this 12 of October 1560,

Yor freynd assuredlye,

---

[146] Exiled in Emden since 1554 (Garrett, *Marian Exiles*).
[147] Cuthbert Hughes, of Yorkshire, arrived in exile in Zürich with Thomas Lever on 10 Mar. 1554; Bentham arrived in April; Hughes attended Basel university late in 1554 and 1555; Bentham was a student there in 1555.
[148] Royal Injunctions, 1559.

102. [*To George Lee*[149] *of Shrewsbury, 12 Oct. 1560*]

(fo. 58) Item a letter to Mr George Lee of Shrewsberye signifying that upon hope I am contented to differ the correction of Sir Henry Techoo, howe be yt I can not suffer those that beare ii faces in one hood, to marrye & love images etc.

103. [*To the bishop's summoner, 12 Oct. 1560*]

(fo. 58) Item a letter to my somner to somne and cause William Corbett in the parishe of Shuffnall and Agnes his wyffe from the parishe of Dawley to appere before me upon Thursday next, and also one Beadmaker of Shrewsberye.

104. [*To James Weston, Registrar, 12 Oct. 1560*]

(fo. 58) Item a letter to James Weston to gyve institution to Sir Richerd Tayler of the parsonage of KyrkIreton,[150]

105. [*To Thomas Bickley,*[151] *12 Oct. 1560*]

(fo. 58) Item to Mr Byckley to take the parsonage of Norbery yf it be voyd by lapse.

106. [*To Thomas Chedulton,*[152] *Stafford, 14 Oct. 1560*]

(fo. 58) Item a letter to Mr Chedulton of Stafford to signifye unto me the cause whye he did excommunicat one William Wood.

[149] See item 89. There is a possible reference in Bateson (*Original Letters*, p. 45): 'George Leigh, now bailif' of 'the toun of Salop' who is one of the 'aldermen & counselleres of the toun miet to bear office & miet to be called to office'.

[150] Kirk Ireton, Derbyshire.

[151] 1518–96. Fellow of Magdalen College, Oxford; he went into exile in France; chancellor of Lichfield cathedral in 1560; archdeacon of Stafford in 1567; bishop of Chichester, 1585/6–96.

[152] Vicar of Worfield 1545–62, when he was deprived; prebendary of Denstone; prebendary of Pipa Parva, 1552–60, deprived; vicar of St Mary's Stafford, 1548–?60, deprived; L.J.R.O., B/V/1/2 gives him as official of the Stafford archdeaconry in 1558.

107. [*To William Beche, 15 Oct. 1560*]

(fo. 58) Item a letter to Sir William Beche to appere before me at Eccleshall upon Saturday next to answere to suche thyngs as shall be obiected agaynst hym then & theyr etc.

108. [*To Mr Webster, Chester, 21 Oct. 1560*]

(fo. 58) Item a letter to Mr Webster of Chester to helpe me to some lynge[153] & saltfyshe and to let me understand the pryse thereoff, and also what store of heryngs ther ys.

109. [*To the Dean and Chapter, Lichfield, 23 Oct. 1560*]

(fo. 58) Item a letter to the deane and chapiter concernyng the reformation of Eccleshalles churche,[154] boyth to examine the churchewardens of theyr othe taken at Lichefeild and also of the regester whiche they shold kepe accordyng to lawe, of mariages, chrys[t]nyngs & buryalls.

110. [*To Lawrence Nowell, Dean of Lichfield, 23 Oct. 1560*]

(fo. 59) Item a letter to Mr Dean of Lichefeild to take order whith Eccleshall churche and to favor Huxlays cause so moche as in such troblesome matters he may.

111. [*To John Cocke, 24 Oct. 1560.*]

(fo. 59) Item a letter to brother Cocke to be diligent in my suet and to gett the best counsell he can, among whome I am gladd he haithe reteaned Mr Forsett.[155] And yf he lacke money, to go unto my brother Raphe Egerton; also, that he shold consult with Mr Brom-

153 Ling, a fish of the cod family.
154 A dean and chapter peculiar jurisdiction.
155 R. Forsett signed letter to Nicholas Bacon on Hanbury, on Bentham's behalf (P.R.O., C/3/13/63).

ley and Mr Fletewood with Mr Sollicitor & bestowe a dynner or supper upon hym. Moreover to wathche wether Cragge[156] doethe medle any thyng privelye in the behalffe of Sir George Blount and Mr Swynnerton who purpose to gett forth processe agaynst me this terme. And to call upon Mr Bolt[157] for my quiets ese & to see in what case of arrerages I stand in thexchecker for tenthes & subsydeyes. And as towchyng Hanberye they be nowe at London to ask counsell for the same; and in any case not to forget Towcester. To bye one hondreth hoppes and some sak cloythe, a rean for a brydell for my selffe, a sursinglett & an horse combe & a rondlett of malvesey & of renyshewyne.

112. [*To Ralph Egerton, 25 Oct. 1560*]

(fo. 59) Item a letter to Mr Egerton concernyng the payment of certane money: fyrst to discharge that whiche I do owe unto hym selffe privatlye & then the rest to runne to the payment of Mr Brasey and hym joyntlye.

113. [*To Mr Sale or to Mr Weston, Registrar, 26 Oct. 1560*]

(fo. 59) Item a letter to Mr Sale or Mr Weston regester to graunt a licence to mary withowt the banes askyng.

114. [*To Mr Sale, 28 Oct. 1560*]

(fo. 59) Item a letter to Mr Sale concernyng a divorcement wherein because I have no skyll I remytt the matter to his iudgement to be ordered as lawe wyll.

115. [*To Dr Weston, Chancellor, 28 Oct. 1560*]

(fo. 59) Item a letter to Doctor Weston in the behalffe of Robert Hill that where he is called up by order of lawe for the probation of

---

[156] Thomas Cragge, alias Underwood, was made bailiff of Eccleshall for his natural life on 19 Jan. 1559 (L.C.L., Dean & Chapter Act Book IV, fo. 161v).
[157] The bishop's collector, Thomas Bolt.

a testament, he may fynd suche favor as equytye wold consideryng
yt was his fathers testament, wherein nature semethe to crave favor
etc.

116. [*To Thomas Brasey, at London, 31 Oct. 1560*]

(fo. 59) After my harty commendations unto you gentill Mr Brasey
and to good Mrs Brasey allso. Allthoughe I have no great matters to
wryte off besydes my hartye thankes for your gentillnes at all tymes,
yet one thynge mencioned in the latter end (fo. 60) of your letter
wyll not suffer me to neglect the same, because that yt towchethe
some my honestye, which ys in denying a copye of Mr Bedels accusation sent unto me from my Lord Stafford. The trueth whereoff yf
you heard you wold not thynke me so worthye blame as I perceave
I am now made, for the case sent unto me as yt was I cold not,
savyng my honestye, geve forth a copye of suche an honorable manes
letter. And yet dyd I reade planelye and truely everye word of the
complaynte unto Randell that he might declare unto his brother
wherein he was cheyflye accused, but of this I will spayre to speak,
because you have so gentilly signefyed unto me what you heare. Yf
either yt be my chaunce to come to London or yours to come into
thes partyes, whereof I wold be very glad, then shall you understand
more. In the meane tyme yf Mr Bedell wold be more familiare than
hitherto he haithe bene, he shold be wellcome to me. An other thyng
I have nowe to remembre by occasion, that the xvth day of Septembre comyng frome Muglestone[158] homewhard, your eldest brother[159]
dyd over take me by the waye and, talkyng together, he asked me
wether I was acquaynted with the lord presydentt of Wayles or not,
for he desyred me to wryte a letter unto hym on his behalfe. Whereunto I answered thus symplye and with owt all flaterye that I was
neither familiare not yett well acquaynted whith hym: howe be yt I
wold wryt my letter so well as I cold in the mornyng and desyred
hym to take a pece of mutton with me to supper, whiche he had
doen, save that your sister fetched hym away to her house, and yet
I send for hym to breakfast in the mornynge, meanyng to have
delivered my letter wryten in his behalffe, but either he ryd to Coventrey or els homeward, so that I saw hym not sence. Nowe yf any
thyng shall come unto you by report hereoff, you hearre the truethe
playnelye. Whereunto I doubt not but you wyll give credyte. Thus

[158] Mucklestone, Staffs.   [159] Richard Brasey; see item 66.

desyring you to iudge of me even as the trueth is & shall beare me in
all thyngs and no further, I commytt you to almighty God, who blesse
you & yours to his pleasure. Wryten this laste off October at my
castell of Eccleshall,

yours assuredly to commaund,

117. [*To Clement Throckmorton, (?) London, 31 Oct. 1560*]

(fo. 60) My harty commendations remembred to your good worshippe, thes may be with thanks for your paynes hitherto, to desyre
your further helpe and furtherance in my suets now at London yf
you tarrye there this terme tyme, and especiallye concernyng Hanberye, which yf I do not obteane I shall not be able to contynue
here for lacke of corne. I here say that my brother Cocke reteaned
some counsell with owt your consent. Whereof I am sorye, howe be
yt I pray you, for this once, beare therewhithe for I wyll wryte to
hym that he shall use your counsell more hereafter. And one thynge
I must desyre you to tak paynes in: that ys to mak a iust survey of
the parsonage of Towceter[160] at your comyng agayne frome London.
And yf you tarye a day or ii about yt, I wyll alowe your charges
(fo. 61) for I must indue a vicare there and, therefore, I wold knowe
what glebe lande or pasture there ys to allott some reasonable portion forthe for the vicars lyvynge. As yet I have not receaved one
penny of Mr Harcourt but I have a letter frome my Lord Treasorer
unto hym whiche I doubt howe yt wylbe taken. For lack of good
officers and good instructions I have lost at my court kepynge xx^{li}
as some do tell me: here is nothyng to be gotten but by extremytye.
Thus commyttyng my causes to yor good helpe and you to the good
gwydyngs of all allmighty God, I bydd your worshipp fayre well.
Wryten this last of October at my castell of Eccleshall,

your good worshippes at commandment.

118. [*To Thomas Lever, Archdeacon of Coventry, 31 Oct. 1560*]

(fo. 61) Item a letter to Mr Levir concernyng an answere to his
letters sent unto me, whiche I purpose to send unto hym by Mr
Sampson.[161] In the meane I have sette my hand to Mr Mullins

---

160 Towcester rectory, Northants.
161 Thomas Sampson, an exile. See Garrett, *Marian Exiles*.

reqest,[162] desyryng God to blesse theym boyth and hym to gett the handes of good Iustices there because there ys none here.

119. [*To John Cocke, London, 31 Oct. 1560*]

(fo. 61) Item a letter to my brother Cocke to London that he shold conferr whithe Mr Throkmorton, who ys my freynde, and that he shold cheyflye regard the matter of Hanberye, for that he dyd put back Grene whome I wylled to repayre unto hym, he dyd not well. And also to learne what ys best to be doen in the matter of Hanberye & to send me word whithe spede.

120. [*To Lawrence Nowell, Dean of Lichfield, 31 Oct. 1560*]

(fo. 61) After my harty commendations unto you worshippfull and gentill Mr Deane, as I have bene a meanes to cause divers of Eccleshall to appere before you and the rest of the chapter, so nowe the matter fallethe owte that I must requyre in you & the rest with you more diligence and severyty then haithe hitherto bene shewed. For suche sygnes and tokens of open sedition and manifest rebellion this weyke in wycked wemens doynges haithe bene used that yf it be not in tyme corrected yt wyll growe to suche a scabbe that you and I and[a] all the godlye in this contrey shall not be able to cure, besydes the danger that we shall incurr towardes the Quene yf we do not whithestand ytt. And frely I must desyre you to sygnifye thus moche unto your bretherne, that yf yt be neglected of theyr part I wyll not onelye present the fact sediciously commytted but allso theym to the counsell, and that whithe spede. The matter ys so heynous and longe that I can not wryte yt shortlye: but this berer, my man, can signifye partlye unto you the wycked interprise, and the names of the cheyfe offenders I have sent here inclosed because that I thynk yt best they be called to answere to theyr doynges. And yf they be cited I wyll be there my selffe at your next court day to obiect, but this I pray you kepe secret for they have not intended agaynst me more then they

---

a Word repeated.

[162] John Mullins, fellow of Magdalen College, Oxford, was deprived with Bentham and escaped to exile in Zürich with him; he was appointed archdeacon of London in December 1559.

have agaynst you yf you knew all theyre sayngs & doyngs. Thus trustyng that you wyll cause this matter to be loked unto, I commytt you to God. Wryten this last of October at my castell of Eccleshale etc.

your freynd assuredly to command,

121. [*To Edmund Grindal, Bishop of London, 31 Oct. 1560*]

(fo. 62) My harty commendations had unto your good lordship thes may be partly to signifye unto the same amonge what troblesome peple I dwell and partly to desyre helpe agaynst theyr pretended malyce. Whiche helpe may be greate yf yt please your lordshippe with some other of the commyssioners to wryte your letters unto the deane and chapter movyng theym so to order theyr churches that I be not more whithe stande and defaced in theym then in any other churche of my whole diocesses. For where I dwell at Eccleshall, the churche belongyng to one of the prebendaryes and so withowt my iurisdiction, I fynd more wyllfullnes then any where els, So that I come in no place to preache or to do any thynge but they lay Eccleshall in my waye. Howe sediciously the wemen of the towne have wrought this weyke the berrer hereoff can declare to your good lordshippe, whiche I pray you consyder, as my trust ys you wyll. I am farr frome good counsell and destitute of lerned men for lack of lyvynge to geve theym and I can gett no helpe of any Iustice. Thus commyttynge thes busy matters to allmightye God and your good helpe, I pray god to blesse and preserve your lordshipe in healthe. Wryten this last of October at my poore castell of Eccleshall.

your good lordships at commandment,

122. [*To Richard Walker, Archdeacon of Stafford and Derby, Lichfield, Nov. 1560*]

(fo. 62) A letter wryten to Mr Walker at Lichefeild, fyrst concernynge a lease to be made to Sir Androwe Corbett[163] yf Mr Dean wold confyrme the same and in the behalffe of Mr Augustyne and allso concernynge the offyce of Mr Chedulton.[164]

---

[163] Andrew Corbet, of Moreton Corbet, is known o have been a puritan.
[164] See item 106.

123. [*To James Weston, Registrar, Nov. 1560*]

(fo. 62) Item a letter wrytten to James Weston concernyng the sirvey or vew to be taken for dilapidations and for the benefyce of North-wynkfeild nowe in controversye betwene Mr Sale & Mr Cooke,[165] whiche matter I wold have differred untyll Mr Doctor Westons comyng home.

124. [*To Lawrence Nowell, Dean of Lichfield, 6 Nov. 1560*]

(fo. 62) Item a letter to Mr Deane in the behalffe off a yonge woman whiche was maryed to Robert Snellson, that the case may with expedition be determined etc.

125. [*To Christopher Grene and Christopher Baynes, Hanbury, 8 Nov. 1560*]

(fo. 62) After my hartye commendations etc. Where as I do nowe understand your meanynge by your doynges: which as they lacke discretion, so doo they also lacke sobrietye. I am moved, partlye for dewtyes sake and partlye for conscience, to move and exhorte you to use henceforthe more honestye and reason in your talke of me then hitherto you have done. Verely yf your doynges and sayngs dyd hurt me so moche as they hurt your selves I (fo. 63) shold iustly be angre thereat: but seynge that you bable but to your owne foly, I thynke yt sufficient to warne you thereoff, whiche shalbe in thes poynts: first not to bragge to moche either of your title or of your counsell, for I have as good as you; secondarylye, not to threaten me so moche as you do, lest the payne thereof faule to your owne parte; and last of all, not to abuse my folkes as you doo at this present, for I wyll have boethe so many persons in the house and so good romethe and ease as you have or els I shall make you pay dere for your lodgynge. I have shewed you nowe so moche gentilnes that therefore nowe you crack me with extremytye, but I wyll suffer no longer: take hed to your doynges. I have bene readye quyetlye to have the matter de-bated, either by freyndes or by counsell in the lawe, withowt either checkyng or threatnynge, but nowe beynge thus moche abused no reasonable man can blame me yf I seke a redresse. Thus whysshinge

[165] Instituted to Northwingfield rectory, Derbyshire, on 28 Dec. 1560. (P.R.O., Bishops' Certificates, E. 331 C. & L. (2) 4).

unto you boythe suche quietnes as I wyshe to any freynd, I wyll you consyder your case, whiche with troblesome behaveyore can not be made better, and so you shall the rather serve God, who kepe you to his pleasure. Wryten this viii^th day of November at my castell of Eccleshall.

your freynde assuredlye,

126. [*To Thomas Bickley, 10 Nov. 1560*]

(fo. 63) Item a letter to Mr Byckley in the behalffe of one Raphe Cotton for one part of his tythes off Alderwas[166] yff he may spare yt for the man wyll geve as moche as an other.

127. [*To Ralph Egerton, London, 11 Nov. 1560*]

(fo. 63) Item a letter to my brother Raphe Egerton concernyng the delaye of his money, which was because that I have long loked for the returne of Thomas Constantyne, his servant. Howe be yt nowe I send the same to Coventrey to have yt conveyd unto hym from thens desyring hym to use yt as my former letters do declare etc.[167]

128. [*To John Cocke, 11 Nov. 1560*]

(fo. 63) Item a letter to my brother Cocke to declare what they doo at Hanberye and howe they speak evell off me and threaten me allso when theyr bondes ende. Wherefore I wold knowe what I may doo agaynste that tyme. And concernyng my other matters to do what my counsell shall thynke good.

129. [*To Mr Over, Coventry, 11 Nov. 1560*]

(fo. 63) Item a letter to Mr Over of Coventrye to helpe me to convey some money upp to London to my brother Raphe Egerton and I wylbe glad to deserve his pleasure.

---

[166] Alrewas, Staffs; a prebend.   [167] Presumably item 112.

130. [*To Lawrence Nowell, Dean of Lichfield, 11 Nov. 1560*]

(fo. 63) Item a letter to Mr Deane of Lichefeild signifyinge that I have stayed the citation because I wyll not troble the chapter, beyng either fearfull or dowtfull what to do, and to declare that Cragg threateneth to sue theym, agaynst whome they must arme theym selffes with theyr statutes.

131. [*To an unknown correspondent, 11 Nov. 1560*]

(fo. 64) After my harty commendations unto you, thes ar to signifye that as in your absence I was at Swynnerton to preache so seynge some thynges worthye reformation I differred the same to your comynge thither. Wherefore for better understandynge of the same, I wyll that you repayre to Eccleshall castell to morowe, there to heare and learne what ys to be doen concernyng the premysses and thus fayre you well this xi^th of November at my castell of Eccleshall.

yor freynd assuredlye,

132. [*To Mr Vescott, Bailiff of Lichfield, 14 Nov. 1560*]

(fo. 64) Item a letter to Mr Vescott baylye of Lichefeild to thank hym for his payns takynge, willyng hym allowe his charges fullye of the receapts yf he receave so moche: yf not, I wyll by the grace of God remembre yt otherwyse. And as towchyng Willford medowe & suche parcells of pasture, allthoughe I heare say that some of the leases be forfeat for lacke of payment, yet I wyll use no extremyty agaynst any of theym but contented to receave as you thynke best and also I wold gladly call for the rent of the palace of Coventrey etc.[168]

133. [*To Simon Harcourt, 15 Nov. 1560*]

(fo. 64) Item a letter to Mr Harcourt to commytte one John Kroke[a] clearke of Whitchurch[169] to prison for speakyng sedicious woordes agaynst the lawes of religion.

[a] *Followed by* eke, *struck out.*

---

[168] Let in 37 Henry VIII (1546) for 99 years (L.J.R.O., CC. 124100).
[169] Whitchurch, Shropshire.

134. [*To Edwin Sandys, Bishop of Worcester, 16 Nov. 1560*]

(fo. 64) Item a letter to my Lord of Worcetor thankyng hym for his paynes takyng in my diocese as I am informed by one Cole, whome as he haithe licensed to read within his diocese, so I pray hym to helpe the said Cole in to the ministerye yf he geve orders before me and I shall acknoweledg yt a pleasure for I lack many good ministers. Allso I desyre his counsell agaynst the tyme of my visitation because I am destitute of counsell & lerned men etc.

135. [*To Dr Weston, Chancellor, 18 Nov. 1560*]

(fo. 64) Item a letter wryten to the chancelor or his deputy for spedye iustyce to be ministred in divers cases of matrimonye, especiallye for one John Collier, who as he saythe haith bene deceaved by the inconstancye of an old woman. Suche cases mo there be wherein I must shortlye wryte for the uniust dealyng of divers persons notwithstandynge accordynge to iustyce.

136. [*To John Cocke, 20 Nov. 1560*]

(fo. 64) Item a letter to my brother Cocke to ask counsell concernyng Hanberye for I wold sue a forfeyture of theyr lease because they have broken divers & sundrye covenaunts, and also towchyng a *quare impedit*[170] and last of all concernyng Sir George Blounts lease of Gnosall & rent which my steward hayth receaved, under the valewe moche etc.

137. [*To James Weston, Registrar, (?)15 Nov. 1560*]

(fo. 64) Item a letter to James Weston for his counsell concernyng Lonforthe[171] and to helpe hym to some processe for his tenthes, so moche as lawe wyll beare, for because I use soo moche sofftnes, yt makethe the proud & pevyshe papistes stowt & bold, but I must

[170] A case brought against the bishop in the court of Common Pleas for rejecting the patron's presentee to a living.
[171] Longford rectory, Derbyshire; possibly the occasion of the *quare impedit* mentioned in item 136.

begynne to traveise with theym and purpose, God wyllynge, to do with the proudest of theym. Also for a copy of a precept or mandate and last of all to declare what day I wold geve orders, that is the 15 of November.

138. [*To Dr Weston, Chancellor, Nov. 1560*]

(fo. 64) Item a letter to Doctor Weston towchyng the same matter of Longforthe & Northwynkfeild.

139. [*To Ralph Egerton, 20 Nov. 1560*]

(fo. 65) Item a letter to my brother Raphe Egerton for that he and Mr Lane ys bond for his first fruyts for Longforth to contynue his freynd styll and they shalbe no losers therein God wyllyng.

140. [*To the farmer of Densford parsonage, Northants, 20 Nov. 1560*]

(fo. 65) Item a letter to the fermer of the parsonage of Densford in the countye off Northampton for my rent that yt may be prepared either agaynst the day of payment or els so shortly after as may be, wherein his diligence shall not onely deserve thankes but lyke pleasure as shall lye in my poore power to shewe yt.

141. [*To the farmer of Belgrave and Long Buckby, Leicestershire and Northants, 20 Nov. 1560*]

(fo. 65) Item to the fermer of Belgrave and Bugbye for my rent off boyth, wyllinglye hym to use suche diligence as may deserve thankes & lyke benefyte or pleasure.

142. [*To Mr Lord, official of Leicester, 20 Nov. 1560*]

(fo. 65) Item a letter to Mr Lord officiall at Leicester to desyre hym to send mye letter to the fermer off Belgrave and to signifye that I have one lying att London this terme for the discharge of subsidyes

& tenthes whiche shold have bene this terme yf that the collectors
of Leicestershire and Northamptonshire had bene at London.

143. [*To John Barker, 20 Nov. 1560*]

(fo. 65) Item a letter to John Barker thankyng hym for his gyffts and
desyryng hym to come & to be payd hym selffe, wrytyng merely to
hym in this poynt.

144. [*To Thomas Lever, 21 Nov. 1560*]

(fo. 65) After my harty commendations to you gentill Mr Lever, thes
ar to signify unto you that as towchyng your last letter I purpose,
God wyllyng, to geve orders the xv^th day of December, yf I have no
other lett then at this tyme I knowe off: wherefore yf I send you no
contrary worde prepare those whome you have mete agaynst that
day. And as concernyng those which were apoynted deacons the last
tyme, I wyll allso receave and minister unto theym accordynglye yf
they come at that tyme. As towchyng my dett to Mr Ryley, I have
yt in remembrance very well for yf that other detts were met I wold
not be so moche blamed of negligence & so moche suspected of
coldnes as I perceave I am with those whome I take to be my dearest
freynds. Last of all I desyred Mr Sampson to call for a citation at
Lichfeild, and so I thought that he had done; howe be yt, I wyll
cause one to be send downe so shortlye as may be yf then my Lord
of Canterberyes visitation be ended.[172] And thus commyttyng you
to allmyghtye God, I commytt me to your godly prayers. Wryten
this xxi^th of November at Eccleshall castell.

145. [*To John Audley, steward of Hanbury, 28 Nov. 1560*]

(fo. 65) Item a letter to my steward to Hanbery for to go to Sallowe[173]
and demaund my rent and in the way to signify to the baylye off
Derbye that I have received his letter and concernynge an answere
I must take deliberation because I have received letters to the contrarye before.

---

[172] Metropolitical visitation.
[173] Sawley, Derbyshire, an episcopal manor.

146. [*To John Beeche, vicar of Sheriff Hales,*[174] *29 Nov. 1560*]

(fo. 65) Item a letter to the vicare of Sheriff Hayles that he provyd some body to the cure of Woodcote,[175] controversye dependynge betwene hym and Mr Coote that upon Tuesday next I may common with boyth partyes.

147. [*To John Cootes, esquire, Woodcote, 29 Nov. 1560*]

(fo. 66) Item a letter to Mr John Cootes esquier of Woodcote, to signifye unto hym that I have apoyncted the vicare of Sheriffe Hayles to be with me upon Tuesdaye next at what tyme & place I wold have hym also to be for the better endynge of all matters of controversye.

148. [*To the parson of Stoke Copnal, 29 Nov. 1560*]

(fo. 66) Item a letter to the parson of Stooke Cappnall for that he maried one John Mosse, beyng contracte before to an other woman, that he signifye unto me either wether they be married or ells come and answere to that which shalbe obiected.

149. [*To the Summoner of Shrewsbury, Dec. 1560*]

(fo. 66) *In primis* a letter to the somner of Shrewsberye to call and somen the vicare off Upton Magna,[176] one Morres,[177] whith divers others to appere before me at Eccleshall the Fryday beyng the xiii[th] day of this monethe.

150. [*To Sir John Savage, 'Fradsom Castle', 4 Dec. 1560*]

(fo. 66) After my harty commendations to your good worshippe, as thes may be to thank you for the sendyng of your rent nowe at my nede to pay the Quene, which caused me to demaund yt the rather:

---

[174] Vicar 1556–86.　　　　[175] A chapel in 1563, otherwise unrecorded.
[176] Upton Magna vicarage, Shropshire.　　　　[177] Robert Morris.

so also to signifye unto your worshippe that you have no cause iustlye (as I tak yt) to marvayle at my doynges, or thynke that I use you
strangly in sendyng for my rent. Yf yt were not asked where yt shold
be, the fault ys not myne and you must geve me leave to understand
where you dwell before I can send to your house. For before this
present tyme I dyd not knowe the contrarye but that your worshippe
had dwelt upon the lordshippe. Yf I had either shewed any straungnes or els bene medlynge where I might have taken good advantage,
then you might well have admoneshed me thereoff, for at the last
payment I told your servant that there was a forfeitt of fyve markes
because yt was not tendered within twoo monethes accordyng to the
indenture. And nowe peruse your indenture what I myght doo: and
then I trust you shall understande that I sett more by your favor and
freyndshippe then fyve markes thryse tolde. This I wryt to the end
that I wold your worshippe shold neither conceave any opinion of
straungnes nor of any sinistrall meanynge in my simple & playne
doynges and thus I commytt your good woorshippe to the goodnes
of God. Wryten this iiii^{th} of Decembris at my castell of Eccleshall.

your freynd assuredlye,

151. [*To the bishop's servants at Hanbury, Nov. 1560*]

(fo. 66) Notes of remembraunce for Hanberye.

1. First quietlye to use your selves, nether sufferynge then doyng
   wronge whithe force or violence.
2. Item to take upp my chamber agaynst my comynge, whiche
   shalbe in suche tyme as I can covenientlye. (fo. 67)
3. Item to learne whether theyr horses have bene accostomed to be
   sett in the stables and yf they have to sett yours there also, pro-
   vydynge for theym otherwyse then of the hey gathered in.
4. Item upon Monday next to hyer some bodye to threashe forthe
   the corne and then to send yt home to Eccleshall whithe spede.
5. Item to mak some provision for your table rather then to goo by
   meals.
6. Item in any case to look well to the kepynge of possession.
7. Item when they put theyr cattell in to freshe pastures to putt
   yor horses in to the stables and yf they pound your horses or
   dryve theym forthe serve theyr cattell with the same measure.

152. [*To Lawrence Nowell, Dean of Lichfield, Dec. 1560*]

(fo. 67) Item a letter to Mr Deane of Lichefeild to signifye that as I wold be gladd to se hym at my cold castell, so divers matters in theyr churches here about me nede great reformation, whereoff I wyll talke with hym at our next metyng. Also that I am desyred to request his favor agayne for this poore man so farr as he may lawfullye doo etc.

153. [*To Mr Audley, steward of Hanbury, and others there, Dec. 1560*]

(fo. 67) Item a letter to Mr Awdley, Mr Manley and to the rest of my servants at Hanberye to use sobrietye in theyr doyngs for I purpose that they shall answere for theyr rashe doyngs. Wherefore I wold that onely you shold kepe possession unto I send you further worde, which I wyll doo yf I may have any counsell or helpe to put theym forthe. I look for the comyng of my brother Coke, before the whiche I can not say so moche as I wold.

154. [*To Ralph Egerton, London, 10 Dec. 1560*]

(fo. 67) Item a letter to my brother Raphe Egerton desyryng hym to helpe me in a case towchyng my dewty and honestye whith yerely payng of the Quens newyers gyfft, which after that my brother Cole of Bowchurche[178] have learned of my freynd Mrs Asheley for a certantye, then to prepayre xx^{ti} marks in gold yf I send not some of my folks to London before that day and he shall receave what soever shall be geven agayne unto I mak hym a iust recompence with the payment of his owne, whiche god wylling shalbe shortly for my matter be so full of busynes and troble that I must come to London for the dispatch of theyme & thus fayre you well.

155. [*To Simon Harcourt, 10 Dec. 1560*]

(fo. 67) Item a letter to Mr Harcourt to desyr his helpe yf ned shalbe for I am lyke to be wronged at Hanberye.

---

[178] Robert Cole, rector of St Mary-le-Bow, 1559–76, and All Hallows, Bread St, 1569–76; M.A. Cantab. 1550; an exile and purveyor of heretical books who acted as go-between between fugitive London congregation and the exiles; model of conformity in Elizabeth's reign; will proved in P.C.C., 1576, 7 Daughtry. See Garrett, *Marian Exiles*.

156. [*To Thomas Bickley, 12 Dec. 1560*]

(fo. 67) Item a letter to Mr Byckley to signifye that I have talked with the undersheriffe whome I fynd a gentill and lovynge man and one that promisethe to be my freynd where so ever a [   ] thynge [shalbe done,] for as yet he haithe nothyng and he (fo. 68) told me allmost the lyke that you dyd, that the generall sessions beyng so nere there ys not lyke to be any before. Howe be yt yf there shalbe he wyll boethe geve me knowledge thereof and also bryng to passe that some of my freynds maybe impanaled; yet I purpose, God wyllyng, to proced and make so manye freynds as I can. And so do you I pray you in lernynge some counsell and thus fayre ye well 12 Decembris.

157. [*To Lord Stafford, 13 Dec. 1560*]

(fo. 68) My harty commendations remembred unto yor good honor, may yt please the same to geve me leave so moche to be bold as to desyre your good Lordships favor so farr as my cause shall seme reasonable to aequitye and right. So yt is that there haithe bene a litell busynes betwene my servants and others at my parsonage of Hanberye for the witche my adversaryes seke secretelye (as I am crediblye informed) to indite either my men or els me at some privey sessions. Wherefore yf your good honor do heare and understand any thyng thereof, I shall thynke my selfe greatly bound unto yor Lordshipe to be put to knowledge of the same. The matter ys so long that yt can not be contend in a fewe lynes and therefore I wyll wayte upon your honor at a more convenient tyme to open the same. In the meane season this my servant can declare the case unto your Lordshippe, yf it please you to heare the same presentlye. And thus I commytt your good honor to the goodnes of allmightye God. Writen this xiii^th of December at my castell of Eccleshall.

158. [*To John Audley, steward, Hanbury, 16 Dec. 1560*]

(fo. 68) My harty commendations had to you all etc. Thes ar to wyll you use your selfes quietlye and soberlye in all thyngs boethe for your owne commendation and myne also for moche rumor goethe of the fact and therefore be of fewe wordes. And as concernyng Marchington, I wold have you medle no more there untyll I send you other worde, for Mr Adderlay hayth bene with me, and I look for word frome hym shortly. In the meane tyme what so ever shalbe doene there suffer yt. Further prepayre your corne agaynst Weddesday at nyght for then, God wyllyng, I purpose to send a wayne. I wold allso have some pease for to mak horsebread. Yf you have non threshed then look yf you can borowe some of any man and he shall have so manye agayne whithe thankes. I wyll send for some of my folkes when the wayne comethe. I have here sent you xl⁸, where-whithe you must play the better husband or els I must geve over all. Thus I commytt you all to God this 16 of December at Eccleshall.

159. [*To Simon Harcourt, 16 Dec. 1560*][179]

(fo. 68) After my hartye commendations to your good worshipp etc. thes may be to signify unto the same that where as ten pownds of my rent for the (fo. 69) prebendaries of Gnosall ar behynd unpayde, I wold have you as my balyf to aske or send for the same. Wherein I pray you use boeth suche diligence and order that may stand in lawe for a lawfull askynge and in so doyng you shall do me suche pleasure as I trust upon and suche as I wyll not forgett to recom-pence, as knowethe allmightye God, to whose good pleasure I com-mytt yor worshipp this xvi[th] of December at my poore castell of Eccleshall.

yors etc.

160. [*To Simon Harcourt, 16 Dec. 1560*][179]

(fo. 69) After my hartye commendations, for so moche as there re-manethe in the handes of Sir George Blount thenn pounds of my rents for the prebendes of Gnosall dew at Michaellmas last, thes ar to desyre you to demaund yt and to use suche diligence and order that may stande with lawe in lawfull askyng the same. Whitche to doo I trust you wyll consider to be your part for that you ar my offycer and balyfe. And yf you shall refuse this to doo, then I pray you thynk me not unkynd to place an other that wyll most gladly exercyse to my contentation. And what you shall do herein I pray you with sped advertyse me, for that he is nowe at his house nere you.

---

[179] This is a draft of the previous item; there is no indication of which version was sent.

Thus commyttyng you to Gods pleasure, do reste, from my castell of Eccleshall this xvi[th] of December at iiii of the clocke of the evenyng in haste, 1560.

> yor very lovyng freynd assured,

161. [*To Ralph Adderlay,*[180] *18 Dec. 1560*]

(fo. 69) After my harty commendations to yor worshipe. Whereas I have receaved your letters desyryng a permission quietlye to occupye and enioye the tythe of Marchyngton thes may be to answere in fewe wordes that as I am nowe in controversye with Christofer Grene & Bayne for the whole parsonage of Hanberye, I wold be very sorye to do any thyng in part which myght hurt my right and interest either in part or in whole. And the saide tythe ys so necessarye that I shall never be able to kepe house my selfe with owt yt. Yet for as moche as yor request ys in no part to hurt my right and title, nor in any part to streyngthen theres, as I understand yor letters, I wylbe contented to permitt you therin for your present necessitye of corne, so that you stand my freynde and answere me therefore, as reason of lovyng freyndes shall hereafter iudge, and thus I have wryten to my steward to deliver you the key of that locke which he sett on the barne dore at Marchyngton, trustyng that you wyll use my good meanyng as you wold have me to use yors, all for the best, God directyng us boethe who kepe and blesse us boethe, this xviii[th] of December at my castell of Eccleshall.

> your freynd assuredly to commaund,

162. [*To John Audley, steward, Hanbury, 18 Dec. 1560*]

(fo. 70) May hartye commendations etc. Whereas Mr Adderley hayth requested me for the tythe of Marchyngton[181] I have upon certane poyncts consented thereunto. Wherefore yf he send unto you for your keye, I wyll that yo deliver yt and thes letters shalbe your discharge in so doynge. I wold have you to sett[182] forthe some of that grassynge to make some money whereof I have greate nede. Thus fayre ye well, this xviii[th] of December at my castell of Eccleshall.

> yors assuredly,

---

[180] 'Rafe Adderley of the Holt'. In 1564 Bentham considered him an adversary of religion but among the more learned J.P.s in Staffs (Bateson, *Original Letters*, pp. 42–3).   [181] See item 47.   [182] In the sense of 'let'.

163. [*To John Gifford,*[183] *esquire, 19 Dec. 1560*]

(fo. 70) After my hartye commendations to your good worshippe, whereas I wrote unto the same heretofore in the behalfe of my poore neighborres and tennaunts of M[   ] for a percell of ground called Sidawyfe, whereof then I dyd take your worship to be lord, nowe beynge better certifyed thereoff, I am a sueter unto you agayne that yt may please you stand so moche the poore mens good freyndes and worshipfull master as to be a meanes to Robert Byll your servaunt that he might so consider theym that at his handes they may obteane for theyr money the use and occupation of that whiche they have longe had amongest theym. I am certane they wyll be gladd to geve as an other man wold. And herein what pleasure or benefyt your worship shall helpe theym unto, you shall not onely bynd me to deserve yt but allso make me readye to shewe what pleasure I can to any tennaunt you have when lyke occasion shalbe offered, as knowethe allmyghtye God, to whose good guydynge I commytt your worship this xix[th] of December at my poore castell of Eccleshall.

your good worships to commaund,

164. [*To Alderman Ryley of Coventry, 19 Dec. 1560*]

(fo. 70) After my harty commendations to your worshipe Mr Ryley, thes ar to thanke you for your lovyng gentillnes and freyndshippe shewed unto me at my necessitye and to signifye that I have sent unto you by this messinger my servant part of the some of money whiche I do owe unto you, desyryng you most hartelye to beare with me a litell for the rest, whiche God wyllynge I wyll send unto you so shortly as I can gett the same of my tennaunts. In the meane season yf you shall take this in good part you shall pleasure me greatlye and cause me to remember you when so ever I shalbe able to shewe the lyke, as knowethe allmightye God, who kepe you to his pleasure in healthe, this xix[th] of December at my castell off Eccleshall 1560.

yor freynd assuredlye,

165. [*To Mr Jeffcock of Lichfield, 19 Dec. 1560*]

(fo. 70) My harty commendations had unto you etc. thes ar to signifye that as towchyng the yers fee which was dew before my

[183] John Gifford of Chillington, Staffs.

tyme, I wyll not pay yt but for one whole yere I am contented, so that you take an acquitance of the same. I shold have sene the paten before I do pay any money, howe be yt, because Mr Walker ys my freynd I wold that you shold pay the whole yers fee whiche was nowe dewe; you receave of my servant so to doo. Conceryng the synages of Hanberye, I do not well understand theym: yf Mr Walker have disbursed theym of his owne, he shall have theym agayne whithe thankes. And thus fayre you well this xixth of December at my castell of Eccleshall,

yor freynd assuredlye,

166. [*To Lawrence Nowell, Dean, and the Chapter of Lichfield, 24 Dec. 1560*]

(fo. 71) My hartye commendations had unto yor worshippes, where as I sett my seale unto ii leases nowe restyng under your custodye and am supposed to be the one stay of the same at this present, thes ar to signifye that as I thought yt not my part at that tyme to move any man further then his owne reason shold perswade hym: so that whiche I then dyd I can not nowe revoyke, but am contented for myne owne part to lett theym passe upon suche reasons as then moved me to seale theym. Yf any of you have better reasons to stay theym, I contend not. Use your libertye and hereafter I shall use myne with better advysement. In the meane tyme I thought yt good to signifye thus moche unto yor worshippes, even so commyttyng you to the goodnes of God, whome I beseche to kepe us all in the bonds of peace and love this xxiiiith of December at my castell of Eccleshall.

yor lovyng freynd to his poore power,

167. [*To Thomas Sampson, Coventry, (?)24 Dec. 1560*]

(fo. 71) *Salutem in Christo* etc. Where as I do perceave by your last wryting unto me that you ar greatley offended with me for suche slackyng of myne offyce and executynge of my dewtye as you loked for at yor departure. Whereunto what I shall answere I am in dowbt onelye because yor letter berythe no day of datynge. Yet this I must say that either you wryte your letter in post hayst after yor departyng

G

frome me or els you have heard and beleved that whitche ys most
untrewe for whith suche spede as I cold possiblye, I sent one of
myne owne servantes to call boeth the curate and the clerke of
Whitchurche before me.[184] And the clerke came at his daye, whome
I sent to the next iustyce to be punyshed accordynge to the lawe.
So that in this when you shall heare the ende I trust you wyll not
blame me so moche as you do. As towchyng the curate, who then
alledged greate sekenes and sorenes I cold do no more by order of
lawe then hitherto I have done, and therein I have done moche
more then you heard off, yet have I bene more defaced with that
stoborn parson then with any that ys within my diocese sence that
tyme. Howe be yt, I can not streyght way correct his wyllfullnes.
Wherefore I praye you gentil Mr Sampson use me charitablye and
blame me iustlye and I wyll (as I must nedes) take yor wrytyng
boyth freyndlye and lovynglye whitheowt either troble or greyfe.
In the meane season I desyre you (*in visceribus Christi*) to admonyshe
me (fo. 72) a freynde of that which you knowe yor selfe certanly or
els of that whithe you hear of others godly[a] crediblye, and you shall
not troble me in so doynge but do me most freyndlye and godlye
pleasure. And as concernyng[b] thes thynges whereof you have nowe
blamed me, I wyll most hartelye to talke and conferr whithe you
here at Eccleshall to thend that I might onely knowe myne accusers
and my wyfes but allso most charitablye to desyre your counsell and
use the same for the reformation of my familye. Whitche thynge yf
you shall do, you shall do me most comfortable pleasure. So you
shalbe most hartelye welcome unto [me] as knowethe the Lord,
who kepe us boethe in his feare and favoure. Writen this 2[ ][c] of
December at my poore castell of Eccleshall 1560.

　　　　your lovyng & poore freynd to his smale powre,

addition postera

Thes ar to signifye that as I am sorye to offend any godlye man
willinglye, so I must stay for pleasure of polityke men, nor perilos
displeasyng of suche as you iudge whithe what spede I colde
convenientlye after yor departyng frome me I sent etc. Howe be yf
as concernyng the parson hym selfe I had no byll of any accusation,
but have burdened hym with more then he was able to answere
unto and more then you told me of hym, yet have I bene etc.

　a Word interlined.　　　　　　　　*b Two words interlined.*
　c The second figure of the date is lost in the binding.

[184] See item 133.

168. [*To James Weston, Registrar, 27 Dec. 1560*]

(fo. 72) After my herty commendations unto you etc. thes may be to signifye unto you that concernynge Northwynkfeild my mynd was longe ago that this messinger Mr Cook shold have yt and therefore the best way you can use therein I pray you doo. Yf his presentation wyll not serve, then I am contented he have yt by collation.[185] I am sorye that he shold be thus driven to labor to me in this plane case. Allways provided that you take bonds for my idemnity in collatynge the same.[186] And thus fayre you most hertelye well this 27 of December at my castell of Eccleshall.

169. [*To Sir Ralph Bagnold, 2 Jan. 1561*]

(fo. 72) My hartye commendations remembred to your good worshippe, thes may be to signifye thereunto that as I have a litell busy controversye about my parsonage of Hanberye, so I most hartelye desyre your worshippe of your favor, when the case shall come before you, no further then the aequitye of my cause shall requyre. Whereof allthoughe I doubt nothyng, yet I acknowledge yt my dewtye boeth to signifye my case unto you and allso to desyre your lovyng favor, as a freynd especiall, whome in thes partyes I iudge I may be bold whithe. Where as I am bold thus moche to request at your worshippes handes, even so I desyre you most hartelye to take my poore house in your way. In the whitche allthoughe your worshippe shall not have so great chere as whith other yor worshipfull freynds, yet shall you be so wellcome to suche as my poore hability can make as to other places, as knoweth allmyghty God to whose [good] (fo. 73) guidance I commytt yor worshippe this second of Januarye at my poore castell of Eccleshall.

yor good worships at commaundement,

---

[185] Presentation is the process whereby a patron offers a cleric to the bishop or ordinary for institution to a living; collation is the act by which the bishop admits and institutes a clerk to a living in the bishop's own gift, or to one where he has the right of patronage *pro hac vice*, in which case there is no presentation.

[186] The presentee was normally required to enter into a bond guaranteeing resignation should the right of patronage be proved to lie elsewhere than in his patron; the bond also provided the bishop with indemnity should the title be disproved.

170. [*To Lawrence Nowell, Dean of Lichfield, 3 Jan. 1561*]

(fo. 73) My hartye commendations had unto yor worshippe, thes may be to signifye that I wold have wryten an answere unto your letter by the messinger whiche brought yt, but that I [had not] leasure. Wherefore in few wordes thes ar nowe to lett you understand that as concernyng the twoo leases whitche I sealed, I have boyth done and spoken so moche as I purpose to do, whitche as I partly declared unto you so at our next metyng I wyll more fullye satisfye you on my behalfe. In the meane season I pray you thynke no ungentillnes in my wrytyng before for I ment nothyng of you. As towchyng Chedulton,[187] I purpose to use an other way with hym then he lokethe for. And therefore yf you do but observe what they do or say yt shalbe suffycient for the tyme for I purpose God wyllyng to go upp to London this terme but I pray you kepe this to yor selfe. Yf we myght go to gether I wold be gladd but I wold have you and Mrs Nowell to come and mayk merrye whith me some day the next weyke and then we shall talk more fully of all thynges further. I wold that you cold learne what evell and papyste stuffe Walkaden[188] uttered in his sermon for surely he shall answere for yt for he haythe no licence of me to preache any where. He was never my houshold chaplayne nor shall be but how he hangethe on me otherwyse you shall understand when I have more leasure to wryte or els when we mete to talke. In the meane tym I commytt your worshippe and good Mrs Nowell unto allmightye God and me to yor godlye prayers. Wryten this thyrd day of January at my poore castell of Eccleshall.

yor freynd assuredly,

171. [*To Lord Stafford, Stafford Castle, 5 Jan. 1561*]

(fo. 73) My dewtye remembred in humble wyse unto yor good honor, thes maye be not onely in my troblesome state to desyre your assistance so farr as aequitye and truethe shall defend my cause but allso to be so freyndly and good lord unto me at this present as to wryte yor letters unto Robert Plummer of Lichefeild, your honors

---

[187] See item 122.
[188] William Walkeden, rector of Clifton Campville, Staffs, 1558–?1607. He was also prebendary of Whittington. Noted in 1593 as 'scholaris ruralis et praedictor publicus'.

servant and sergiant, to come and brynge whithe hym his patient unto the sessions nowe at Stafforthe. For so yt ys that one of my menne beyng so wounded in the head contynuethe whithe hym at Lichefeild in caryng, whose presence ys and wylbe necessarye unto me that day: and except I might have your servant to come whithe hym he shalbe more in daunger, and I lacke suche instructions and informations in my cause as ar most necessarye to be had. Wherefore yf yor honor shall herein wryte your letters, movyng your said servant to come and bryng his cure: you shall not onelye do me great pleasure but also heare and understand the whole truethe of my cause, whithe owt color or [   ] (fo. 74) as knowethe all-myghtye God, whome I beseche to blesse your good honor in health and longe lyffe to his pleasure, this fiffth day of Januarye at my castell of Eccleshall.

Your good honors at commaundement,

172. [*To Sir Edward Aston,*[189] *6 Jan. 1561*]

(fo. 74) My harty commendations had unto yor good worshipe, as one unacquaynted with the same thes may be not only to begynne or desyre acquayntance with yor worshippe but allso most hartelye to thanke you for that good wyll and syngulare affection whiche I understand divers wayes you beare towardes me. Whitch allthoughe I have not well hitherto con[sid]ered yett I pray you impute the same rather to my rudenes and shamefaced nature then either forgettfull-ness or wyllfullnes. And what hayth bene straunge hitherto shall whithe to moche boldnes be amended hereafter. In the meane tyme and especially this present I must desyre yor worshippe to be so moche my freynde yf any more be promoted agaynst me nowe at Stafforthe as to helpe me with yor counsell but even as the aequity of my cause shall seme reasonable. Wherein I wold have requested yor favor before this tyme but that I was thorowlye perswaded yor worship to be my verye freynd, as presently I do most certanely perswade my selfe. Even so com[myttyng] your good worshipe to the goodnes off allmyghtye God, who blesse and preserve you in healthe to his pleasure. Wryten this vi[th] of Januarye at my poore castell of Eccleshall.

yor good worshippes at commaundement,

[189] Sir Edward Aston of Tixall. In 1564 advisers regarded him as one of a 'knot hurtfull to Justice & great Mainteineres' (Bateson, *Original Letters*, p. 42). He died in 1568.

173. [*To Sir William Gresley,*[190] *7 Jan. 1561*]

(fo. 74) Althoughe I have not deserved so moche to be bolde nor recompensed that whitche I have receaved at your worshipps handes yet, knowyng your gentill nature and seyng your good wyll towardes me divers and sundrye wayes, I can not omytt whithe rebuke & shame but most thankfully acknowledge yor gentillnes and most the hartely thank you for the same. Especially for that whitche yor good worshipp shewed unto my servants at Hanbery: for the whitche allthoughe I have not writen unto you heretofore accordyng to my dewtye yet verely I had yt in remembrance and wyll have, God wyllyng, untyll I shalbe better able either to deserve or recompence the same. Wherefore as I trust yor worship wyll beare with my slacknes therein, so allso with this my boldnes in troblyng you agayne, to desyre yor favorable counsell in my troblesome matters if you shall perceave theym either to be worthy or ned any part thereof. Wherein as your worshipe shall do me most acceptable and thankfull pleasure, even so you shall bynd me to acknowledge the same, as knoweth allmighty God, who kepe and preserve your good worsshipe in health and prosperyty to his pleasure. Wryten this vii[th] day of Januarye at my poore castell of Eccleshall.

yor good worships at commaundement,

174. [(?) *To an incumbent, 13 Jan. 1561*]

(fo. 75) After my hartye commendations unto you etc. Where as I do understande by past information that George Torperlay havyng of long tyme a convenient seate or forme in the churche for the hearyng of devyne servyce to hym and his wyfe of custome belongyng and nowe of late ys put forth of the same: thes ar to wyll and requyre you to see the same George and his wyfe placed as they have bene accostomed in theyr said seate untyll I may have the hearyng of the ma[tter] betwene all partyes contendyng about the same. And this as you tender q[uiet] and love unytye, fayle not to do. Wryten at my castell of Eccleshall this xiii[th] of Januarye.

your lovyng freynd,

[190] Sir William Gresley of Colton, who, in 1564, was seen as one of a 'knot hurtfull to Justice & great Mainteineres' (Bateson, *Original Letters*, p. 42).

175. [*To Dr Weston, Chancellor, at Lichfield, 13 Jan. 1561*]

(fo. 75) After my hartye commendations unto your worshippe thes ar to signifye that I sent my clearke to serve the citation, who could not fynd the curate o[f] Whitchurche but he haithe cited the woman withe whome he ys suspected,[191] al[lthough] she was not wryten before, for the whitche woman I have had greate suett mad[e] unto me that she might not appere before you, whitche in no case I wold h[ave]. Some of theym can not be found and therefore we had not leasure to serve [   ] the rest. You shall have a poore woman, Margarett Wendlock, alias ap Edward, before you, whose suett I pray you tender for I knowe her husband to be a wyllfull man: he dyd greatly abuse me at Eccleshall when I fyrst talked w[ith] hym.[192] I sent you a letter wryten unto me conteynyng the iniuryes done unto [the] said woman by her yester daye. I wold have bene at your court but I could not dispatch my matters at Eccleshall: howe be yt, I purpose on Weddensday, God wyllyng, to be at Lichefeild, and so to go towardes London. And thus fayre you most hartely well this xiii[th] of Januarye at my poore castell of Eccleshall.

your loving freynd,

176. [*To Simon Harcourt, 16 Feb. 1561*]

(fo. 77)[a] After my hartye commendations to your good worshipe, thes may be with thankes for your gentillnes at all tymes, to signifye that as I discharged Mr Bolt at Lichefeild when I cam upp, even so I stande whithe hym at this tyme. Howe be yt he is no yet thorowe whithe his accompte, And as for his collection whiche he haithe made, he told me that his preceptes were goen forthe so farr before I gave hym a discharge that he cold not revoyke theym in tyme but I iudge he wyll gather no more. Wherefore as my mynde was before my comyng uppe, even so yt is nowe that you shold collect the same upon suche order as you and I shall agree and apoynct. Wherein because we dyd conferr nothynge, I have stayd hitherto lokyng for you at London. Notwhithestandynge yf you can not come, upon your letters of assurance, untyll we may take order by

[a] *The pagination goes directly from fo. 75 to fo. 77, as fo. 76 is blank.*

[191] See items 133 and 167.   [192] See item 32.

communication together and other ways, I wyll direct my letters
unto you for the collection of the same tenthes, because yt is more
then tyme yt were begonne. And whatsoever Mr Bolt haith receaved
I wyll cause hym to deliver yt in to your handes. Thus for lacke of
more leasure, I commytt your good worshippe unto God. Wryten
this xvi^th of Februarye.

your freynd to his power,

177. [*To Thomas Lever, Archdeacon of Coventry, at Coventry, 17 Feb. 1561,
from London*]

(fo. 77) After my hartye commendations in our Lord Jesus etc. thes
may be to signifye that as I do perceave the godly zeale and affection
of your flocke daylye to increase, so I pray unto allmyghtye God
that in suche godlynes they may not onelye be fervent but allso
constant to the end. As you have moved me to make hayst and
dispatche my busynes: truely my affection and conscience towardes
my charge movethe me no lesse, but my state ys so troblesome and
my charges so great everye waye that I knowe not howe or wherewith I shall lyve when I come. Althoughe I have nothyng here to
lyve upon, yett thorowe myne acquayntance in London I can nowe
and then borowe somethyng to helpe me, whiche in the countree I
can not doo. Althoughe in some part off my busynes I hope well,
yet in the greatest of all I se no suche towardnes, but I must stand
to the tryall of the lawe: whiche as yt wyll delay tyme, so yt wyll put
me to no smale charges. Howe be yt, yf I were any thyng eased in
thes thyngs I wold make suche shifte as I could to come awaye.
In the meane tyme, as I wyshe most hartelye the increase of Christes
kyngdome, so I wysche the defence and protection off God con-
tynuallye to be over all theym that labour and studye in the same.
And thus commyttyng your godlye doyngs to the blessinge off God,
I commytt me to your godly prayers. Wryten this xvii^th of Februarye
at London.

your lovyng freynd assuredlye etc.

178. [*To John Audley, steward of Hanbury, 22 Feb. 1561, from London*]

(fo. 77) After my hartye commendations to you and the rest of my
familye, thes ar to signifye that in and by the order whiche my Lord

Keper of the Greate Seale haythe taken betwene me and Christopher Grene, yt is agreyd that he shall have pasture all this sommer unto the feast of St Michaell next (fo. 78) folowynge for syxe kyne in my pasture grounde aboute Hanberye. Wherefore thes ar to wyll you suffer the same Christopher Grene or his servants boythe to brynge the saide syx kyne in to the pastures amonge myne owne, and allso to suffer his maide to have free passage to mylke the same kyne at theyre pleasure. And hereoff see that you fayle not, usynge your selfe towardes hym so that you may have commendation therefore and I no blame. Further as concernyng his goodes, delyver theym as they were receaved at his pleasure, kepyng a note of remembraunce of the same, that yf he take any thynge whereunto he haithe no ryght, I may iustly by order of lawe call for yt agayne, for as I purpose to whithold nothyng of his, so I wold gladly reteane or recover myne owne. I do remembre that there ys a litell dytche and hedge beynge in decaye, I wold have quycke sett where yt is nedefull. As towchyng Marchyngton barne, yf you have not as yett delivered the key to Mr Adderlay I wyll that you kepe yt styll untyll he and I have commoned to gether for when he was att London he wold not see me and therefore I purpose to talke with hym before he have any thyng at my hande. And I wold not have you to medle any thyng at Marchyngton untyll I come my selffe or els send you further word what to do. And thus fayre you well etc. this 22 of February.

179. [*To Matthew Parker, Archbishop of Canterbury, 22 Feb. 1561, from London*]

(fo. 78) Dewtyfullye commendynge me unto your grace, thes may be to desyre the same be so favorable unto this messinger Edward Hayles my chaplayne as his sute in this greate scarcytye off good and lerned ministers shall seme to your graces order reasonable. Where in you shall not more pleasure hym then bynde me to acknowledge the same benefyte, as knowethe allmyghtye God, to whose good protection I commytt your grace this 22 of Februarye.

                    your graces at commandement etc.

180. [*To Robert Aston, rector of Mucklestone,*[193] *22 Feb. 1561, from London*]

(fo. 78) Commendyng me most hartelye to you and to all with you, thes ar to signifye that my Lord Keper of the Greate Seale of England purposethe verye shortlye to take order in my matters. As towchyng Hanberye he haithe concluded yester daye that I shall have and enioye the possession of the whole and that Christopher Grene shall have some recompence in consideration of his hurt and losses. And yf either Mr Adderlay or els Bayne put me to any busynes, I shall have processe agaynst theym boythe. My Lord Keper haithe bene my very good lord in all my suetts whitche I have allready in Eccleshall Castell etc. agaynst Mr Swynnerton and Sir George Blounte. Whereoff I will wryte unto you when yt is done. In the meane tyme, I thought good to signifye this moche unto you of my procedyngs whiche hitherto I have no cause to mislyke, prase be to God, who kepe you all in health this xxii[th] of February at London etc.

181. [*To Simon Harcourt, 27 Feb. 1561, from London*]

(fo. 79) After my harty commendations unto your good worshippe, thes may be to signifye that where as I have made promyse unto you for the collection of the tenthes whithin my diocesse, so yt ys that divers honorable personages of the Quens maiestyes most honorable counseall have wryten earnestlye to me for the same collection to be bestowed upon one Mr Highame. And althoughe I have answered that my promyse thereoff ys past unto you (whiche in no case savyng myne honestye I can revoyke) yet I am moved to assay what may be done whithe you in this case. Wherefore as I doo understande that in this behalffe there shall be letters addressed unto you for your good wyll herein, so my wrytynge in the same ys to knowe your pleasure that I may either staye yt for you accordyng to my promise, or else conferr yt at suche request whithe your full consent, whitche in no case I purpose to do whitheowt the same. And thus lokynge

---

[193] Rector of Mucklestone, Staffs, 1546–53, deprived; vicar of Sandon, Staffs, 1530–53, deprived; restored to both *c.* 1560: until death in 1577. Made prebendary of Freeford, 1561–76; no record of university career; origins unknown. Not to be confused with vicar of Alstonefield and rector of Stanton who died 1604.

for a spedye answere hereoff, I bydd you most hartelye fayre well this xxvii[th] of Februarye at London.

your freynd assuredlye to his power,

182. [*To Robert Aston, rector of Mucklestone, John Audley, and William Critche, 27 Feb. 1561, from London*]

(fo. 79) Whereas I doo understande certane of my neighbours and tennaunts to have nede of some wood and in part suethe haithe bene made unto me therefore, besydes the necessitye of moneye whiche presentlye I shold pay unto the Quene, thes ar to wyll and autoryse you three to gether or two of you at the least to sell and suffer to be fallen and caryed awaye whithe in my woods called the Byrkylls, the Songles and Bloore parke, or else where whithe in my maner or lordshippe of Eccleshall, to the some or valor off one hondrethe poundes, usyng suche circumspection and diligence therein that so lytell wayst or spoyle be made therebye as may possiblye be avoyded and apoyntyng the tyme of fallynge at your discretions provided that the last day of payment be no longer then to mydsommer next commyng and the tyme for caryng away the same no longer then unto the feast of Sanct Michaell next insuyng the date hereoff. And in so doynge thes my letters to be a sufficient discharge for you in that behalffe. Wryten att London this 27 of Februarye by me your freynd.

183. [*To Robert Aston, rector of Mucklestone, 27 Feb. 1561, from London*]

(fo. 79) My harty commendations with lyke thankes remembred unto you gentill Mr Aston, thes may be to sygnifye that nowe I purpose to praepare my selffe homeward yf I had my horse here. Howe be yt, I wold remayne at Hanberye yf that there may be made any provision for woode. Yt is longe to wryte howe I have spedde, and therefore I omyt allthyngs untyll my commynge, save that I wold you shold understande that I am kept in possession of all and shalbe untyll they have better titles then hitherto can be shewed. Of my commyng downe I have wryten my mynde to my wyfe desyryng you to peruse her letter. Concernyng the collection of the tenthes, you shall understand here by thes iii letters whiche I have purposelye sent unto you boythe to reade theym your selffe and allso to shewe the same to Maister (fo. 80) Harcourt, to thintent that he may wryte me a spedye answere: for I am called upon by divers others then by those who wrytt theyr letters. I knowe that I shall have greate displeasure aboute yt: howe be yt, I wyll not revoyke my promyse wyllynglye wherefore I pray you take a litell paynes to conferr with Mr Harcourt, that I may understand his pleasure herein before I come downe. I have wryten to my steward boythe to send up my horse and also to signifye unto me what provision may be had att Hanberye. And thus beyng occupyed other wayes very earnestlye, I byd you most hartelye fayre well. Wryten this 27 of Februarye at London.

your freynd assuredlye,

I have sent my letter allso for wood sellyng, prayng you to use your wysedome therein for the fallynge of yt. I have ioyned with you my steward and William Critche that in the absence of one you may use the other. Also I pray you, when you have let Mr Harcourt see those iii letters, to kepe the same for me.

184. [*To Matthew Parker, Archbishop of Canterbury, 28 Feb. 1561, from London*]

(fo. 80) Where as I am moved in the behalffe of one Sir George Vernon knyght of Darbyshire, within my diocesse, and Maud his wyffe, to be a meane unto your grace for your graces favor in this request. That whereas by reason of divers and sondrye infyrmities whereunto theyr bodyes be subiecte and can not contynue whitheowt good diett, fysche beynge hurtfull for theyr diseases, thes may be to desyre your grace to extende your favor so farr towardes the saide Sir George Vernon, Maude his wyffe with some ii or iii of theyre freynds for theyre better ease and comforthe, that for the recoverye and preservation of theyr healthe you wolde graunte theym libertye that whitheowt daunger of the lawe they may use and eate suche meats as they have experience to be most holsome for theyr bodyes. In whitche doynge your grace shall bynd theym boythe to pray for the preservation of yor honors healthe, as knowethe God, who have your grace in his kepynge this last of Febryarye.

your honors at commaundement etc.

185. [*To John Audley, steward, at Hanbury, 11 March 1561, from London*]

(fo. 80) After my hartye commendations to you etc. Whereas you have wryten to me to understand what you shold do at Hanberye, concernynge divers thyngs; the tyme of the yere requyryng some consideration to be had for hedgyng, dychyng and suche other labors: thes ar to signifye unto you that I can not so well instruct you therein beyng absent as you may be daylye experience learne beyng present. Howe be yt as I wold have no maner of waystfull charges nor unnecessarye expenses, so wold I have you well looke into that whiche must necessarylye be done. As for money, I thought that you wolde have made some of those peasen, boythe to helpe your selves this tyme of my absence and to ease me in thes my great and importable expenses. Further whereas you wryte unto me that you can not as yet make anye provision for your wyfe, I wold be verye sorye to use suche extremitye therein as I am boythe suspected and reported to use. My meanyng was to ease my selfe of my great burden and yet therewhithe to shewe what pleasure I cold to theym that cold understand what pleasure ys, but of this at my commyng downe we shall conferr more. In the meane tyme, I wold neyther have you nor your wyfe discomfeted for lacke of house romethe, seyng that my mynd was not to thrust any owt of the dores but to geve theym convenient tyme to provyde for theym selves. As towchyng the parsonage of Towceter, I have allreadye promised yt to Mr Manley,[194] so that I can make you no answere therein to your contentation, but here after as God shall bryng thynges in to [my] handes, I shall so use theym that I trust nether to be forgetfull nor unthankfull. Con(fo. 81)cernyng all other mye matters, I doubt not but you wyll use suche diligence as may deserve thankes: whereof you shall not fayle by the grace of allmightye God, to whose good orderyng and guydyng I commytt you this xi[th] of Marche at London.

yors assuredlye,

---

[194] William Manley, rector of Hamstall Ridware.

186. [*To Adrian Hawthorne, Principal of Magdalen Hall, Oxford,*[195] *13 March 1561, from London*]

(fo. 81) After my hartye commendations unto you, gentill and lovyng freynd Mr Hawthorne, thes may be in a very freyndes case of myne to be a suter unto you. That whereas for thencrease of learnyng, he haithe sent his sonne with a tutor unto hym to studye at Oxforthe and, amonge other places, ys moche desyrous to have hym in your hall for that yt ys nighe unto the grammer schoole and, havyng smale acquayntance either with you, or any of your hall, moved me to speake somethyng in his behalfe. Wherefore, knowynge my said freynd to be a man of worshipp and by Gods blessyng wealthye and also to be verye myndfull and thankfull in pleasuryng his freyndes, I desyre you hartelye and earnestlye to shewe theym so moche favor as to appoynt theym some mete and convenient chamber for theyr quyet studye in your hall. And what pleasure you shall shew hym in this godly cause you shall not onely deserve the lyke at his freynds handes but also bynd me to remembre your gentill doynge when so ever lyke occasion shall be offered to pleasure you or your freynds, as knowethe allmyghtye God to whose good guydyng I commytt you this xiii[th] of Marche at London.

yor freynd assuredlye,

187. [*To John Mullins, Archdeacon of London, 13 March 1561, from London*]

(fo. 81) *Salutem in Christo*, whereas I am moved to wryte in the behalfe of this messinger that the rather he might fynd some favor at this present tyme to enter in to the ministerye, understandyng that my Lord purposeth to minister unto some this weyke. Thes may be to request you, after the tryall of his learnyng and manors, which I leave to your judgment, to shew what favor you can conveniently do yf that for the foresaid qualytyes you fynd hym mete. The cause movyng me to wryte unto you in his behalfe ys for that I perceave he teacheth the grammer schole where I was borne and shold minister there,[196] where I wyshe as moche good as to any

---

[195] Principal of Magdalen Hall, 1558–70. See Foster, *Alumni Oxonienses.*
[196] Sherburn, Yorkshire.

place for that they have nede of a good man. And thus fayre you well this present xiii off March.

yors assuredly,

188. [*To Simon Harcourt, 17 March 1560/1, from London*]

(fo. 81) My commendations considered to yor worshippe, thes may be to signifye unto the same that as concernynge my promisse made unto you for the collection of the tenthes, I neither have nor mynde to revoyke the same but, beyng earnestlye requested of divers honorable personns to move you therein, I cold do no lesse then wryte as I dyd. Nowe therefore, knowyng your mynde in the same, I shalbe better able to make answere when I shall be requested agayne. In the meane tyme, as I have begonne so I trust at my next comyng to Lichefeild to go thorowe. At which place and tyme, yf you convenient leasure to mete me, you shall well understande that I ment no defraud nor dislykyng of my former promisse. And before I come there I can not geve forthe any order because I must have my chauncellors counsell and my regesters helpe thereto. And this shalbe as shortlye as I can have my horses come unto me. Of your great heavynesse and losse, as I am right sorye so I wold wryte, yf that my wrytyng shold not be rather a renewyng of yor greyfe then mitigation of your sorowe. Howe be as I trust you understand thereby the visitation of God, so I doubts not butt you take yt thereafter, which in all greyves ys best to do. And thus I commytt your worshipp to allmightye God, who send you moche comforthe to his pleasure, this xvii^th of Marche at London, 1560.

your freynd assuredlye,

189. [*A Bill of Acquittance to Thomas Fisher, esquire, 22 March 1560/1, made at London*]

(fo. 82) This byll of acquitaunce made at London the xxii^th day of Marche, 1560, in the third yere of the prosperous reagne of our soveraygne ladye Quene Elizabeth etc. wytnessethe that I, Thomas, bysshoppe of Coventree & Lichfield, have receaved & [had] the day of the date hereoff, of Thomas Fisher, Esquyer, one hondrethe three scoore and fyve pounds of lawfull money of England, beynge the rent off certaine lordshipps called Tachebrooke and others whithe theyr members and appartenaunces in the countye of Warwyke, dew at Christemasse last past before the date hereof for two hoole yers then ended, and commaunded to be payd by order of warrant, beryng date the tenthe day of February, 1560, frome the Lord Treasorer of England, Sir Richerd Sakvyle and Sir Walter Mildmay to the said Thomas Fisher in that behalfe directed. Of the which saide some of one hondrethe three score and fyve pounds, beyng the rent of two hoole yers as is aforesaid, I do acknowledge my self to be well and truly satisfyed and payd, and therefore do acquyte, discharge and save harmelesse the said Thomas Fisher, his heyres, executors and administrators by thes presents. In wytnesse whereof, I the said bysshoppe have herunto sett to my seale and subscribed my name at London the day and yere first above wryten.

190. [*A warrant licensing Henry Cumberford, late Archdeacon of Coventry, to travel to London, 9 March, 1560/1, from London*]

(fo. 82) Whereas Henry Cumberford late archdeacon of Coventry standith bounden by recognizans by him acknoleged before the Quiens majesties commisioners the last of April last past that he shuld within six wieks affter the same day continu & remain in the countie of Suffolk (reserved not withstanding unto him liberties to travil into the countie of Stafford twys every yere concerning his necessarie affairs ther to be doon, touching thexecucion of the last wil and testament of his brother lately decessed to whom he was executor, with vi wieks space for ether iourney in the yere) we in consideracion that the right reverend father in God the bishop of Coventry & Lichfield intendith to attempt and prosecute a caus of dilapidacion agaynst the said Cumberford, hav licensed and by thys praesent warrant subscrybed with our hands do licens, the said Henry Cumberford to travil to London or els where, as well for the answering of the said caus as also to use such defens for his parte as iustis shall requyr, without any penaltie by him to be susteinid or otherwys of hym recovered by reason or force of the said recognizans. Given this ix^{th} of March, 1560.

Matthue Cantuarr   Walter Haddon
Edm. London   Tho. Huick.

191. [*Receipts of synodals and procurations*]

Mr Thomas Fysher Receiver.[197]

Comitatu Warr'	Episcopo Coven' et lich' pro diversis sinodis et procurationibus exeuntibus de diuersis ecclesiis videlicet de possessionibus pertinentibus prioratu Carthusiani iuxta Coventre xxii*s*. ii*d*. *ob*. et de ecclesia de birley parcella nuper monasterii de Nuneton' iii*s*.[a] ii*d*. *ob*. in toto per annum xxv*s*. v*d*. videlicet in allocatione huiusmodi pro vno[b] anno integro finito ad festum sancti Michaelis Archangeli. Anno secundo domine Elizabeth nunc Reginae	xxv*s*. v*d*.

Examinata per Johannem Swyffte Auditorem.

To Master John Mershe receiver

Comitatu Salopp'	Episcopo Coven' et lich' pro Sinodis et procurationibus exeuntibus de diuersis ecclesiis, videlicet de ecclesia de Nessestraunge xiii*s*. iiii*d*. de ecclesia de Riton xlv*s*. v*d*. de ecclesia de Riton xii*s*. ii*d*. *ob*. de decimis pertinentibus nuper monasterii de hamproud xxii*s*. ii*d*. *ob*. et de decimis pertinentibus nuper prioratu de wombrydge xv*s*. in toto per annum Cviii*s*.	Cviii*s*. ii*d*.
Debentur	ii*d*. videlicet, in allocatione huiusmodi pro uno Anno integro finito ad festum sancti Michaelis Archangeli. Anno secundo domine Elizabeth nunc Regine.	

a Followed by iiii*d*., *struck out.*
b Word interlined.

---

[197] Rec' has been transcribed as receiver. For Fisher, see item 189.

Comitatu Wigorn'	Eidem Episcopo pro confectis Sinodis et procurationibus exeuntibus de possessionibus pertinentibus nuper monasterii de Bordsley in Comitatu Wigorn' videlicet de ecclesia de Kynvare vi*s*. viii*d*. et de Aliis possessionibus xii*d*. in toto per annum vii*s*. viii*d*. videlicet in allocacione huiusmodi per tempus predictum	vii*s*. viii*d*.

examinata per Johannem Swyfte Auditorem

To Master harrington' receiver

Comitatu Derbie	Episcopo Coven' et lichef' pro diversis pencionibus exeuntibus de diversis Ecclesiis videlicet Ecclesia de Dronefeild parcella nuper monasterii de Beachieff xiii*s*. iiii*d*. Ecclesia de Ikellston' et haynor xiii*s*. iiii*d*. parcella nuper Monasterii de Dale, ecclesia de hathersage parcella nuper prioratus de Land v*s*. ecclesia de Churche- broughton' parcella nuper prioratus	lis. viiid.
Debentur	de Tutbery xiii*s*. iiii*d*. ecclesia de Makeworthe parcella nuper monasterii de Derleighe vi*s*. viii*d*. In toto ad li*s*. viii*d*. per Annum de [ ] pro vno anno integro finito ad festum Michaelis anno ii° domine Elizabeth regine	

Examinata per me Thomam Neile Auditorem.

To Master Simon' harcourt receiver

| Comitatu Staff' | Episcopo Coven' et lichef' pro Sinodis et procurationibus exeuntibus de diversis Ecclesiis videlicet de ecclesiis de Audley et bedulphe xxxiii*s*. iiii*d*. de aliis decimis pertinentibus nuper monasterii de hubton[198] xxii*d*. *ob*. de decimis pertinentibus nuper prioratus de Trenthame' xxv*s*. ix*d*. de decimis pertinentibus nuper prioratus de Stone xxxv*s*. vi*d*. *ob*. et de ecclesiis pertinentibus nuper prioratus de Ronton xxxii*s*. x*d*. *ob*. in toto per annum, vi*li*. ix*s*. iiii*d*. *ob*. videlicet in allocatione huiusmodi pro uno anno integro finito ad festum sancti Michaelis Archangeli Anno secundo domine Elizabeth nunc Regina. | vi^{li} ix*s*. iiii*d*. *ob*. |

Examinata per Johannem Swyffte Auditorem.

192. [*To Mr Williamson, (?) parson of Densford,*[199] *Northants, 26 March 1561, from Towcester*][200]

(fo. 84) With my harty commendations to your worshippe etc. Thes may be to signifye that as longe agoo I dyd wryte for my rent of the parsonage of Densford, even so I marvaile that I heare not frome you concernynge the same; whitche thynge causethe me nowe to send this my servaunt, boithe to requyre my right and also to understande the cause of suche longe delaye. Wherefore as you wold have me gentlye to conferme yor doyngs, so use me that I have no cause either to compleane or to seke any other remedye to recover my right. And thus I bydd you most hartelye fayre well this 26 of Marche at Towcester,

your freynd to his power,

[198] Hulton.
[199] The heading in the letter-book reads 'To Mr Williamson or the fermor of the parsonage of Densford. . . .'
[200] *En route* from London to Eccleshall.

193. [*Special preaching licence granted to Thomas Darney, 28 March 1561*]

(fo. 84) Thomas permissione divina Coven' et Lich' episcopus, dilecto nobis in Christo Thomae Darney litterato Salutem. Quia ut accepimus, iuxta sancta matris Ecclesia doctrin[e] semen ad fidei Catholicae cultusque divini augmentum in agro dominico seminare desideras perspectaque nobis tua literarum scientia, vitaeque et moris honestas, aliaque probito [   ] ac virtutum merita, super quibus etiam multorum nobis commendaris testimonio, nos moventibus, ut et te speciali favore pro sequamur, et officii nostri onera tibi imponiamur. Ad predicandum igitur verbum dei in sermone latino vel vulgari, clero et populo, in et per totam nost[ram] diocesim Coven' et lich' in quibuscumque ecclesiis, sive aliis locis honestis, ad hoc congruis et decentibus dummodo te in huiusmodi predicationis officiis laudabiliter gesseris, licentiam in domino concedimus specialem per praesentes, ad nostrum beneplacitum tantum modo duratur[am] Dat' sub sigillo officii nostri, vicesimo octavo[a] die mensis Martii, Anno secundum computationem ecclesiae Anglicanae millesimo quingentessimo Sexagesimo primo.

194. [*An acquittance to Ralph Delves, 31 March 1561*]

(fo. 84) An acquietance made to Rauffe Delves gentillman, sone unto the Ladye Cicilye Delves, for xv^{li} x^{s} viii^{d} beyng the halfe yeres rent of the parsonage of Wibunbury,[201] dewe at the feast of St. Michaell last past. Condicionally, the[b] conference of the lease and counterpayne do agree for the rent of the feast of thannunciation of our ladye.

195. [*To Richard Cliffe, curate of Stone, Staffs,*[202] *9 April 1561*]

(fo. 84) After my hartye commendations etc. whereas I am informed that one Alyce Clyffe beyng brought in bedd of a chyld begotten by Thomas Harvey, haithe by her freynds moved the same Thomas

---

[a] *Followed by a word struck out.*   [b] *Word repeated.*

[201] Wybunbury, Cheshire.
[202] Curate of Stone, 1548–53 and again 1559 until death in 1578; 1553–59 vicar of Sandon.

to gett the chyld christened, as reason wold that he shold, beyng his owne, and he refused so to do. Thes ar to wyll you, yf necessity and peryll of death be suche, to requyre the same Thomas Harvey better to consyder boeth his honesty and dewty, then to contemne the laudable order of the churche, as I am informed he doethe. Which thyng yf he refuse to do, then to christen the same chyld whith such godfathers and suects as can be hadd for I purpose shortlye to call hym before me and thus fayre you well this ixth day of Aprile at my castell of Eccleshall.

yors assuredlye etc.

196. [*To Thomas Bolt at Lichfield, 11 April 1561*]

(fo. 84) After my hartye commendations to you Mr Bolltt etc. thes may be to signifye that where as I dyd sufficientlye dyscharge you of the collection of the tenthes and subsidyes and yet you have proceded in the same contrarye to my mynd and commaundement, now my full mynd and wyll ys that you do not onely cease frome further collection but also that you delyver suche somes of money as you have already collected, whithe your bookes of collection, to Mr Simon Harcourt, whome I have apoyncted my collector, boythe for myne owne indemnyty and, as I do trust, for the Quenes com-modytye. Wherefore fayle you not thus to do as you wyll answere to suche thyngs as shall whithest[203] [   ] (fo. 85) obiected in place and tyme. And thus fayre you well this xith of April at my castell of Eccleshall.

Your freynde,

197. [*To John Barker, 11 April 1561*]

(fo. 85) After my hartye commendations to you gentill Mr Barker, thes ar to signifye that I have sent my servants for the oxen whitch you have provided for me; howe be yt because as yett I have not receaved any part of my rents here at Eccleshall, I am not able to make up the whole some of the pryce. Wherefore I praye you to helpe that the rest of the money may be foreborne but by the space of vii or viii days longer, and I wyll with all spede praepare yt with owt any fayle, God wyllynge, or els I shalbe compelled to take no

---

[203] The document is torn at this point.

mo, then this smale some wyll presently pay for, and thus helpyng me you shall do me greate pleasure, whiche God wyllyng I shall remember. Further I am at this tyme destitute of a cooke, wherein I heare say you can helpe me for a tyme, which yf you can I pray you the sooner the better, thus fayre you well this xi[th] of Apryle at my castell of Eccleshall.

your lovyng freynd,

198. [*To Matthew Parker, Archbishop of Canterbury, 11 April 1561*]

(fo. 85) My dewtye remembrer, with most hartye commendations unto your grace, thes may be to desyre the same most earnestlye to be so favorable unto me in my greate nede, as to lycence Dr Weston towardes the ende of the terme, to make suche spede homewarde, as he doethe well knowe to be verye necessarye for the reformation of divers and sundrye thyngs far owt of order, allmost in my hoole dioces, whereof he is better able to geve your grace understandynge by private talke then I at this tyme by my simple wrytinge, further whereas one Mr Aston[204] a godlye preacher within thes parties of my dioces ys preferred to a benefyce with in the dioces of Lincolne, whereupon he shold by order of lawe be resident, my request and desyre to your grace ys, that yt wold please the same to shewe so moche favor as your grace may lawfullye do unto the said Mr Aston, for that he haithe nowe begonne a good worke to the furtheraunce of a schole in Shrewsberye[205] whiche yf he shold praesentlye departe were lyke either not to procede or els moche therebye to be hyndred. In consideration whereof, yf it may plaese your grace the rather to tender his absence you shall not onelye do a greate pleasure of the towne of Salop but allso to me in thes parties of my dioces, whiche have here no other preacher but hym. Even thus commyttynge your

---

[204] Thomas Ashton or Aston. First headmaster of Shrewsbury; others considered him its virtual founder (Camden, *Britannia*, trans. R. Gough (3 vols, London, 1789), ii, 399). See also B.L., Add. MS. 29,546, fo. 52r, and G. W. Fisher, *Annals of Shrewsbury School* (London, 1899). The Thomas Ashton deprived under Mary for failure to take orders does not appear to be the same (W. H. Frere, *The Marian Reaction* (London, 1896), p. 108). See *D.N.B.*, and Venn, *Alumni Cantabrigienses*.

[205] A charter was granted by Edward VI, on 10 Feb. 1552, in response to petition from bailiffs, burgesses and inhabitants (Corporation Minutes; Taylor MSS., Shrewsbury School Library). The first master was one Mr Morrys in 1551. The school flourished greatly under Ashton's control. This letter provides the only known reference to the school between October 1556 and 21 June 1561.

good grace to the goodnes of God, wryten this xi[th] of Apryle at my castell of Eccleshall.

your graces at commaundement,

199. [*To Richard Walker at Lichfield, 15 April 1561*]

(fo. 85) After my hartye commendations to your worshippe thes may be to signifye that whereas there be certane resolutions consented upon by my Lord of Cantorberyes grace and other bysshoppes whithe hym for the better understandynge and observynge of the Quenes Majesties iniunctions,[206] amongest the which certane of theym ar to be putt in execution by the archdeacons in theyr visitations whitche I wold you shold nowe execute in your visitation.[207] Where of I wold have commoned whithe you before, yf that I had hadd convenient leasure thereto, for lacke of the whitche I am nowe in thes few wordes compelled to putt you to knowledge of the same that you may execute accordyngly. (fo. 86) One matter ys this, that in your visitation you apoynct all curats cer[tane] taxes of the new testament to be lerned withowt the booke; and at your next visitation to execute a rehershall of the same. And as towchyng the perambulation weyk mencioned in the xix iniunction of the Quens iniunctions, they must syng or say the ii psalmes begynnyng *benedyc anima mea domino* in Englyshe with the letanye and suffragyes thereto with some sermon or homelye of thanks gevenge to God and movyng to temperancye in theyr drynkynge yf they have anye. Here you must charge theym to avoyd superstition and suche vayne gaysynge as the used the last yere and in no case that they use either crosse, taper, nor beades, nor wemen to go abowte but men that knowe the bondes of theyr parysh. Other thyngs for lacke of leasure I comytt to your good wysedom. I must desyre you also put Mr Wells in remembraunce of my court daye which is apoynted upon to morow sevenyght. And yf my freynd Mr Aston do in any matter of

[206] Bentham comments on items 3 and 4 of the Interpretations of the Bishops which were ratified in April 1561; these items elaborated on nos. 16 and 19 of the Royal Injunctions of 1559 (W. M. Kennedy, *The Interpretations of the Bishops*, Alcuin Club Tracts, viii, 1908, pp. 29–30).

[207] Le Neve contends that Lawrence Nowell was archdeacon of Derby, 1558–76, but there is considerable evidence that Walker held both Stafford and Derby in plurality until his death in 1567 (B.L., Harl. MS. 594, fo. 173; *Letter-Book*, item 23). However, Nowell was probably reappointed on Walker's death. Luke Gilpin was collated to the archdeaconry of Derby on the death of Nowell in 1577 (L.J.R.O., B/A/1/15).

myne conferr with you, I pray you helpe hym with your counsell as you knowe best in suche cases, and I trust it shall not be unthankfullye taken, as knowethe God, to whose good direction in spirite and truethe I commytt you this 15 of Aprile at my castell of Eccleshall.

yor lover and freynd to his smale power,

200. [*To Mr Wells,*[208] *15 April 1561*]

(fo. 86) A letter writen to Mr Wells to signifye that I have apoynted my court upon Weddensdaye beyng the xxiii of aprile at the which I wold have hym to helpe me or els to send me word of the contrarye etc.

201. [*To the curate of Long Buckby, 16 April 1561*]

(fo. 86) After my hartye commendations unto you, where as at my beynge at Dayntrey I wylled you to cause the perishoners of Bugbye to staye theyr tythes untyll they herd further fro me, thes ar nowe upon certane considerations to wyll you to move and commaund theym agayne to pay all theyr tythes ordinarylye as they were accostomed and ar bound by order of lawe to do, untyll suche tyme as I shall have leasure to take better order for the same. And thus fayre you most hartelye well this xvi[th] of Aprile at my castell of Eccleshall.

your freynd,

202. [*To Edmund Scambler, Bishop of Peterborough,*[209] *16 April 1561*]

(fo. 86) My dewtye remembred unto yor good Lordshippe, Thes may be to desyre the same shewe so moche favor unto my fermer of the parsonage of Bugbye yf he come unto you for some processe agaynst those which deteane theyr tythes, as to graunt hym the same: the rather for that yt is burdened with great payments and the same can not be levied but by dew and iust payment of tythes.

---

[208] See item 64.
[209] Nominated 11 Nov. 1560; consecrated 16 Feb. 1561; translated to Norwich 15 Jan. 1585.

And so your good Lordshippe shall bynd me to acknowledge the same most thankfullye as knowethe God to whose good gwydyng I commytt yor Lordshippe with my hartye commendations to your bedfellowe, as unacquaynted, and to my old familiare freyndes with your Lordshippe this 16 of Aprile at my poore castell of Eccleshall.

yor freynd to his smale power,

203. [*To Mr Lond at London (?), 16 April 1561*]

(fo. 86) A letter to Mr Lond thankyng hym for his paynes in doyng for me wherewith I am contented, signifying that I have done more for Mr Grenewode at his request then I wold do for iiii other mens, movyng hym also to helpe me at London yf he can, my solicitor[210] dwelleth in barbycane besyds Mr Maisters.

204. [*To the Dean and Chapter of Lichfield, 21 April 1561*]

(fo. 87) My hartye commendations had to your good worshipps, may it please the same to understande that where as I have bene greatlye requested of my verye freyndes for the offyce of the regester of testaments and seynge the same offyce to be graunted before my tyme, in as ample maner as yt is nowe required, and also that the graunt now made by me thereoff ys most preiudiciall to my selffe as I take yt I have graunted the same ioyntlye to two persons, whiche before was geven to one, as by the graunt commyng to your worshipps to be confirmed may appere, whiche thyng as I have bene moved in my freyndes behalfe to signifye unto you, even so I leave the rest to be considered of yor wysdoms as you knowe best, commyttyng the same to the direction of Gods holy spirit this xxi[th] of Aprile at my castell of Eccleshall.

your worships assuredlye to command,

205. [*To Mr Critcheley at Lichfield, 21 April 1561*]

(fo. 87) After my harty commendations with lyke thanks to you gentill Mr Critcheley, thes ar to desyre you delyver this letter as accosion shall serve to the worshippfull Mr Deane and chapter, and

210 Mr Playfere.

also to kepe for me boythe the resignation and the former patent or graunt accordyng to my desyre that I may leave yt as a testimonye of my doyngs. And forgett not to lett me have a copye of the same graunt which I have sealed my selfe. I pray you also do thus moche for me as to signifye to James Weston that concernynge the case of diffamation betwene the bayliffe of Derbye and Mrs Grome yet dependyng in the court, I wold have differed untyll Mr Doctors[211] returne yf that great and playne evidence requyre not the contrarye. And thus I commytt you to the goodnes of God this 21 of Aprile at my castell of Eccleshall.

yor lover and freynd.

206. [*To the Dean and Chapter of Lichfield, 23 April 1561*]

(fo. 87) After my hartye commendations to your worshipes, thes may be in the behalfe of my trustye and faythefull servant and freynd Mr Manley[212] to desyre your lawefull favors in helpyng to his smale preferment with your confirmation. Althoughe I have divers tymes wryten unto you yet in no mans cause have I bene more desyrous to obteane my request then in this. And the cause ys for that omyttyng and neglectyng my private gaynes, I have sought to mende the curats stipende, as you maye playnelye perceave, whithe the increase of fyve quarters of wheate, syx quarters of mawlt and ii lodes of hay yerely, whiche I take to be worthe twenty nobles *communibus omnis*, who so ever shall inioye yt. In consideration whereof I am the bolder to request your favors herein. Wherein you shall not onleye pleasure hym, but also cause me thankfullye to consyder the same, as knowethe allmightye God, to whose good governance I commytt you all this xxiii[th] of Aprile at my castell of Eccleshall.

yor freynd assuredlye,

207. [*To Lawrence Nowell, Dean of Lichfield, 23 April 1561*]

(fo. 88) After my hartlye commendations to you, worshipfull Mr Deane, and to good Mrs Nowell, thes may signifye unto you that I

[211] Robert Weston, chancellor, from Canterbury.
[212] William Manley, rector of Hamstall Ridware, Staffs, from 18 Dec. 1558 until 1561, when he was deprived. He had been presented by the recusant Fitzherbert family.

wold have wryten by Mr Crytcheleye agayne by whome I receaved
your letter but that he mayde suche hayst that I cold not then
conveniently wryte. Nowe therefore thes ar boythe to thanke you
for your gentilnes and also to desyre your furtherance in Mr Manleys
sute, which ys to have your confirmation to a lease of the parsonage
of Towcester.[213] I trust yt wyll seem so reasonable, considerynge the
augmentation of the curate stipende, that I ned not to use anye
waye of perswasion. And yett hereof I thought yt good boythe to
put you to knowledge of my request and desyre your helpe therein.
Whereof as I doubt not so I trust that I shall not forgett the same, as
occasion shall serve at any tyme hereafter. And thus I byd you most
hartelye fayre well. Wryten this 23 of Aprile at my castell of
Eccleshall,

> your freynd to his smale power,

208. [*To Richard Walker at Lichfield, 23 April 1561*]

(fo. 88) Commendynge most hartelye the sute of my servant to your
good worshippe gentill Mr Walker, thes may be to desyre your
favor in the same, the rather for that the honest provision for the
servyng of the cure, with owt diminution of my successors portion
maye somethyng move thereto.[214] And as I sought rather the curats
or vicars commodytye then myne owne, even so I wyshe that I were
able to do in all other of my improperations though I receaved no
advantage therbye my selfe. I must also dsyre you that in your
archdeaconrye of Derbye the somners may geve knowledge that the
subsidyes be payd to suche as I shall very shortlye autoryse to gather
the same, because that Mr Bolt haithe not used me well, I have
bestowed the collectorshippe upon Mr Simon Harcourt. If any man
have alreadye payd, I wyll take order that they shall not be trobled,
but for that which ys unpayd, I wold not that Mr Bolt shold receave
any more of yt. And thus thankyng you for your gentillnes & counsell
at all tymes in myne owne matters, I byd you most hartelye fayre
well this 23 of Aprile at my castell of Eccleshall.

> your lover & freynd,

---

[213] Towcester vicarage, diocese of Peterborough. Bentham continued to augment
his impropriate rectories outside the diocese; on 20 Feb. 1571 a grant was made to
the vicars of Pytchley, Long Buckby and Towcester of £10, £10 and £13
respectively (Northants Record Office, Peterborough Ordination Book).
[214] See items 205 and 206.

209. [*To Mr Critcheley at Lichfield, 23 April 1561*]

(fo. 88) Item a letter to Mr Critcheley of Lichefeild to receave the lease and letters yf Mr Deane be not at home, and at his commynge to preferr yt with the other patent which he had at Eccleshall that they may boythe be confirmed to gethere etc.

210. [*To Robert Wharledayle, Bentham's brother-in-law, 23 April 1561*]

(fo. 88) Item a letter to my brother Robert Wharledayle and to my sister to come to me this sommer and make merrye yf they be in healthe and able to ryde.

211. [*To Mr Playfere at the Barbican in London, 25 April 1561*]

(fo. 88) After my hartye commendations to you gentill Mr Playfere and to your lovynge bedfellowe with lyke thankes for your paynes takynge in my busye matters. Thes ar to desyre you contynue your good wyll and diligence untyll I shall brynge the same to effect: And as God shall make me able, I wyll be right gladd boythe to acknow-ledge and to acquyte your travayls therein. Amongest other matters, I wold gladlye have suche diligence as might understande wethere Sir George Blount and Mr Swynerton do attempt any further in theyr sute concernyng Eccleshall; And also wethere Mr Masey do prosequute his action in the Sterr Chamber for Hanberye, but my cheyfe desyre ys to have my tenthes sued forthe in the Exchequer by my patents whiche I leyfft in a chest with my brother Raphe Egerton. Yf you can so begynne the pley that yt may be ended shortlye, I wold have you so to do, for I shall have no quyetnes (fo. 89) with my parsonages untyll the be discharged in the Exchequer, as well of dues as of the payments to come. And here I wold have the sute or playe to go general[ly] for the parsonage of Hanberye (whereof, I have here sent my severall patents) ys [   ] upon for suche arrearages; and also the parsonage of Wolstanton,[215] which ys one of theym which ar in my patents of the recompence. To be short, I have here in a sheall mea[sured] suche thyngs as I

---

[215] *C.P.R., 1547–1548*, pp. 179–80.

wold have remembred, even so commyttynge you to the goodnes of
al myghtye God this xxvth of Aprile at my castell of Eccleshall.

      your lover and freynd to his smale power.

212. [*Notes*]²¹⁶

(fo. 89)

1. First wether Sir George Blountt and Mr Swynerton do folowe
theyr sutes agaynst me or not, as I heare say they wyll.

2. Item wether Mr Masey do folowe his sute in the Sterre Chamber
or not.

3. Item the wrytyngs of *sub pena* for Mr Adderlay & for Christofer
Bayne.

4. Item wethere Mr Clement Throckmorton and you were with
my Lord Pagett for the prebends which he promised to graunte,
and also to seale, as my lerned counsell dyd thynk most mete.

5. Item wether you were lykewyse with Sir Walter Myldmaye for
the xl^s which he shold pay owt of the duchye, a note whereoff I
leyfft with you.

6. Item to remember well the suts of my benefyces impropriate,
as of Belgrave, Boigbye, Towen, Towcester, Wolstanton and of
all others in those my patronage, Pightesleye onely excepte,
which ys not as yett fallen voyde.²¹⁷

7. Item the sute of Hanberye in thexchequer lykewyse for the
tenthes thereof, whereof I have sent up my letters patents.

8. Concernynge the wrytts which were taken forthe of the Kyngs
Benche they ar all served save one and the partyes have sub-
mytted theym selves to my orderynge and to my officers.

213. [*To Ralph Egerton at London, 25 April 1561*]

(fo. 89) Commendynge me most hartelye unto you brother Raafe
Egerton, to my sister Anne your wyfe and to my god daughter
Sarah, whome I pray God to blesse, Thes ar to thank you al for
your gentilnes towardes me, for the which I pray God make me
boythe myndefull and thankfull. Althoughe I dyd perceave at my

---

²¹⁶ Notes 'of remembraunce' intended for Playfere.
²¹⁷ Pytchley, Northants, did not fall vacant until 1563 when it was let for
twenty-one years.

H

commynge awaye that you were somethyng in body diseased yet
thought I that with a litell warme kepynge you shold well have
recovered, but sence understandynge howe lowe you were brought,
and in what daunger, I shold greatlye and worthey have sorowed, yf
I dyd not nowe heare howe God haithe geven you to overcome the
extremity and begynnethe to restore you to your former estate of
healthe. I doubt not but that as God h[ath] thus lovyngly chastened
you lyke a father, even so you have patientlye and obedientlye
receaved yt lyke a child; And nowe thanke hym no lesse for his
fatherlye correction then at any tyme before for his favorable and
mercifull preservation. In that I have not wryten unto you all this
tyme was because that before Mr Manleys commynge I dyd not
heare of your case in the extremytye of seknes. I pray you commend
me to good Mr Brasey and [to all] other my freynds with you.
I must also desyre you, yf nede shalbe, to lett John Flowde or Mr
Playfere have foure or fyve markes in moneye for my sutes this
terme and (fo. 90) by the grace of God I shall with thankes repay it
agayne. And thus wisshinge your fu[ture] and stable healthe, I
commytt you to God and me to your godlye prayers this xxv^th of
Aprile at Eccleshall castell,

yours assuredlye,

214. [To Clement Throckmorton, 25 April 1561]

(fo. 90) My harty commendations remembred to your good worshippe with lyke thankes for your carefull affection of my state,
which never had more nede then at this present yt haithe, Thes
m[ay] be to signifye that I wold gladlye understande wethere you
have commoned with Mr Whyttyngham or not,[218] and what
answere you have for, yf he can not come unto me, I must as I ever
have ment and presentlye wyll provyde for some others. Also I wold
gladlye knowe wether that you have bene with my Lord Pagett for
the release which he haithe promised me or not of certane prebendes[219] in Lichefeild churche. I shold have had theym my selfe
at my beyng at London but that my Lord Pagett was then at his
house in the countrey.[220] So that nowe for suche matters as I cold

---

[218] ? William Whittingham, 1524–79. Exiled in Frankfurt 1554; elder of
church in Geneva 1555; chaplain to the Earl of Warwick 1561; dean of Durham
1563–79.
[219] Baswich and Longdon.
[220] Beaudesert, Staffs.

not dispatche before I have sent upp John Floude. And especiallye his sute or not in the Sterre Chamber. Wherein and in other matters, yf nede shall requyre, I pray you of your helpe that I may the rather folowe my vocation, whitche ys my cheyfe desyre as knowethe God, to whose goodnes I commytt your worshippe this xxv[th] of Aprile at my castell of Eccleshall.

your lover and freynd,

215. [To Sir John Fermor, 26 April 1561]

(fo. 90) My hartye commendations had to your good worshippe, thes may be to signifye that where as I dyd understand and ment by conference betwene your worshipe and me, that you shold look to take in ferme the personage of Towceter at Mr Manleys hande and not at myne, I do nowe by information learne that for this yere you clay[me] the same by promise of me as you say. Wherein I may boldly affirme that absolute[ly] yt can not be so for I dyd ever differ the cause with gentill words untyll I might have convenient tyme and leasure with counsell to resolve thereupon. Notwithstandyng yf you rest upon that promyse then I trust you wyll aswell take my pryce, f[or] I never agreyd to the rent of your lease, thoughe of gentilnes I dyd accepte the same because that I wold boythe freyndlye begynne and freyndlye end with your worshippe. Wherefore, yf your worshippe do not agrey with Mr Manleye for this yere, I wyll then that you agrey with me boythe for the yere and for the rent before you take or receave any further commoditye, and thus I commytt your worshippe to the goodnes of God this xxvi[th] of Aprile at my castell of Eccleshall.

your freynd to his smale power,

216. [To Peter Morweyn[221] at London, 26 April 1561]

(fo. 90) My harty commendations had to yo and to your wyfe etc. thes ar to wyll you gett knowledge where Comberforthe lyethe in

[221] B.A. of Bentham's old college, Magdalen, Oxford; ordained deacon at London, aged 34, 25 Jan. 1560; priest 25 April 1560; appointed Bentham's personal chaplain; instituted to Norbury rectory, Staffs, in 1561 on the deprivation of Henry Cumberford, and to Longford rectory, Derbyshire, on the removal of John Ramridge, late archdeacon of Derby, in July 1560, on collation by the bishop.

Suffolke,[222] that John Floud may ryd thither to serve the citation. And yf he can not there be spoken with to be served, then to conferr whithe Dr Weston to have forthe a citation *viis et modis* (as they terme yt) to call hym in to answere.[223] And the same to be served in the paryshe churche where he continuethe. Herein I pray you use diligence for my matters slepe on everye syde. And use suche counsell as you can for the dispatche of your owne sutes, because I have [nede] of you at home. Commend me to Dr Weston and desyre hym to geve you his (fo. 91) best counsell boythe in my matters and in yours allso. Yf I had any stoore of money I [wold] have sent you some but verelye I am moche behynde whithe my rents. Commend [me] to all my freyndes at London this 26 of Aprile at Eccleshall castell.

yours assuredlye,

217. [*To John Floude, 26 April 1561*]

(fo. 91)

1. *In primis* to looke for the matter in the Sterre Chamber wethere Mr Masey have replied.
2. Item to gyve attendance upon Mr Playfere for the dispatche of those matters conteaned in his letters.
3. Item to learne of Mr Morwynge where Mr Comberforthe lyethe in Suffolk and to ryde thither to serve the citation.
4. Item to knowe of Mr Bentley whye he doethe not send me the rest of my livereys, which I dyd bespeake & he promised to sende.
5. Item to wyll Mr Wayre to sende me the glasse which he promised me and the prunes.
6. Item to knowe wether Mr Hyll the upholster have made me a cople of fether bedds or not and to send all thes downe by the waynemen.
7. Item yf ned be to desyre my brother Raphe Egerton to lay forthe iiii or fyve marks to Mr Playfer and you.

---

[222] See item 190. Cumberford had lately been precentor of Lichfield Cathedral as well as rector of Norbury, and had been reported to the Privy Council by the bailiffs and burgesses of Lichfield for 'lewde preaching and misdemeanour' in Feb. 1559 (*Acts of the Privy Council, 1558–70*, pp. 60, 64, 71, 87).

[223] Such a citation need not be delivered in person but could be publicly displayed—normally on the door of the parish church.

218. [*To Mr Fleetwood, 26 April 1561*]

(fo. 91) Considerynge your greate deservynge and myne unthankfull recompensynge thereof, gentill and w[or]shipfull Mr Fletewood, thes ar to thanke you (which ys all that presently I am able to do) f[or] your greate payns taken in my troblesome matters and to desyre you continue my lovy[ng] freynd styll yf I shall have nede of lyke helpe and counsell. Wherein you shall more str[ongly] bynd hym that is alreadye bound, more then in one yere he is able to loose. Yf you have, as my hope ys you shall, occasion to come downe this sommer, I wold thynke me [happy] to see you in my poore house at Hanberye wether you shalbe most hartelye welcome wh[ith such] other chere so ever God shall send. Havynge occasion to send my man John Floude up to L[ondon] to understand howe suche thyngs proced as I leyft undone, I must as my dewtye byndeth me boyth salute you and also desyre your further helpe when nede shall requyre. Whereoff [al]thoughe I neither doubt nor have any cause to doubt (yf myne owne unkyndnes and r[   ] be not the onely cause) yet my very dewty and reason wyll not suffer me to for[get] your gentilnes. I pray you commend me to Mr Solliciter and to Mr Bromeley m[ost] hartelye in the Lorde, to whose godly direction I commytt you all, and your godly st[udy?] this 26 of Aprile at my castell of Eccleshall.

yours most assuredlye to command,

219. [*To Mr Masey[224] at Whitehall, 3 May 1561*]

(fo. 92) After my harty commendations to your worshippe, thes may be to signifye that as I have moche to be payd,[a] unto the Quens majestie for first fruytes and otherwyse and [have] no wayes to pay the same but by and with my rents, I shall desyre you to lett me have the rent for Burton dew at aester last, wherein as presentlye you shall pleasure me, so I wylbe right gladd to acknowledge the same, as knowethe God, who kepe you and yours in healthe this third of Maye at my castell of Eccleshall.

your lover & freynd,

---

[a] to be payd *repeated*.

[224] He was pressing a suit against Bentham in Star Chamber.

220. [*To Mr Barker, 4 May 1561*]

(fo. 92) After my hartye commendations with lyke thankes gentill Mr Barker, as I am sorye that I [have] thus moche steaned my poore honestye, even so verelye the onelye cause thereof ys for that I am greatly disapoynted of my rents, as well here at Eccleshall as elswhere. Wherefore I pray you thynk no disceat in me because I have not kept apoynctment whithe you as my promise was, for surely there ys no day but I send one way or other for money. I pray you also have in good remembraunce[a] my cooke, that I may (as shortlye as he can) understand wether he wyll come unto me at mydsommer or no for I purpose to stay for hym untyll I have an answere. And thus I bydd you most hartelye fayre well, this iiii[th] of May at my castell of Eccleshall.

your freynd assuredly,

221. [*To Thomas Boseley, 4 May 1561*]

(fo. 92) After my harty commendations etc. understandynge that of late you had a yonge woman in your house and servyce called Elizabeth Kowall, who haithe had a child, and the same chyld nowe to remayne with you, and the mother thereof goen frome you, Thes ar to wyll you to appere at Eccleshall on Fryday next beynge the ix[th] day of May, there and then afore none to answere unto suche thyngs as in that behalfe shalbe obiected. And hereof fayle ye not. This iiii[th] of May at my castle of Eccleshall.

your freynde,

222. [*To John Wacklett, Isabelle Butterton and Douse Hunt of Trentham parish,*[225] *5 May 1561*]

(fo. 92) Where as we do understand amongest divers and sondrye abuses and faults[b] commytted agaynst the right of your churche, you do deteane certane sommes off money dew unto the same, where

---

[a] *Followed by* yer, *struck out.*   [b] *Word interlined, with caret.*

225 Trentham, Staffs.

whithe the decay of your churche shold be repeared, thes ar to wyll & commaund you and everye one of you to appere at Eccleshalls churche on Fryday next beyng the ix[th] day of Maye, betwene ix and x of the clocke afore none, there and then to answere to suche thyngs as shall be obiected in that behalfe. And hereoff fayle ye not. This fyvethe day of May frome Eccleshall Castell.

your freynd,

223. [*To Roger Wolriche, Thomas Brett, Margery Parker, Raufe Cleton James Unton, Roger Smythe, in Seighford parish, Staffs, 5 May 1561*]

(fo. 92) Where as I have travayled with some of you for certane detts dew unto the churche of Seighford by reason of burying your freyndes in the same, And as yet you have (fo. 93) not satisfyed in that behalfe, Thes ar agayne to admonyshe and commaund you and [every] one of you to appere in Eccleshalls churche on Fryday next beyng the ix day of M[ay] betwene ix and x of the clocke afore noone, there and then fully to answere [suche] thyngs as shalbe obiected aswell in that behalfe as for your contempte. And hereof fayle ye not. Wryten this v[th] day of May at my castell of Eccleshall.

your freynde,

224. [*To Dr Yale, Chancellor to the Archbishop of Canterbury, 6 May 1561*]

(fo. 93) Commendyng me most hartelye to your good worshippe, thes may be to desyre your favorable helpe or counsell (yf you be not iudge on the case) to this my neighboure and freynd, the berr[er] hereof, Thomas Hanley, who beynge put to greate troble and brought to great daunger in the late tyme of Quene Marye by the means and workynge of one William Yonge, gentilm[an] or esquier, commensed his action agaynst the same William Yonge in my court at Lichefeilde, And nowe the same matter ys removed from thence up in to my Lord of Cantorberyes grac[e] court, as I suppose either suspectynge myne officers or els to delay iustyce yf he can by any means. Wherefore I pray you use the matter as to your wysedome shall seme most expedient, helpynge this my freynde to spedye ende, because longe sutes ar chargeable. And th[us] I commytt your worshippe to the goodnes of God, this vith of Maye at my castell of Eccleshall.

your freynd to his smale power,

225. [*To Mr Playfere at the Barbican, London, 6 May 1561*]

(fo. 93) Concernyng your letters & the effect thereof gentill Mr Playfere, this you shall understande that as I send you some instructions by John Floude: so to supplie the rest. Mr Maseys lease was planelye surrendered and delivered upp when Pope tooke his seconde lease.[226] Wherefore in that poynt, I wyll neither yeld nor agree with Mr Masey. As towchynge the matter in the Sterr Chamber, I wold yt shold be answered by lawe as you thynke best. And as for Mr Adderlay & Christofer Bayne, you had nede to consyder what tyme wyl be sufficient to serve the wrytes upon theym when you shall sende theym downe. I thynke yt must be agaynst the next terme. As concernynge suche instructions as I leifft at London Mr Manley dyd take theym to have delivered unto you: or els I had lefft theym either with Mr Egerton or els with Mr Morwynge. Wherefore I praye you wyll Mr Manley to deliver you the notes whiche he tooke at my handes in Mr Wayrs house: of other thynges you may take instructions by my patent, aswell of the names of the prebendes, Whereof I shold have a graunt frome my Lord Pagett: Longdon, Berkeswyche & others mencioned in the begynnynge of the patents: as also of the benefyces impropriate, for the whiche I wold have my sute begonne in the exchequer. Other thynges I must leave to your godlye and freyndlye diligence. Commyttynge you and your lovynge bedfellowe to the goodnes of allmightye God, this vith of may at my castell of Eccleshall.

your lover and freynd,

226. [*To Thomas Bolt, 6 May 1561*]

(fo. 93) Commendynge me unto you Mr Bolt, mervalyng therewith that you procede styll, contrarye to my commaundememt, litell regardynge either your owne estimation and honestye or my degree and callynge; and the great charge hangynge over my heade,

---

[226] For the confirmation of the lease of Hanbury rectory to William Pope, see L.C.L., Dean & Chapter Act Book IV, fo. 155v.

BISHOP THOMAS BENTHAM 225

havynge no assurance of you; And also the undeserved trobles which throughe your means the cleargye of my diocese ys lyke to susteane. For the avoydance whereoff, I wyll and commaund you to be whithe me att Eccleshall castell upon Thursday next beynge the viii[th] day of May betwene [   ] (fo. 94) and xi of the clocke afore none there and then to understande more of that matter. In the meane tyme also wyllynge you to do nothynge but that which [by] iust lawe may be allowed. Even so wysshinge unto you and your doyngs, as to myne owne, the prosperous assistance of God, to whome I commytt you this vi[th] day of May at my castell of Eccleshall.

your freynde,

227. [*To Sir William Cecil, Secretary to the Queen, 7 May 1561*]

(fo. 94) Right honorable, my dewtye well considered, as occasion ys presentlye offered, even so I am bolden, but with confidence of your gentilnes and hope of your furtheraunce, to desyre your godlye & ever redye helpyng hande in the sute of this messinger, Mr Simons,[227] the vicare of St Michaels in Coventree. Who as he is greatlye charged with the arrerages of his vicaredge (whitche as I can learne hitherto dyd onelye growe in the tyme of the late intrusor) so sence his restitution made in the Quens Majesties visitation, he haithe sought occasions diversleye boethe to me and otherwyse to leave and gyve upp the saide vicaredge agayne, for that he is not able to paye the arrerages demaunded. Wherefore yf yt may please your honor to helpe the said vicare to a release thereof, as they shall appere by divers particularyties, you shall not onelye ease hym of a greate burden, but allso do a greate pleasure to the cytye of Coventree, and a singuler benefytt unto me, whiche have greate nede of suche ministers in my hoole diocese for he ys learned, godly and sobre in his doyngs. Thus desyrynge your honors favorable furtheraunce in his cause, I commytt the same to your goodnes, and all your doyngs to the good wyll and favor of allmightye God, who ever kepe your honor in healthe to his pleasure this vii[th] day of May at my poore castell of Eccleshall.

your honours at commaundement,

[227] Hugo Symons: originally instituted to St Michael's vicarage, Coventry, 17 March 1551 (on vacation by John Ramridge, archdeacon of Derby); he was deprived in 1553 (L.J.R.O., B/A/1/14ii). Symons died in 1577.

228. [*To Thomas Lever, Archdeacon of Coventry, at Coventry, 7 May 1561*]

(fo. 94) *Salutem in Christo* Althoughe I have not answered by wrytynge your letters of late writen unto me, yet I have neglected no poynt of theym, for immediatelye I dyd wryte to Lichefeild boethe towchyng the vicare of Colshyll,[228] and the other accused of simonye.[229] Concernynge gevyng of orders, I suppose the day ys apoynted and sett up at Lichefeild to be the xviii[th] day of this monethe, for so I wyll my register to do. And at Hanberye I purpose God wyllynge to minister theym. Howe be yt, I shall verye hardlye have my thyngs thither agaynst that day. As concernynge my visitation, I wyll by the grace of God hasten yt so spedely as I can. Whereof you shall understand more at the day of gevyng orders. In the meane tyme commendynge me to all my freyndes whithe you, I commytt you to God this vii[th] of May at my castell of Eccleshall.

yours assuredlye,

229. [*To Peter Morweyn, chaplain, at London, 7 May 1561*]

(fo. 94) Commendynge me to you & your wyfe etc. thes ar to wyll you learne what my Lord of London doethe in his visitation, besydes his articles whiche you sent me. I wold also have those articles or iniunctions and homelyes, whiche I heare saye ar sett forthe by my Lord of Cantorberyes. And yf you can gett me the table of the degrees of mariedge I wold have yt. What other thyngs you see to be nedefull for me to knowe, lett me understande by your letters from tyme to tyme, so longe as you shall tarrye there. Speake to Mr Seres to gett me the Statuts of Kynge Edward, and also the statutes of Quene Marye well bounde severallye: And at Michelmas he shall have money for theym and suche thyngs as I shall send for hereafter before that tyme. Commend me to my brother (fo. 95) Rauffe Egerton and to his wyfe. And to all other my freynds in Christ, who prosper all theyr doyngs, this vii of May at Eccleshall.

yours assuredlye,

---

[228] See item 58.
[229] Thomas Stoneinge of Nuneaton.

230. [*To the Queen, 8 May 1561*]

(fo. 95) In most humble wyse, shewethe and enformethe your most excellent majesti your poore orator and obedyent chaplayne, Thomas bysshope of Coventry & Lichefield, that where the vicaredge of St Michaell within your majesties citye of Coventry is charged and chargeable with the payment of certane arrerages of a certane pension, subsydies and tenthes dew to your maiestye in the tyme of certane intrusors there. And where also the nowe vicare beynge restored to the said vicaredge, in your m[ajesties] late visitation, beyng a lerned, godlye and discrete minister can not be able nor wyll contynu[e] and take upon hym the charge of so greate a cure & ministerye and payment of suche arrera[ges] beynge daylye required and commaunded to pay the said arrerages of the said pencion, s[ub]sydyes and tenthes and thereby moche trobled and disquieted. And where also the lyvyng of the said vicare ys of late also moche impered & decayed by reason[a] of the decay a[nd] impoveryshement of thinhabitants of the said citye. Whereby the said citye shalbe utterlye destitute of a godlye and lerned minister,[230] especiallye of suche one as he ys, onles yt wo[ld] please your most excellent majesty of your graces pytye and favor toward your said poore citye, beyng the cheyfe citye of all thes parties of your majesties realme,[231] and for that there ys no other minister within the whole citye,[232] and your majestie patrones of the said vicaredge and also the said vicaredg beyng the greatest cure of any one benefyce within my whole dioces,[233] to pardon and remytt aswell the said arrerages as also the said yerelye pencion, yerelye dewe and payable out of the said vicaredge. As in the tyme of your ma[jesties] late sisters reagne

---

[a] by reason *repeated*.

---

[230] A somewhat strange statement in view of Lever's position as archdeacon of Coventry and minister of St John's, Bablake.

[231] Coventry had a population of perhaps 2,200 in 1563 (Harl. MS. 594); the parish of St Michael was larger than that of Holy Trinity—503: 49 households.

[232] Holy Trinity was vacant.

[233] The living was not valued in the same form in the *Valor Ecclesiasticus*, St Michael's being the church of the Priory of Coventry and also the cathedral church. So far, no post-reformation particulars of the assessed income of the living, now a crown impropriation, have been forthcoming, but P.R.O., E.331, Institutions Books, MS. Index Ser. A. vol. 4 (entry regarding institution of William Panting to St Michael's on 22 May 1633) indicates that the assessment was reviewed in the vicar's favour: 'refor' in 2 et 3 Eliz. per Annum 26[li] 15s. 4d', presumably as a result of this appeal by Bentham.

Quene Marye, the late intrusors there should have had the said pencion, arrerages of subsydyes & tenthes upon the takynge upon theym the reall possession of the said vicaredge pardoned and remytted*a* whereby your said orator and chaplayne and your said citizens and minister shall as of dewtye they ar most bownden*b* pray to allmightye God for your ma[jesties] most prosperous reagne longe to contynue etc.

231. [*To Dr Weston, Chancellor, 8 May 1561*]

(fo. 95) Item a letter to Dr Weston to signifye that I must kepe my visitation before his commyng, that ys shortlye after wytsontyde, wherefore I wold have hym to mak spede downward, and in the meane tyme to speake yf there be any appels mad forthe of my court at Lichefeild, but especiallye in Hanleys case etc.[234]

232. [*To William Paulet, Marquis of Winchester and Lord Treasurer, 8 May 1561*]

(fo. 95) My dewe and humble commendations to your honor havynge receaved your Lordships letters by par[son] Bolt for answere whereof your good Lordship shall understand that in somer last after I h[ad] receaved commaundement frome your honor aswell by word of mouthe beynge present as al[so] by letters, which yet I have to shewe, for the collection of tenthes and subsydyes, whith tharrerages of the same. At my commynge downe to Lichefeild I called the deane and chapter for that end and there understandynge that parson Bolt had the collectyng of the [same] I charged hym therewith accordynglye, who in the presence of the chapter promised me t[he] terme next folowynge (which was michaelmas terme past) he wold discharge all thy[ngs] and brynge me my *quietus est*, which yet in no poynt he dyd fulfyll. Where upon & also for that divers complaynts were mad to me of his uniust dealynge with s[uche] (fo. 96) poore men as were unable to beare yt, I dyd discharge hym

---

a Followed by in consideration whereoff, and for that also there ys, *struck out.*
b Followed by day.

---

in Januarye last at my commynge upp to London, wyllyng hym for my savetye no more to medle in that offyce but to clere the old [ac]comptes, and to bryng me a *quyetus est*, whiche he promised me shold be done in Hyllarye terme then next folowyng. Att the whiche tyme I dyd desyre my very good freynd & neighbore Mr Simon Harcourt to use & exercyse the offyce. And parson Bolt contrarye to this order & his promyse, after my departure entred in to thoffyce, makyng more hast to leavye the moneys then ever had bene accostomed, usyng suche wrongfull wayes amongest the poore curats that the clamour thereof caused me once agayne to desyre Mr Harcourt to take the offyce in hande, who then at my request wrote to hym in the Quens highnes name not any further to medle therewith but to come before me for the dew answeryng off suche somes of money as he had withowt my consent levied, which I trust your honor thynekethe not to be evell done. And what his letters patents ar, I knowe not but suer I am that in the tyme of Quene Marye for his untoward servyce therein my last predecessor Bysshope Bayne wold neither suffer hym to enioye the fee nor exercyse the offyce but placed others in that romethe, whereby yt may appere unto your honor that he haithe untrewlye reported to have gathered the dewtyes withowt lett for xv[th] yeres. Assuryng your good Lord-ship that the poore men wold be loythe to be any more trobled with hym. Even so besechyng your honor that I may with your favor apoynt suche a one as I knowe to be of hability and credyte to discharge me for that I stand bound by statute to answere the same. And also that yt may please your honor to direct your commaunde-ment by letters to hym for repayment thereof to me, that I may with more diligence dispatche that which ys to be payd. And he to m[ake] an end with the old accompte in that receipte and not whithe this newe as I am informed his common custome ys to do, whiche thynge causethe me to feare the end greatlye as knowethe God, to whose gracious protection I commytt your good honor this viii[th] day of May at my castell of Eccleshall.

your good honors at commaundement,

233. [*To Mr Ryley, Alderman of Coventry, 11 May 1561*]

(fo. 96) Commendynge me unto your good worshipe, as I am sorye that I have so longe disapoyncted you of your money which most freyndlye at my nede you lent me: even so you shall understande

that I am greatlye disapoynted in that case my selfe for, I assure
you, that I dyd delyver the said money to one of my servants John
Flood and that with an earnest charge to pay unto you a fortnyght
agoo when I sent hym to London aboute certane busines which I
have there this terms. If you were at home when he came through
Coventree, he ys moche to be blamed, as at his returne shall understand, for I made for suche shyfft as then I cold to send yt unto you.
Notwithstandyng seyng the matter ys thus standyng, I wyll send
unto you the fyrst money that comethe to my handes; in the mean
season desyryng you not to iudge this to be done of purpose on my
part, for in deed I wylled my man to pay you your money as he cam
by you. And thus God blesse you & yours this xi[th] off May at my
poore castell of Eccleshall.

your freynd assuredlye,

234. [*To James Weston, Registrar, at Lichfield, 13 May 1561, from
Hanbury*]

(fo. 96) Receavyng your letters to knowe what articles I purpose to
sett forthe for inquisition in my visitation, you shall understande
that I am nowe aboute the same: howe be yt, I must take deliberation and have some consultation wethere yt be better to have theym
writen or printed. And therefore I stay the more at this present,
but so shortlye as I am resolved herein, you shall then fully understand, as knoweth God, to whose kepyng I commytt you this xiii[th]
of May at Hanberye.[235]

yours assuredlye,

235. [*To Edwin Sandys, Bishop of Worcester, 18 May 1561*]

(fo. 97) Item a letter to my Lord of Worceter thankyng hym for
his paynes takyng in those partys of mye diocese, and signifying unto
hym howe werye I am of mye seate and knowe not where [to] compleane for the amendment of the same etc.

---

[235] Bentham apparently used Hanbury as his summer residence.

236. [*To Thomas Sampson, 18 May 1561*]

(fo. 97) Item a letter to Mr Sampson declaryng that I thought he had bene offended with me, for that he cam not to me at London, but nowe by his wrytyng I am perswaded the contrarye, wyllyng hym to iudg the best of me, for my state beyng knowen wyll rather move all good men to lament then any man to accuse or complayne of my sofftnes and also movyng hym to come by me when he comethe in to the countree.

237. [*To Thomas Lever, 18 May 1561*]

(fo. 97) Item a letter to Mr Levyr signifyings that althoughe I have not answered to all his letters, nor to all partes of theym, yet I have neglected no part of theym. Concernyng a relaxation for his court, I have wryten to my regester, and as for Stonynges matter,[236] I differ to do any thyng therein before I talke with hym, further that I look for his helpe in my visitation. I wold be sory that his goyng to Brystowe[237] shold be an occasion to leave Coventre. Of other matters we shall talke more fully at my next commynge to hym etc.

238. [*To the Dean of Lichfield, 18 May 1561*]

(fo. 97) Item a letter to Mr Deane of lichefeild desyryng hym to common whithe my register[238] in certane poynts, cheyfly concernyng Mr Levers relaxation, and that by the institution of Stonynge I susteane more dishonestye that ever I shall have honestye by his servyce,[239] wherefore I wyll that he mak no mo institutions before the partye come to me or els before Mr Deane do examyne theym yf he be at Lichefeild when suche come for[a] institutions.[240] Also to the

---

[a] *Followed by* orders, *struck out.*

---

[236] See item 238.   [237] Bristol.

[238] James Weston, registrar.

[239] Thomas Stoneinge. On 5 May 1561 Stoneinge was instituted to Nuneaton vicarage, Warwickshire, presented by the Queen (L.J.R.O., B/A/1/15).

[240] In future presentees to benefices were to be examined by either the bishop or the dean in person. For a similar case of simony, see the deposition of Katherine Dyott, Weston's sister, in a case against Henry Trickett, vicar of Doveridge, Derbyshire, in 1598/9 (L.J.R.O., B/C/5).

end that he wyll be my freynd in suche matters as my right liethe
in and when Mr. Aston[241] shall come thither to use his counsell.

239. [*To James Weston, Registrar, 18 May 1561*]

(fo. 97) Item a letter to my register to geve credyte to Maister
Deans instructions whiche for lacke of tyme I was compelled to
wryte etc.

240. [*To Mr Marrow, 21 May 1561*]

(fo. 97) Item a letter to Mr Marowe signifying that I wold be glad
to satisfy his request and the inhabitants of Knole[242] but not beyng
acquaynted with the matter I feare lest in my wrytyng I shold not
towche the effects of the same. Wherefore yf yt wyll please hym to
wryte the matter conteanyng theyr request & his meanyng with a
certantye of truethe I wyll be readye to subscribe & send the same
with all diligence, as knowethe God etc.

241. [*To Mr Critcheley at Lichfield, 22 May 1561, from Hanbury*]

(fo. 97) Commendyng me unto you most hartelye gentill Mr
Crutcheley, thes ar to desyre you helpe a litell. So yt is that of
necessitye, by apoynctment, I must pay upon Sonday next xxv[li]
And, lokyng to have receaved more then that at this tyme, I am
disaponted of my espectation. Wherefore, yf you can by your selfe
or by your freynd helpe me to so moche but for the space of viii or
x dayes, you shall do me suche a pleasure as, God wyllyng, I wyll
not forgett to requyte and have your money within x dayes with
most hartye thankes as knowethe God, to whose kepyng I commytt
you, this xxii[th] of May frome my house at Hanburye.

                                        yours assuredlye,

241 Robert Aston, rector of Mucklestone, Staffs.
242 Knowle, Warwickshire.

242. [*To Thomas Bickley, 23 May 1561, from Hanbury*]

(fo. 97) My hartye commendations to you Mr Byckley, thes ar to signifye that Mr Aston haithe brought me no money And I dowbt wether I shall have any before the tyme, wherefore I pray you helpe to make shifft for so moche, And in my name make theym some assurance. Wherewhith by thes presents I wyll stand chargeable, God wyllynge. And to that end shewe this my request & promise this 23 of May at Hanberye.

243. [*To William Fleetwood at London(?), 26 May 1561, from Hanbury*]

(fo. 98) Item a letter wryten to Mr William Fletewoode, signifyinge that I have not understandyng of the matter whereof he wrote, but nowe I wyll (God wyllyng thereto) use diligence in the same, and thes weike I mynd to send for the popishe prelate and charge hym with his dewtye or els blame my negligence therein worthelye. Also I am sorye that you cold not come to me & that I am not able to deserve or recompence your gentillnes notwithstand to increase myne owne dett, I must crave your helpe this terme at London wether God send you prosperouslye.

244. [*To Robert Aston, surveyor, 26 May 1561, from Hanbury*]

(fo. 98) So yt is that I sent for a copye of the letter which was brought downe to the deane & chapter, whiche copye I have sent you here inclosed, wyllyng you to take some paynes to common of the same with Mr Harcourt, as this copye doeth proport, whiche as yet I have not receaved yf you cold come to me upon Thursday or Fryday next to talke of this and other matters, I trust we shold come to some quyett. The matter goethe so that I must of necessitye take order for the Quens certanty of payment, for my owne savetye and honestye, and also for the quietnes of my clergye, whose troble in no case I wold procure. James Weston wyll not alter his dayes which I knowe wyll troble us in my visitation, especiallye rydyng frome Busshburye[243] to Shrewsberye upon one day. Thus with my commen-

243 Bushbury, Staffs.

dations to Mrs. Aston I byd you fayre well this 26 of May at Hanberye etc.

245. [*To James Weston, Registrar, 28 May 1561, from Hanbury*]

(fo. 98) Where as ther ys a controversye dependyng in your court betwene Sir William Tarleton parson of Brelisforde[244] in the countye of Darbye and the inhabitants of Osmaston, grevous complaynte ys made unto me of the longe delay thereof by worshipfull & lerned men. Wherefore I have promised to convent the parson my selff and with spede bryng theym to some quiett end. So that in the mean season I wold not have the said inhabitants called any further to your court before yt shall appere what I can do in the matter. And thus I commytt you to God, this 28 of May at Hanberye.

your freynd,

246. [*To William Tarleton, rector of Brailsford, Derbyshire, 29 May 1561, from Hanbury*]

(fo. 98) Where as we do understande a certane controversye to be betwyxt you & the inhabitants of Osmaston for servynge of the cure there: and the same cause nowe longe dependynge in the court at Lichefeild to the greate charges of the same inhabitaunts, Thes ar for the more quiett and spedye end thereof, to will & commaunde you to be at Hanberye upon Monday next beynge the seconde day of June, betwene ix and x of the clocke, there and then to answere such thynges as in that case shalbe obiected and hereof fayle ye not, this 29 of May frome my house at Hanberye.

your freynd,

247. [*To Simon Harcourt, 29 May 1561, from Hanbury*]

(fo. 98) Commendyng me to your good worshippe Mr Harcourt, Thes may signifye unto you that receavyng the copye of my Lord Treasorers letters sent to the deane and chapter of Lichefeild in a farr other sence and meanynge then that whitche Robert Bu[tler?]

[244] Brailsford, Derbyshire.

brought unto me, immediatly I sent the other copye to my sur-
veyour[245] partly to peruse but cheyfly to conferr with you therein.
And after to come to [   ] (fo. 99) that with good consultation,
I myght for the present state, take some good order which I thynke
to be most mete for all partyes. Howe be yt, be you assured that mr
Bolt shall knowe that he haithe abused me. I have not as yet
receaved those letters which I suppose he haith brought for me,
neither have I receaved any word from Mr Deane and chapter
towchyng this matter. Wherefore I differ to wryt unto theym un[til]
by theyr letters I shalbe moved to wryte after that tenor do you
understand. And thus I bydd you most hartelye fayre well this 29
of May frome my poore house at Hanberye.

your freynd assuredlye,

248. [*To Thomas Bolt, 29 May 1561, from Hanbury*]

(fo. 99) Dowbtyng what waye I may best use to move & exhorte
those whitheowt suspicion of iniurye, whome I thought I myght in
my private matters at all tymes commanded, nowe in weightier
matters then either to dalye or trifle in, I am inforced moche contrarye to my nature to signifye howe unkyndlye &[a] frowardly I am
abuse in the greatest matters of my charge towardes my most
gracious & soveraygne ladye the Quene, for yf you had come unto
me when I sent for you to take order in the matter, you had saved a
greate deale of labor besydes your charcges, and happely as neighe
your purpose as nowe and also kept in stoore your complaynts &
slaunders, where whithe you have towched and colored me, untyll
you had better occasion to utter suche wayres, but for that you then
neglectyng your dewtye & obedience nowe gard your selfe with
other means, I thought good once agayne (respectynge herein my
bownden dewtye & charge towards the Quene) to wyll you as
before be whithe me at Hanberye upon Fryday next beyng the
xxx[th] of May betwene ix & x[th] of the clocke there to take a better &
a more quiett waye then I see you seke. And hereof fayle you not
this 29 of May at my house in Hanberye.

your freynd,

[a] *Followed by* un, *struck out.*

---

[245] Robert Aston.

249. [*To James Weston, Registrar, 29 May 1561, from Hanbury*]

(fo. 99) Item a letter to James Weston to make a citation to cause one Sir Richerd Sherer clerke to appere before me or my deputye at Shrewsbery on Tewsday nexte in the cheiff churche to be examined of a matter towching my Lord of Hereford[246] & me, before Mr Thomas Aston preacher.

250. [*To Thomas Aston at Shrewsbury, 29 May 1561, from Hanbury*]

(fo. 99) Where as I have a cause of examination to be herd at Shrewsberye by reason the parson is aged & impotent thes ar not onely to wyll you but also therewhith to autoryse you in my name to tak his examination accordyng to suche articles as the berer hereof shall minister or exhibyte unto you. Wherein I praye you most hartelye to use your diligence and so I do[ubt] not but the wicked shalbe put to confusion. Thus trustyng to your good & diligent discretion herein I commytt you to God this 29 of Maye frome my house of Hanbery.

your freynd assuredlye,

251. [*To Mr Playfere at London, 30 May 1561, from Hanbury*]

(fo. 99) Concernynge the *subpenais* which you sent me, you shall un[derstand] the one was served upon Christofer Bayne[a] on the Ascension da[y] [   ] must take some paynes to see that the byll of complaynts my be p[   ] Suche instructions as I thynke most mete you shall receave nowe [   ] I pray you helpe boethe in this and also in the case of my te[nthes . . .] (fo. 100) personages may be discharged, seyng that I am bound for the whole in my livyng. Con[cerning] Mr Adderlay, I have not served his wryte, for that I am by my counsell willed to the contrarye because he doethe not interupte me at this present. Christofer Bayne wyll in h[is]

---

[a] *Followed by* of, *struck out.*

[246] John Scory, Bishop of Hereford, 1559–85.

answere (as I suppose) alledge that I kepe frome hym his goodes & suche thyngs [   ]. Whereunto you shall easely answere that he haithe conveyd awaye my goodes (besydes the decay of my houses, with wayst of my groundes) to a greater some then he is able to paye, and that you may perceave by the articles of instructions whiche I tr[ust] wyll helpe you in many thynges. As towchyng Sir Ge[orge] Blounte & Mr Swynerton I knowe not what to do before they make any more suett. Howe be yt the matter standynge as yt doethe, I trust my Lord Keper of the Great Seale wylbe my good lorde. To be short, I desyre you hartelye to helpe this terme boethe as con-cernynge Sir George Blounte & Mr Swynerton and also Christofer Bayne. Wherein I wold gladlye h[ave] my Lord Keper moved of the lease of Hanberye that yt may be delivered unto me for as moche as I have payd the first part of my payment to Christofer Grene. And yf I sh[all] not have the lease delivered in to my handes after all this labor & charges my successors may be lykewyse trobled with yt as I am. And thus I commytt you to God this 30 of May at my howse in Hanberye.

your freynd to his smale power,

252. [*To Nicholas Bacon, Keeper of the Great Seal, 30 May 1561, from Hanbury*]

(fo. 100) Right honorable and mye verye good Lord as I have heretofore moche agaynst my wyll trobled your honor with my busye matters: so I am inforced styll to desyryng your charitable ayde & helpe for the finishynge of those cases which yet depend in your honorable court, that ys of the castell of Eccleshall & the par-sonage of Hanberye, about the wiche as I have had greate trobles & sustened greate charges besydes the losses of divers commodityes otherwyse: so I wold be verye glad nowe to have the hearynge of theym, whiche ys my cheyfe desyre as knowethe God. So that yf I may be so bolde as to desyre this helpe and especially for the deliverye or cancellynge of boethe the leases I meane of Eccleshall & Hanberye, then I shall thynke my selfe in very good case and be bounden to pray for the preservation of your good honor in healthe long to contynue. This 30 of May at my poore house at Hanberye.

your good honours at commaundement,

253. [*To Ralph Egerton at London, 30 May 1561, from Hanbury*]

(fo. 100) Beynge no lesse glad for your recoverye then thankfullye acknowledgynge y[our] good wyll readye towardes me alwayes, gentill and lovyng brothere, Raufe Egerton, thes may be partlye to salute you and all my freyndes whithe you [and] partly to thank you for your gentilnes, the contynuance whereof, as I greatlye desyre [it], so I pray God make me boethe worthye of yt and also able either to recompence or deserve yt. I wold be very glad to se you and my sister Anne at my p[oor par]sonage of Hanberye nowe after greate trobles. Commend me to Mr Braysey and [to his] bed-fellowe and to my god daughter, whome I pray god to blesse [li]ke a good old Sarah, thus for this present I byd you fayre well and [   ] whome I had all most forgotten this 30 of May frome my house at Hanberye.

INDEX

[References are to pages unless otherwise stated]